JEAN MICHEL BASQUIAT BORN DEC 22/1960/BROOKLYN/N Y)

MOTHER PUERTO RICAN (FIRST GENERATION)
FATHER ~~HA~~ PORT AU PRINCE, HAITI
(DIVORCED)
[NAME OF THE TOWN]

ST ANNS
?
PS 6
PS 101
PS 45
IS 293 ← (SOME CATHOLIC SCHOOL DURING YEAR + ½ IN PUERTO RICO)
CITY AS SCHOOL

11 TH GRADE DROPOUT
① PUT A BOX OF SHAVING CREAM IN PRINCIPAL'S FACE AT GRADUATION
NO POINT ~~IN LOOT~~ IN GOING BACK

FIRST AMBITION FIREMAN
FIRST ARTISTIC AMBITION CARTOONIST

EARLY THEMES WERE ~~THE~~

① THE SEAVIEW FROM "VOYAGE TO THE BOTTOM OF THE SEA"
2 ALFRED E NEUMAN
3 ALFRED HICTHCOCK (HIS FACE OVER + OVER)
4 NIXON
5 CARS (MOSTLY DRAGSTER)S
6 WARS
7 WEAPONS
⑧ MADE DRAWINGS OF OOPICK + FRITZ + HAIR + YABOO WITH MARC PROZZO

Ⓐ SENT A DRAWING OF A GUN TO J EDGAR HOOVER IN ~~3rd~~ Grd THIRD GRADE
(NO REPLY)

TAUGHT SECOND GRADERS WHEN I WAS IN THE FOURTH GRADE (CARS MADE OF PAPERCLIPS MASKING TAPE + FASTENERS

SCHOOLING SOME ^ACADEMIC^ LIFE DRAWING IN NINTH GRADE
(WAS THE ONLY CHILD THAT FAILED)

EARLY MUSIC INFLUENCES WEST SIDE STORY
THE 'WATUSI"
ROUND 'BOUT MIDNIGHT
WALKING HAPPY
BLACK ORPHEUS

CHAÉDRIA LABOUVIER

BASQUIAT'S DEFACEMENT

THE UNTOLD STORY

GUGGENHEIM

Defacement (The Death of Michael Stewart) is not the official title of the painting at the core of this catalogue and exhibition but rather represents a hybridization of early references to the work. When bequeathing this painting to its current owner in 1990, Keith Haring cited it in his will as *Defacemento.* When exhibited in 1992 at the Whitney Museum of American Art in a retrospective of Basquiat's work, the painting was published in the catalogue as *Untitled (Defacement).* It is listed as *The Death of Michael Stewart* in Galerie Enrico Navarra's estate-sanctioned, two-volume catalogue raisonné, *Jean-Michel Basquiat, 1960–1988* (1996). In the present volume, the painting is referred to as *Defacement (The Death of Michael Stewart)*, or simply *Defacement*, and the official title is used in captions corresponding to its reproduction.

CONTENTS

THE SOLOMON R. GUGGENHEIM FOUNDATION

LENDERS TO THE EXHIBITION

AMA Collection

Arora Collection

Brooklyn Museum

Nina Clemente, New York

George Condo

Eric Drooker

East Village Eye

Estate of Jean-Michel Basquiat

Patrick Fox

Monique and Ziad Ghandour

Franck Goldberg

The Keith Haring Foundation

Lyle Ashton Harris

Carl Hirschmann Collection

Allison Marvin and Emily Moyer,
courtesy Gary and Jean Cohen

The Museum of Modern Art, New York

Patricia Pesce, New York

Private collection

Luc Sante

The Stewart Family

Andrew L. Terner, New York, São Paulo

Van de Weghe, New York

DIRECTOR'S FOREWORD AND ACKNOWLEDGMENTS

Jean-Michel Basquiat may be one of the best-known and most beloved contemporary artists in the world today, even though he passed away in 1988 at the age of twenty-seven. Basquiat's prodigious output has been the subject of numerous large-scale exhibitions since his untimely death, and his imagery permeates the visual data bank of popular culture. But only recently has art-historical scholarship turned its investigatory lens toward understanding the complex and sophisticated iconography about race, the Middle Passage, and African-diaspora culture in his work. This tightly conceived exhibition focuses on a formative chapter in Basquiat's brief career, demonstrating how the artist, and others of his generation, responded to a racially charged, violent event in New York City in the early 1980s. It takes as its starting point the painting *Defacement (The Death of Michael Stewart)* (1983), which Basquiat created in response to the death of the young, black aspiring artist Michael Stewart at the hands of the New York City Transit Police in the East Village on September 28, 1983, after being arrested for allegedly writing graffiti on the wall of a subway station. This event had a tremendous impact on the social fabric of the city, galvanizing a sense of political urgency and a demand for justice among the black community as well as the community of downtown artists for whom Stewart was a peer. For Basquiat, Stewart's death brought to the surface his own conflicted status as a black artist in a city roiled by racial tensions and an art world largely immune to the social and economic inequities at their source.

Guest curator Chaédria LaBouvier's original and groundbreaking research on this painting has contributed new scholarship on Basquiat's practice as well as the context in which he worked. In 2016–17 she presented *Defacement* in the Reading Room of the Williams College Museum of Art as the catalyst for a program of dialogues around issues of identity, institutional racism, and criminal justice. Following this single-work exhibition, Nancy Spector, Guggenheim Artistic Director and Jennifer and David Stockman

Chief Curator, astutely invited LaBouvier to expand her research to situate *Defacement* within Basquiat's oeuvre as well as within the downtown New York art community. We are grateful to LaBouvier for curating the exhibition and contributing to this accompanying catalogue, which provide a new and incisive perspective onto a historical moment of cultural struggle, one that still resonates today.

This project benefited from the contributions and close collaboration of a talented team at the Guggenheim. Nancy Spector and Joan Young, Director, Curatorial Affairs, expertly advised LaBouvier on all aspects of organizing the exhibition and publication and contributed markedly toward their success. Terra Warren, Curatorial Assistant, provided valuable support along with curatorial interns Elizabeth Akant, Ana Alvarez de Rosenzweig, Jules Gabellini, Blythe Poor, Ashleigh Smith, and Zijie Zhou.

LaBouvier's meaningful research is joined in this publication by numerous discerning voices. Nancy Spector and cultural historian J. Faith Almiron consider Basquiat and *Defacement* in a broader cultural context, and I would like to thank them for their thoughtful contributions. We are honored to have the opportunity to reprint Greg Tate's seminal essay "Black like B.," which originally appeared in the catalogue of the 1992 retrospective of Basquiat's work at the Whitney Museum of American Art and remains a highly relevant statement on the way race operates in and around Basquiat's work. Recollections from individuals who knew Basquiat and Stewart, or were part of this episode in New York City's history, create a powerful portrait of the tragic event; we are indebted to the following for sharing their memories: Leonard Abrams, Fred Brathwaite, Dianne Brill, George Condo, Reverend Herbert Daughtry, Jeffrey Deitch, Eric Drooker, Ronald Fields, Patrick Fox, Franck Goldberg, Lyle Ashton Harris, Carlo McCormick, Peter Noel, Annina Nosei, Patricia Pesce, Luc Sante, Kenny Scharf, Tony Shafrazi, Michelle Shocked, Carrie Stewart, Seth Tobocman, Michael Warren, and Lou Young. We are grateful to Diana Murphy, Publisher, for her incomparable instincts and guidance and to Elizabeth Zechella, Managing Editor, for her careful oversight of all content. Cullen Gallagher, Editorial Assistant, provided photo research and other essential support. David Jenkins adeptly transcribed hours of conversation conducted by the curators. Alison Chipak, Photographer and Studio Manager, deftly photographed materials for inclusion in the catalogue. These varied materials have been thoughtfully compiled into an artful form by designer Loidë Marwanga, with production skillfully managed by Melissa Secondino, Associate Director, Production, and Shiori Kawasaki, Assistant Production Manager.

Numerous other individuals have aided research and shared their insights, and for this we extend our sincere thanks: Sharon Matt Atkins, Diego Cortez, Maggie Dalla Tana, Carrie Goteiner, Julia Gruen and Anna Gurton-Wachter of the Keith Haring Foundation, Nancy Elizabeth Hill, Fred Hoffman, Rashid Johnson, Laura Levine, Spencer Rumsey, David Schmidlapp, Kate Simon, Franklin Sirmans, Andrew Terner, and Jane Weissman of Artmakers Inc.

I am exceedingly grateful to the private and institutional lenders who graciously parted with their artworks and ephemeral materials to create a time capsule of this historic moment. Their names appear elsewhere in this publication, but I would like to extend special thanks to Nina Clemente, owner of *Defacement*, for her commitment to LaBouvier's research on this painting. I would also like to thank the following friends and colleagues who have provided advice and shepherded loans on our behalf: Josh Baer, Alison Brant, Yana Rovner of Francesco Clemente Studio, Rose Dergan and Kara Vander Weg of Gagosian Gallery, Benjamin Provo of George Condo Studio, Jeanne Greenberg, George Lindemann, Christophe Cherix and Emily Edison of the Museum of Modern Art, Cecile Le Paire, Arnold Lehman and Scott Nussbaum of Phillips, Margot Bird and Jennifer Grimyser of Salon 94, Aaron Shraybman, Amy Cappellazzo and Eliza Ravelle-Chapuis of Sotheby's, Emily Tsingou, and Erin Batson and Jenn Viola of Van der Weghe.

I would like to especially recognize the sincere support and assistance of Artestar, particularly David Stark and Sara Citarella, who work closely with the Estate of Jean-Michel Basquiat to ensure the artist's legacy. We are also grateful to Jeanine Basquiat, Lisane Basquiat, and Nora Fitzpatrick for their gracious support of this project and support for Jean-Michel Basquiat's enduring legacy.

At the Guggenheim Museum, numerous colleagues were crucial to the realization of the exhibition. Kim Bush, former Director of Licensing and Traveling Exhibitions, aided by Lauren Robbins, Associate Manager, Exhibition Management, deftly handled the exhibition's budget and logistical details under the guidance of Clare Bell, Director of Exhibitions. Lucie Reyberol, Junior Exhibition Designer, conceived a discerning design that treated the myriad materials with clarity and sensitivity. Jae-un Chung, Director, Graphic

Design, with the assistance of freelance designer Brette Richmond, and Janice Lee, Associate Director, Graphic Design, contributed adroit conceptual and formal insight. Chiyong (Tali) Han, Archivist and Manager, Library and Archives, and Jillian Suarez, Associate Librarian, provided vital assistance with research. Eliza Stoner, Registrar, Collections and Exhibitions, ably coordinated the intricate details of transporting works in the exhibition and collaborated closely with Julie Barten, Senior Conservator, Collections and Exhibitions, and Jeffrey Warda, Conservator, Paper and Photographs, to ensure all objects were handled with the greatest care. Elizabeth Jaff, Associate Preparator for Paper, attentively prepared the ephemeral materials for display, while crews led by Paul Bridge, Senior Manager, Exhibition Installations, expertly handled the installation of all the works in the show, which were finally illuminated under the flawless supervision of Mary Ann Hoag, Head of Exhibition Lighting. Alan Seise, Associate Manager, Public Programs, capably organized the accompanying film program. And Sarah Eaton, Director, Media and Public Relations, sensitively crafted the press strategy for the show. Sarah Austrian, Deputy Director and General Counsel, provided critically important advice throughout the creation of the exhibition and catalogue, for which we are most grateful.

We also thank Corinne Godsall, Director, Corporate, Institutional, and Global Partners, and Mary Anne Talotta, Senior Director, Individual Development and Campaign, for their steadfast fund-raising efforts. With the aid of development consultant Lili Rusing, applications for grants from the National Endowment for the Arts and the Keith Haring Foundation were generously awarded, and we appreciate the support of these organizations.

Finally, I wish to extend my sincere appreciation to the Stewart family, who have granted the museum the profound privilege of sharing Michael's story.

Richard Armstrong

Director, Solomon R. Guggenheim Museum and Foundation

THE "EXIT ROUTES OF MAJESTY"

EXALTATION OF THE NOBLE, EXCEPTIONAL, AND PROGRESSIVE ACHIEVEMENTS

IN THE COLLECTIVE BODY OF EXPERIENCES OF A PEOPLE SERVES AS A MEANS OF EXAMINING TRAUMA THAT IS SO VISCERAL

THAT A PROTECTIVE GESTURE IS REQUIRED.

CHAÉDRIA LABOUVIER

DEFACEMENT: MOMENT, HISTORY, AND MEMORY

The burnt child dreads the fire.

BEN JONSON, *THE DEVIL IS AN ASS*[1]

Ancestral murderers and poets, more perplexed
In memory now by every ulcerous crime.
The world's green age then was a rotting lime . . .
The rot remains with us, the men are gone . . .

Ablaze with rage, I thought
Some slave is rotting in this manorial lake,
And still the coal of my compassion fought:
That Albion too, was once
A colony like ours, 'Part of the continent, piece of the main'
Nook-shotten, rook o'er blown, deranged
By foaming channels, and the vain expense
Of bitter faction.

All in compassion ends
So differently from what the heart arranged:
'as well as if a manor of thy friend's . . .'

DEREK WALCOTT, "RUINS OF A GREAT HOUSE"[2]

It could be argued that *Defacement (The Death of Michael Stewart)* (1983) **[PL. 1]** is Jean-Michel Basquiat's most personal painting. A first among equals in an oeuvre noted for its intensity and intimacy, no other work from Basquiat's body of work has surfaced with more unfiltered feeling and vulnerability, nor has depicted a current event that touched his life so directly. The location of the work's primary pulse as decidedly emotional rather than strictly political is remarkable, for Basquiat mostly favors temporally distant subjects over contemporary, nameable, concrete enemies. *Defacement* demonstrates an exceptional if temporary shift in Basquiat's body of work from verisimilar depiction to a more deeply felt, personal veracity. It is a rare painting by the artist that does not portray black masculinity and its traumas with the heroism and valor that he so deeply admired—at times relied on—as a bulwark against the marginalization of racism and the threat of its violent enforcement, the legacy of colonialism and slavery. Though an outlier among the artist's highly singular output in terms of style and substance, *Defacement* has the potential to serve as a Rosetta stone to help us better understand Basquiat's work as a whole.

Nineteen eighty-three, the year of *Defacement*'s execution, was a whirlwind year for the artist. The Annina Nosei Gallery in SoHo opened a solo show of his work in February, his second with the gallery since joining in 1981, and in early March he returned to Los Angeles for his second solo show at the Larry Gagosian Gallery. As if there were any question of the new star's ascent, a few weeks later Basquiat joined Keith Haring, Cindy Sherman, David Salle, and Barbara Kruger, among others, as a participant in the Whitney Biennial. It was also a year in which the artist executed arguably some of his best paintings, including *Notary*, *Horn Players*, and *Hollywood Africans*. He also began spending months at a time in L.A. in order to paint without the pressures of the New York art world, a practice that Basquiat would continue for the rest of his life.

In many ways 1983 was the beginning of the 1980s as it later became defined. Though Basquiat had moved on from graffiti[3]—in 1980 his collaboration with Al Diaz, tagging New York City streets as SAMO©, had come to an end—1983 was the year that announced graffiti's official entry into the mainstream: *Wild Style*, Charlie Ahearn's popular film about New York graffiti and hip-hop artists, was widely released early that year. Graffiti artists such as Zephyr and Futura 2000, now represented by art dealers, could expect their works to sell for as much as $1,000 to $4,000—upward of $10,000 in today's market.[4]

Larry Kramer published his essay "1,112 and Counting," warning of the epidemic potential of AIDS and its disproportionate impact upon gay men. Nationally, the American economy slowly began to find its footing after the off-and-on recessions of 1977 through 1982, freeing up capital that would pour into SoHo art galleries through the decade. Nineteen eighty-three was also the year that Basquiat and Andy Warhol began a more organic socialization, a fact reflected in the increased mentions of Basquiat in Warhol's journals that year. Though the pair were introduced years before when Basquiat sold Xeroxed postcards in SoHo, it was Keith Haring's close friendship with Basquiat and Warhol that offered the two artists more meaningful and chance encounters to build an actual rapport. The deepening friendship would prove to be an important relationship for both artists, personally and professionally.

It was also the year that Michael Stewart, a thin, quiet, twenty-five-year-old, African American aspiring artist from Clinton Hill, Brooklyn, leased his first art studio in the Anderson Theatre, at 66 Second Avenue. According to Patrick Fox, the building's then-proprietor: "We shook hands on it, like, 'Can you do $25? Okay, great.'"[5] It was that second-floor studio that Stewart left on the night of September 14. "It was around nine o'clock, 9:30 or so. . . . I remember he was upset and slammed that gate, which was unusual for him, and then he didn't say goodbye," recalled Fox in an October 2018 interview with the author.[6] Stewart's subsequent path through the East Village and the Lower East Side can be roughly pieced together from the accounts of several other friends and acquaintances he encountered that night. He left a friend at the East Village bar Lucky Strike at around 12:30 a.m. "I remember saying to him, like I always did, 'Hey man, be careful,' and he nodded and left," recalled the friend.[7] At some point, Stewart also met up with the artist George Condo and another friend, nicknamed Haitian Freddy, and dropped by Haring's Broome Street loft for a party.[8] Refused at the door, they then made their way to the Pyramid Club, on Avenue A, where Condo recalls seeing Basquiat hanging out in front of the club. Patricia Pesce, a recent acquaintance of Stewart's, joined him at the Pyramid following her shift at a restaurant uptown, The Noodle.[9] The two continued talking outside the club and ambled through the East Village, with Stewart showing Pesce his new design for a T-shirt he was making and talking excitedly about an art show he was going to have. They then got into a cab heading uptown, which stopped at the southeast corner of Fourteenth Street and First Avenue so that Stewart could take the L train back to Brooklyn.

PLATE 1

Jean-Michel Basquiat

The Death of Michael Stewart, 1983
Acrylic and marker on plasterboard
25 × 30½ inches (63.5 × 77.5 cm);
34 × 40 inches (86.4 × 101.6 cm) framed
Collection of Nina Clemente, New York

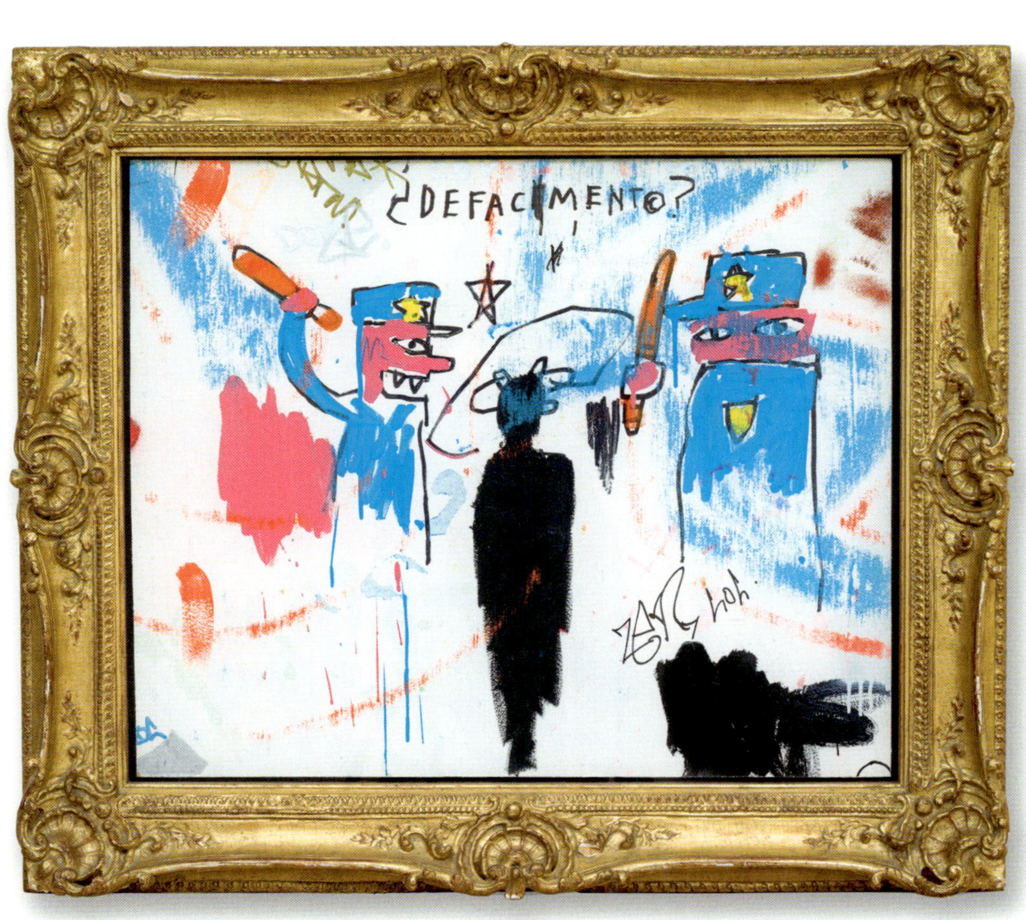
¿DEFACIMENTO?

According to Pesce, it was around 2 a.m. when Stewart kissed her on the cheek and descended the stairs of the subway station.[10]

What happened next, in the early morning of September 15, 1983, remains officially unsettled thirty-six years later. According to the 1984 grand jury testimony of John Kostick, the transit police officer who first encountered Stewart in the subway station, Stewart was caught tagging the wall of the Brooklyn-bound platform with a marker at around 2:30 a.m.; Stewart surrendered without resistance, saying, "Hey, man, you got me";[11] but while being led out of the station in handcuffs, he attempted to run and fell face-forward on the ground at the top of the subway stairway.[12] Testimony from a station token clerk, Robert LeBright, seemed to challenge Kostick's allegation that Stewart attempted to flee.[13] Another witness, a former auxiliary police officer named Robert Rodriguez, who was across the street from the station entrance when Stewart was arrested, testified that he saw Stewart thrown to the ground by officers outside the station, while handcuffed, and then saw an officer kick Stewart, whose body then "ricocheted."[14] Kostick described restraining Stewart with a nightstick after his attempted escape but maintained that he and the other arresting officers had neither beaten nor abused Stewart; however, Kostick alleged that Stewart became "very violent" in the van that was used to transport him from First Avenue to the Union Square Transit Police station, where he again attempted to run, shouting, "Help me, help me."[15] Rebecca Reiss, a college student living in nearby dorms, testified to hearing Stewart's screams and witnessing a flurry of kicking and punching directed by a group of officers toward Stewart's prone body on the sidewalk. Reiss then watched a "silent" and hog-tied Stewart being picked up and "thrown into a van."[16] Stewart arrived at Bellevue Hospital at around 3:00 a.m., comatose. His mother, Carrie Stewart, recalled arriving later that morning to find her unconscious son handcuffed to his hospital bed, with a police guard posted outside the room.[17] Michael Stewart never regained consciousness; he died two weeks later, on September 28, 1983.

By all accounts, the news of what happened to Stewart spread quickly through the artistic community of the East Village, which was politically activated by the apparent injustice of his death.[18] In the weeks following Stewart's assault, there were at least two events organized in his name by Haoui Montaug, a well-known club doorman and nightlife fixture: a protest at Union Square on September 26 and a benefit concert at the club Danceteria on October 3, with

Madonna and David Wojnarowicz's band, 3 Teens Kill 4, as headliners. Wojnarowicz created a poster for the Union Square protest that rallied members of the downtown community politically, but also artistically **[P. 135, FIG. 18]**.[19] Artist Eric Drooker recalled seeing the yellow poster taped "all over" downtown and in turn was inspired to create his own works in response to what happened to Michael Stewart.[20] Basquiat also must have seen Wojnarowicz's work, as the composition of *Defacement*, executed afterward, is nearly identical to the yellow poster. Those who knew Stewart were deeply skeptical of the official police account of his arrest being reported—that Stewart was writing graffiti and then became violent with officers. Many who were part of the graffiti scene contend that Stewart, though an East Village regular, was not part of their milieu. Kenny Scharf, who was then an active graffiti artist and close friend of Basquiat and Haring, recalled of Stewart: "He was a very quiet, sweet guy. I don't remember him ever tagging with us, or talking about it."[21] About the police's claim, Haring was also doubtful: "I found [it] very hard to believe. . . . He was an artist, but wasn't known at all as a graffiti artist."[22] A conviction among many of Stewart's friends, and later the Stewart family lawyers, was that Kostick was allegedly triggered by the sight of Michael Stewart kissing a white woman. Pesce has maintained that it was an innocuous kiss on the cheek, and that they were just friends and hadn't known each other for very long.[23]

Exactly when Basquiat discovered Stewart's fate is unclear. The Stewart tragedy seems to have immediately resonated with Basquiat and registered in his art. Haring later said in an interview that on the night of September 28, when Stewart succumbed to his injuries, Basquiat painted red and black skulls; "He was completely freaked out. It was like it could have been him. It showed how vulnerable he was."[24] But it seems unlikely that most of the downtown art community would have been aware of Stewart's death on the 28th, as the Stewart family lawyers, who were tasked with communicating such news to the larger world at the behest of the family, chose to disseminate via news outlets, outside of their tight inner-circle. Others in the scene, including curator and writer Diego Cortez, recalled learning about Stewart's death the next day, on the news.[25] It is most probable that Basquiat painted *Defacement (The Death of Michael Stewart)* on the wall of Haring's studio in the Cable Building at some point in the following days, between September 29, the day after Haring returned to New York from Brazil, and October 5, when Basquiat and Warhol left for a two-week trip in Europe together (later to be joined by Haring).[26]

The pall cast by Stewart's death seems to have lingered on their trip abroad. Warhol wrote in his diary that while he, Haring, and Basquiat were in Milan, Basquiat was visibly upset, though Warhol doesn't explain why.[27] Warhol and Haring would both go on to create works inspired by Stewart: Warhol with a series of three screenprints based on a contemporary newspaper, including *Daily News (Gimbels Anniversary Sale)* (ca. 1983) **[PL. 2]**, and Haring, more explicitly, with the large-scale mural *Michael Stewart—USA for Africa* (1985) **[PP. 70–71, PL. 13]**. *Defacement* remains Basquiat's only artistic statement on Stewart; however, his identification with Stewart continued. Numerous friends recall how, for the rest of the artist's life, when discussion of Stewart's death arose, Basquiat would repeat the refrain, "It could have been me."[28]

Defacement measures approximately 2 feet high by 2½ feet wide, roughly the size of the *Mona Lisa* turned on its side. Its final dimensions, however, were only determined in 1985, when Haring was moving out of his Cable Building studio and cut out the portion of drywall on which Basquiat had created the work. According to Sam Havadtoy, Haring's friend and an interior designer at the time, the ornate gilded frame that today encases the painting was added in the spring or summer of 1989, and was chosen by Havadtoy based on Haring's desire to create a space that was aesthetically inspired by the Ritz Hotel in Paris.[29] Basquiat would not have seen the frame; this was nearly a year after his death in August 1988. In the summer of 1989, Haring hung his friend's framed painting on the wall above his bed at his Greenwich Village apartment, where he lived until his death from AIDS-related causes in February 1990 **[FIG. 1]**.

Michael Stewart, represented as a largely undefined black figure, is central to *Defacement* in terms of composition, narrative, and meaning, for every action and potential signification splays from his body. The outstretched arms of the policemen, who are depicted as wolf-pig hybrids, with fanglike teeth and pink flesh, are extended in violence against the figure's exaggerated inertia; he has no arms for defense nor feet for escape, instead appearing immobile, fixed in space. The scene can be read as Basquiat's encapsulation of a police-state dynamic, with the officers exercising an extreme and unbalanced power in their total control over Stewart, who is defined by a reciprocal lack of agency and the impossibility of determining an alternative outcome. "¿DEFACEMENT©?" occupies the topmost portion of the painting, bookended by

PLATE 2
Andy Warhol
Daily News (Gimbels Anniversary Sale), ca. 1983
Synthetic polymer paint on canvas
24 × 16 inches (61 × 40.8 cm)
Collection of Allison Marvin and Emily Moyer, courtesy Gary and Jean Cohen

Daily News, Wednesday, October 19, 1983

Pet wolf flees pen and kills owner's child

[illegible]

Artist could have been choked: doc

[illegible]

...[illegible] had sustained a force like that of "a choke hold." A final report on the autopsy could come in about 30 days, Wolf said. Gross' office had no immediate comment on the latest tests.

Brandt joins nuke protest

Bonn (Combined Dispatches)—Nobel Peace Prize laureate Willy Brandt will join the tens of thousands of people protesting the planned deployment of United States in Western Europe, officials of the peace movement said yesterday.

The announcement on the former chancellor of West Germany came as thousands of antinuclear protesters, pelted by rain, demonstrated anew across West Germany in the sixth day of a 10-day protest against the missiles.

In New York, nuclear disarmament activists announced plans for more than 130 marches and rallies and at least a dozen demonstrations involving [illegible] civil disobedience around the United States this weekend to protest the missile deployment.

question marks in the style of Spanish punctuation. Embedded within this construction is Basquiat's customary copyright symbol, which the artist deployed across his work as an assertion of his own artistic authority, hegemonic capitalism, and his fascination with the machinations of both at play simultaneously. Hanging over *Defacement*'s grim scene, the copyright symbol takes on a darker authority, acting as an imprimatur of the state's assumed right to deface black bodies with impunity. The corporeal defacement is a historical legacy and an institutional American rite of passage reenacted to the present day, a connection visually made and married in *Defacement* through Basquiat's copyright, and the invocation of Emory Douglas's police-as-pigs iconography made famous in the *Black Panther Newspaper*'s protests against police brutality in the late 1960s and '70s. The central figure's lack of individuating characteristics brings Basquiat's identification with Stewart home; it could have been any black man in the wrong place, at the wrong time, which, to the appropriated copyright symbol's point, is at *any* time in America.

While *Defacement* represents Basquiat's most personal engagement with state violence, the artist produced works on the subject throughout his career. An argument could be made that his paintings dealing specifically with police brutality represent a distinct body of work within his larger oeuvre. Among them are such early paintings as *Irony of a Negro Policeman*, *La Hara*, *Untitled (Sheriff)* **[PP. 61–64, PLS. 10, 11, 12]**, and *Untitled (Loans)*, all from 1981. There is also *Untitled* **[PL. 3]**, which Basquiat created in 1987, possibly in response to the August 1987 death of the young Brazilian actor Fernando Ramos da Silva at the hands of police in São Paulo.[30] *Irony of a Negro Policeman* and *La Hara*, in particular, can be read as manifestations of an excruciating imperative felt by the artist to bear witness and acknowledge his own state-instigated trauma. *La Hara* and *Irony* present law enforcement figures that promise via color, composition, and rage a fatal promise that is ultimately fulfilled in *Defacement*. The menacing hostility and escalating immediacy of all three works, coupled with their depictions or insinuations of racialized police engagement, constitute a trilogy of paintings that dialogue in an emotionally sequential and prophetic narrative that exists uniquely within Basquiat's oeuvre-within-an-oeuvre of police works.[31]

Irony of a Negro Policeman depicts a black man as a police officer, which the artist considers an irony and a betrayal. The adjacency is manifestly toxic and a betrayal of racial solidarity; the white paint that unevenly bifurcates the figure suggests that police contact prevents

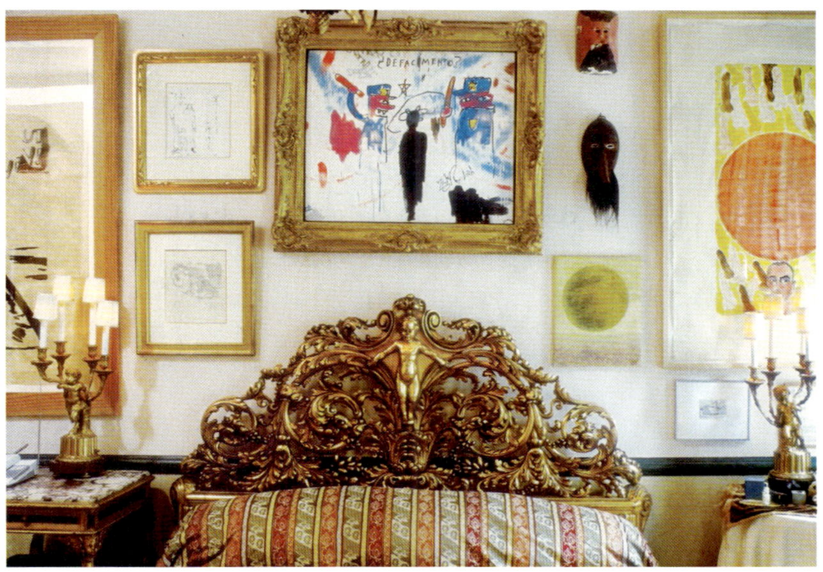

FIGURE 1
Keith Haring's bedroom with *The Death of Michael Stewart*, Greenwich Village, New York, 1989

a lack of proper integration of a whole coherent (black) self. The racial identity of *La Hara*'s figure is underscored by the work's title, a phonetic mispelling of the Nuyorican slang *la jara*, meaning *police*, which is a pun on *O'Hara*, the English language slang with the same meaning that referenced the Irish heritage of many in the police force in the 1970s. Thus "LA HARA" announces a portrait of white-induced terror as seen from and defined by Basquiat's own Afro-Latino perspective, which was undoubtedly informed by what he witnessed and heard of the predominantly white law enforcement while growing up in New York City. The blood-red eyes of the figure in *La Hara* suggest an unstable mental state and an atmosphere of dilating violence, as the color excesses upon the surrounding areas of the canvas. The anger of the figure is uncontained; he is not only red with anger he has gone *rogue*. Basquiat maintains his suspicion and belief that unchecked power corrupts absolutely. Aside from *Defacement*'s uncharacteristic visual economy, the painting's lack of heroism, or of majesty, represents the most striking break from Basquiat's established means of handling personified blackness and black histories. In a 1983 interview with Henry Geldzahler for *Interview* magazine, Basquiat said that "royalty, heroism, and the streets" were his favorite subjects.[32] They are also themes that are fundamentally concerned with power, dominance, and control. The crown is Basquiat's ultimate symbol of majesty, which he deploys to ennoble an assortment of

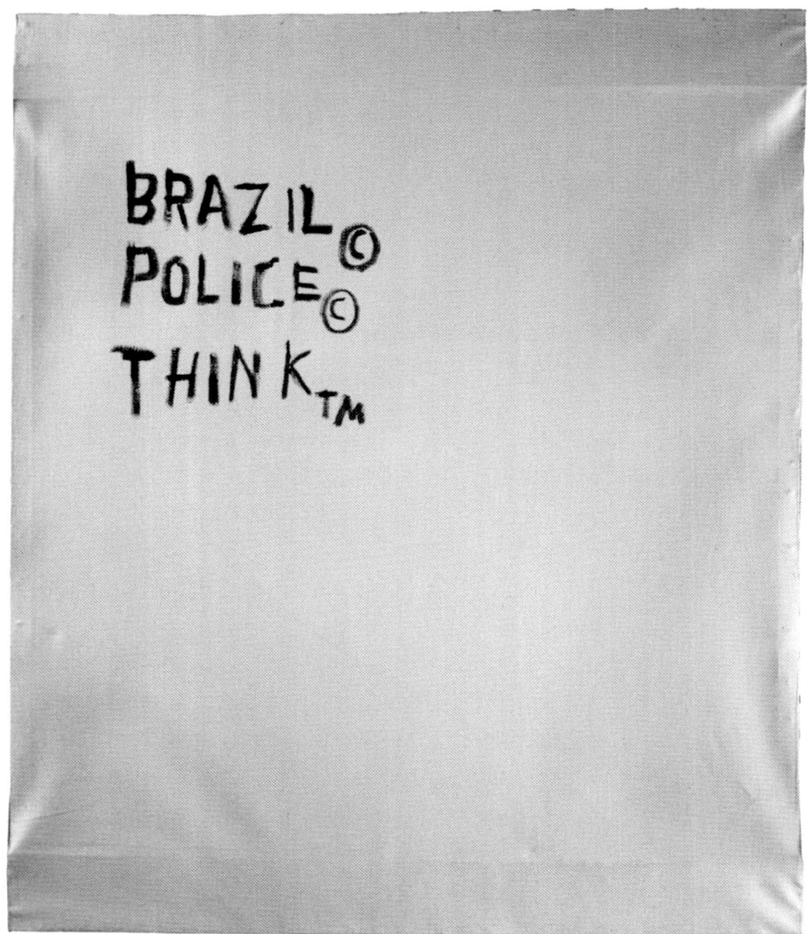

PLATE 3
Jean-Michel Basquiat
Untitled, 1987
Acrylic and oil stick on canvas
47 × 41 inches (119.4 × 104.1 cm)
Collection of Andrew L. Terner,
New York, São Paulo

black male heroes, most often artists and athletes, a symbol of and tribute to the power that the artist so admired them for.

A central strategy Basquiat used to examine the tragic and traumatic chapters of African diasporic histories was a practice that might be called "the exit routes of majesty," in which exaltation of the noble, exceptional, and progressive achievements and histories in the collective body of experiences of a people serves as a means of examining trauma that is so visceral for the participant that a protective gesture is required. To quote art historian Huey Copeland in his writings about the artist Glenn Ligon's work *I Feel Most Colored When I Am Thrown Against a Sharp White Background* (1990–91), majesty takes on the role of the "apotropaic double, a surrogate self that could speak of and for him in a voice not his own."[33]

Across his work Basquiat almost obsessively depicts black achievers and their achievements, and the "high-brow" (white-validated, situationally exotic) aspects of diasporic culture: African American jazz musicians, the African roots of Cubism, particularly in Picasso's work, and the "Black-Atlantic"[34] and continental African gods and religious iconography are themes that Basquiat focused on as he navigated through an art world that has been described as "white wine, white walls, and white people."[35] The black heroes that Basquiat chose as his primary subjects may have eased some of the isolation that the artist must have felt, but his selection also signaled that his mores and tastes were not all that different from those of the art world's gatekeepers. Basquiat's heroes were resolutely rich in social capital, accrued by talent and cemented by fame. The words in Italian and Spanish scattered across Basquiat's canvases suggest trilingualism, but the usages never extend beyond simple yet suggestive phrasing. This linguistic indetermination allowed Basquiat to be anything to anyone and, most crucially, for legend making, to be projected upon. What Basquiat gained from this, and this he knew well, was access to European tastes that, coupled with his own African diasporic core of experience, confounded the most eager attempts to categorize him, especially as a "black artist."

"Black people are never really portrayed realistically. They're not even portrayed in modern art," Basquiat once observed.[36] Using majesty was a means of challenging historical tropes and contemporary stereotypes that flattened black people and rendered them invisible. His majesty is principally about ideals, aspirations, upward social mobility,

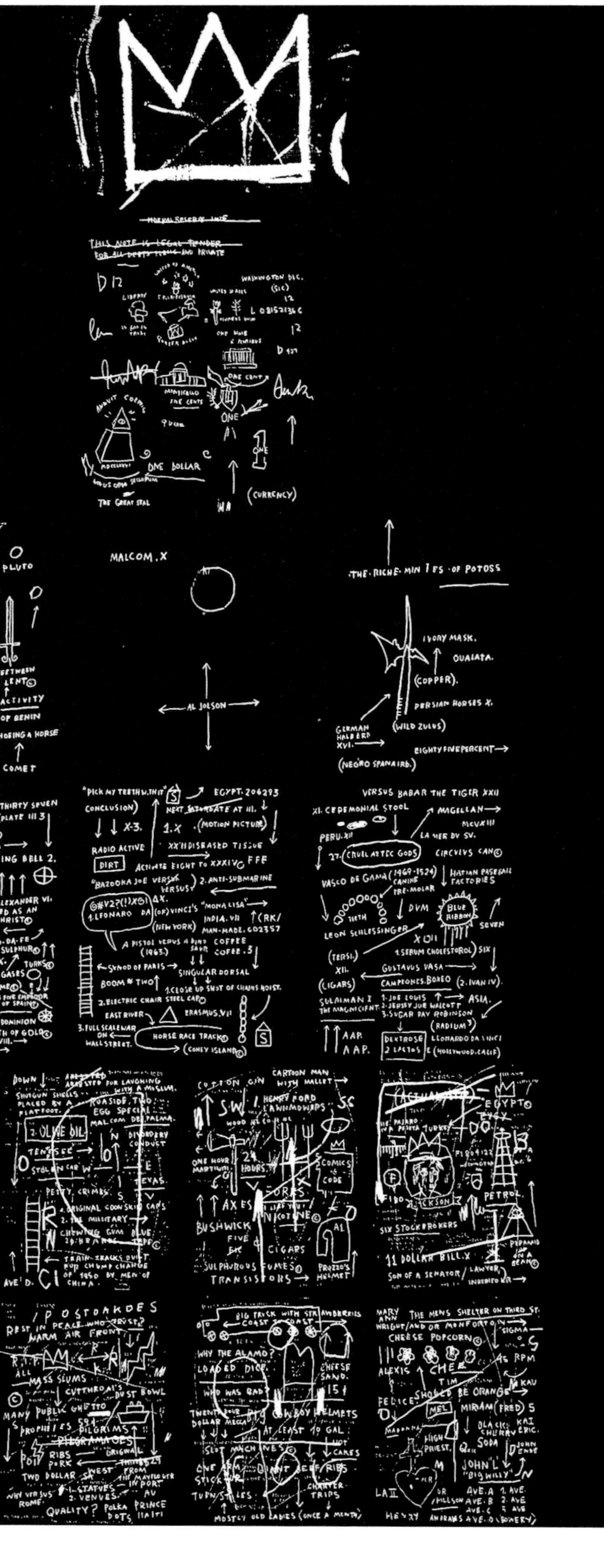

THIS NOTE IS LEGAL TENDER
ONE DOLLAR
(CURRENCY)
THE GREAT SEAL
MALCOM. X
55 LIBERTY©
PLUTO
ROCKET SHIP©
THE BATTLE BETWEEN CARNIVAL AND LENT©
12. DUTCH ACTIVITY
X. TUNISIA
6. BRONZE HEAD OF BENIN
1. ABDUL THE GREAT SHOEING A HORSE
EROK
COMET
AL JOLSON
THE RICHE MINES OF POTOSS
IVORY MASK.
OUALATA.
(COPPER).
PERSIAN HORSES X.
GERMAN HALBERD XVI.
(WILD ZULUS)
EIGHTY FIVE PERCENT
(NEGRO SPANAIRD.)
(FOSSILS)
20. THIRTY SEVEN
EGO SVM PAPA©
DIVING BELL 2.
POPE ALEXANDER VI. DEPICTED AS AN ANTI-CHRIST©
1. A DRUNK
2. A LIAR©
UNINHABITED BY WHITE MEN©
EMERALD CROSS
AUTO-DA-FE
SULPHUR©
VENUS INLAY
TURKS©
NATURAL GASES
SACK OF THE GOTHS (ROME©)
(SEAMONSTER)
HABSBURG DOMINION
CLOTH OF GOLD©
HENRY VIII.
JUNE 1520
LOUIS XII
EGYPT. 206293
CONCLUSION
NEXT SATURDATE AT III.
(MOTION PICTURE)
RADIO ACTIVE
XX III DISEASED TISSUE
DIRT
ACTIVATE EIGHT TO XXXIV© FFE
"BAZOOKA JOE" VERSUS
2. ANTI-SUBMARINE
1. LEONARDO DA (OP) VINCI'S "MONA LISA"
(NEW YORK)
INDIA. VII
A PISTOL VERSUS A DINGO
COFFEE
SYNOD OF PARIS
SINGULAR DORSAL
2. ELECTRIC CHAIR STEEL CAP©
EAST RIVER
ERASMUS. VII
HORSE RACE TRACK©
(CONEY ISLAND©)
WALL STREET.
VERSUS BABAR THE TIGER XXII
XI. CEREMONIAL STOOL
MAGELLAN
PERU. XII
(CRUEL AZTEC GODS)
CIRCVIVS CAN©
VASCO DE GAMA (1469-1524)
CANINE PRE-MOLAR
HAITIAN BASEBALL FACTORIES
BLUE RIBBON
SEVEN
LEON SCHLESSINGER
1. SERUM CHOLESTOROL
SIX
GUSTAVUS VASA
(CIGARS)
CAMPEONES. BOXEO
(2. IVAN IV)
SULAIMAN I THE MAGNIFICENT.
1. JOE LOUIS
2. JERSEY JOE WALCOTT
3. SUGAR RAY ROBINSON
ASIA.
(RADIUM)
DEXTROSE
2 LACTOS
LEONARDO DA VINCI
(HOLLYWOOD, CALIF)
NO SUMMER HOT WATER OSSINING
JOHN
ABUELITA
ABUELA
WOODY
JOHNNY
MARTHA
RUBEN JUNIOR JR.
JOSIEY
MATILDAE
JOSIE
JOSEY
MICHEL
TERESA
GERARD
TIME IN THE SERVICE
JERRY BARRIL
GIN
CASSIUS
JEANINE
AN "A" STUDENT.
ARRESTED FOR LAUGHING WITH A MUSLIM.
SHOTGUN SHELLS PLACED BY A FLATFOOT.
ROADSIDE, TWO EGG SPECIAL
MALCOM DE PALMA.
DISORDERLY CONDUCT
TENSEE
STOLEN CAR
TEXAS.
PETTY CRIMES
ORIGINAL COON SKIN CAPS
MILITARY
CHEWING GUM
TRAIN TRACKS BUILT
FOR CHUMP CHANGE OF 1850 BY MEN OF CHINA.
AVE D.
COTTON GIN
CARTOON MAN WITH MALLET
HENRY FORD
LAWNMOWERS
24 HOURS
COMICS CODE
BUSHWICK
CIGARS
SULPHUROUS FUMES
PROZZO'S HELMET
TRANSISTORS
EGYPT
PETROL
SIX STOCKBROKERS
11 DOLLAR BILL.X
SON OF A SENATOR
LAWYER
PYRAMID
PLAID PLAID PLAID PLAID PLA
PLAID PLAID PLAID PLAID PLAID
PLAIDXPLAID
INFESTED
WESTERN DIET OF SETTLERS IN MOVIES WAS BEANS, MOSTLY LARD
LARD
TRAIN TRACKS BUILT BY MEN OF CHINA FOR CHUMP CHANGE OF 1850
FIVE CENT
TWO CENT
POSTCARDS
REST IN PEACE
WARM AIR FRONT
MASS SLUMS
CUTTHROATS
DUST BOWL
MANY PUBLIC
PROPHETIES
PILGRIMS
RIBS
PORK
TWO DOLLAR
1. STATUES
2. VENUES
ROME.
QUALITY?
POLKA DOTS
PRINCE
HAITI
BIG TRUCK WITH STRAWBERRIES
COAST TO COAST
WHY THE ALAMO?
LOADED DICE
CHEESE SAND.
WHO WAS RAD
TWENTY DOLLAR MECCA
COWBOY HELMETS
AT LEAST 10 GAL
CAKES
ONE ARM
CHARTER TRIPS
TURNSTILES
MOSTLY OLD LADIES (ONCE A MONTH)
THE MENS SHELTER ON THIRD ST.
CHEESE POPCORN
SIGMA
ALEXIS
RPM
CHE
TIM
SHOULD BE ORANGE
FELICE
MEL
MIRAM (FRED)
HIGH PRIEST.
BLACK CHERRY
SODA
JOHN L "BIG WILLY"
LA II
AVE. A
AVE. B
AVE. C
AVE. D (BOWERY)
1. AVE
2. AVE
3. AVE
HENRY

and the highest realization of imagination—*Tuxedo* (1982–83) **[PL. 4]**, as one example, presents a silhouetted, obelisk-like figure comprised of blocks of diagrammatic text resplendent with figures and moments that represent great innovation to the artist: Malcolm X, the Empire State Building, a rocket ship, the American dollar, and copper. *Tuxedo* is a soaring monument to this externalization of majesty, but it also has inherent performative elements. We know nothing about where Basquiat goes for his peace, or where he could possibly begin to look for it. As such, *Back of the Neck* (1983) **[PL. 5]**, similarly silhouetted, acts as the extreme end of *Tuxedo*, the violence and fatalism which along with majesty and (selective) optimism are anchoring themes of much of Basquiat's work. It is also worth mentioning the prophetic quality of this work; the parts of anatomy highlighted in *Back of the Neck* also correspond with Michael Stewart's fatal injuries, despite the fact that the work was executed in February or March of 1983, months before his death.[37]

Paintings that champion historical figures, such as *Charles the First* (1982) **[PL. 6]**, *Horn Players* (1983), and *Toussaint L'Overture versus Savonarola* (1983), send a strong message in their presentation of a black cultural aristocracy and Basquiat's implicit self-alignment with that tradition. In *Charles the First*, Basquiat elevates jazz musician Charlie Parker to the stature of a king, a god, and a superhero, casting him as a peer of the Stuart King Charles I;[38] Thor, the Norse god of thunder;[39] and Superman. Basquiat appropriates and leverages the Superman family crest of the noble El family for Parker, making it clear that every figure referenced in the canvas was not only royalty but dynastic in his heritage and influence.[40] As art historian Jordana Moore Saggese points out, "CHEROKEE," which appears in the upper right-hand corner of the painting, refers to the popular jazz standard from 1938, "the chords of which Parker turned into a regular set of riffs that recur in his improvisation."[41] "Cherokee" is the beginning of Parker's dynastic influence over American popular music; recorded in 1945, Parker's "Ko-Ko" is a contrafact work, based on the chord progressions of "Cherokee," and built upon Parker's mastery of improvisation, swing standards, blues, and sonic total recall. It was also the first recording in which Parker was a band leader and boasted dynastic talent in its musician line-up: "Ko-Ko" was to include a nineteen-year-old Miles Davis on trumpet, who was replaced by Dizzy Gillespie, and the drummer Max Roach, another favorite jazz subject of Basquiat's.

PLATE 4
Jean-Michel Basquiat
Tuxedo, 1982–83
Screenprint on canvas
102 1/4 × 60 inches (259.7 × 152.4 cm)
Edition of 10
Van de Weghe, New York

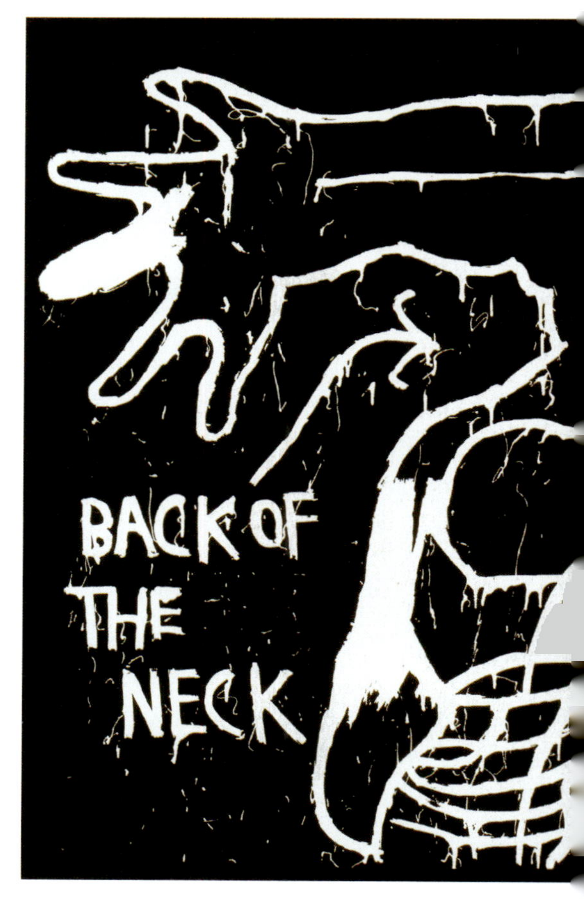

PLATE 5

Jean-Michel Basquiat

Back of the Neck, 1983

Screenprint with hand-coloring on paper

50¼ × 102 inches (127.6 × 259.1 cm)

Edition 1/24

Brooklyn Museum, Charles Stewart Smith Memorial Fund

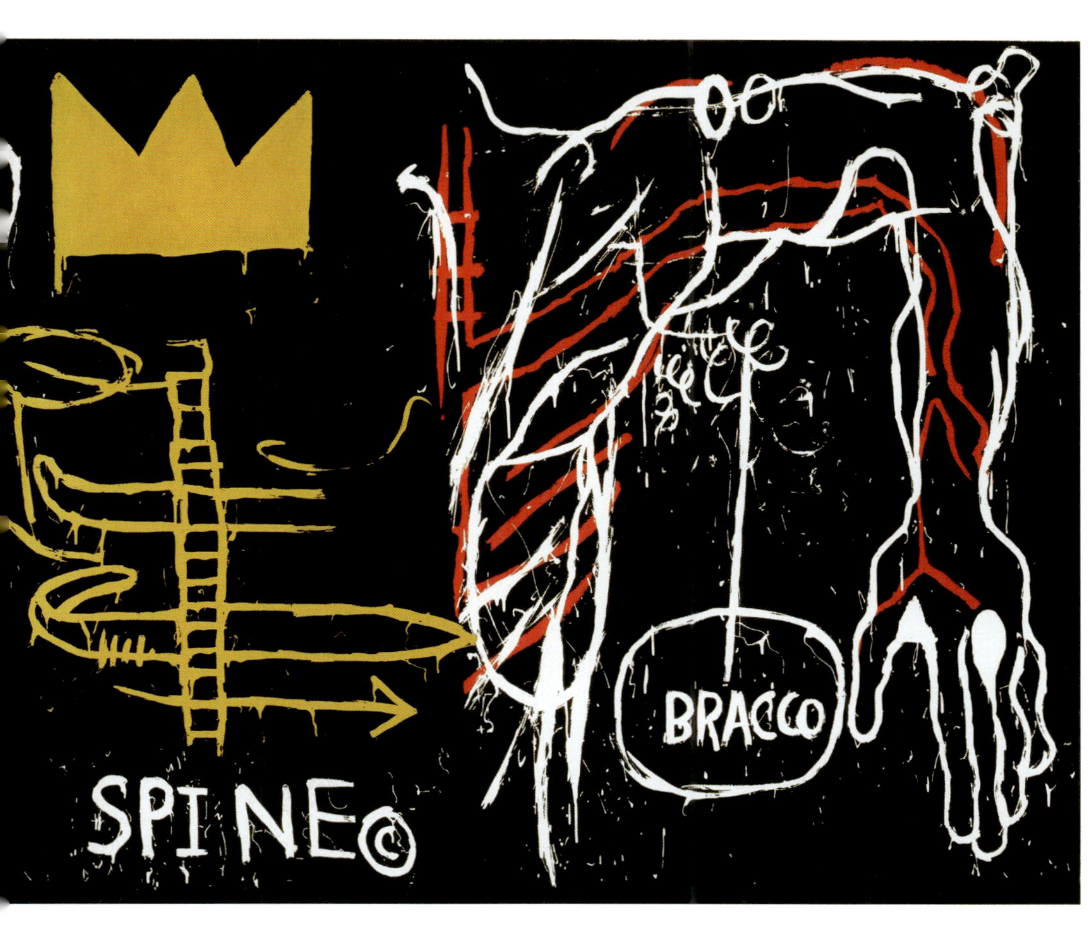

SPINE©
BRACCO

"Ko-Ko" vis-à-vis "Cherokee" marks the demarcation between swing and bebop, which would become influential in the creation of pop music. As such, many jazz scholars and historians in writing about Parker's "Ko-Ko" assert that it is a seminal record.[42] By including "Cherokee," Basquiat distills Parker's monumental genius and places it in historical context for his audience, referencing Parker's kingly role in jazz, popular music, and American culture at large. The 1982 painting *CPRKR* **[PL. 7]** serves as a companion piece to *Charles the First*, again underscoring Basquiat's reverence for Parker. The work is mostly preoccupied with Parker's death and sainthood, but kinghood takes on an anchoring importance via empire: "CPRKR" recalls the ancient Roman emblem for its empire, SPQR. The words "CHARLES THE FIRST" are written below a set of lines and a cross, and below that Basquiat reiterates Parker's place, lineage, and imperial connection by writing the Roman numeral *I* under "FIRST."

The personal life of the maestro musician was famously turbulent and short, and the tragedy of Parker's life abounds in *Charles the First*: the partly obscured name "PREE," above "1951–53" and a black cross, in reference to his daughter, whose death at age two was thought to have hastened Parker's own; the cut-off hands that represent the void left in the music world by Parker's death at thirty-four; and Basquiat's warning, "MOST YOUNG KINGS GET THIER HEAD CUT OFF." Multiple cross-outs populate the canvas, creating a precarious sense of unease. This is balanced by the elements of majesty that Basquiat overlays, which offer both a reminder and a reprieve from the doomed destiny that the artist feels is promised for black genius. For Basquiat, majesty is employed as both a narrative device and a "protective shield" that is meant "to [preserve] the vulnerable underlying layers by absorbing the chief intensity of the energy that assaults the organism."[43] Though the appearance of the word "HALOES" in the upper left-hand corner suggests that while Charlie Parker was also a saint in Basquiat's canon, kinghood and its attendant charms and burdens resolutely takes precedence in *Charles the First*.

In *Defacement*, Michael Stewart's head, too, bears a halo of sorts, but one that offers no exit route. The suggestion of raised bruises (which Stewart suffered all over his body) draws the artist and the viewer closer to the event. The minimalism of *Defacement*'s composition parallels the raw nature of the material object itself: executed on drywall, without priming; unlike many of his works, not painted over or under; and subsequently cut out of the wall. Rawness in and of itself

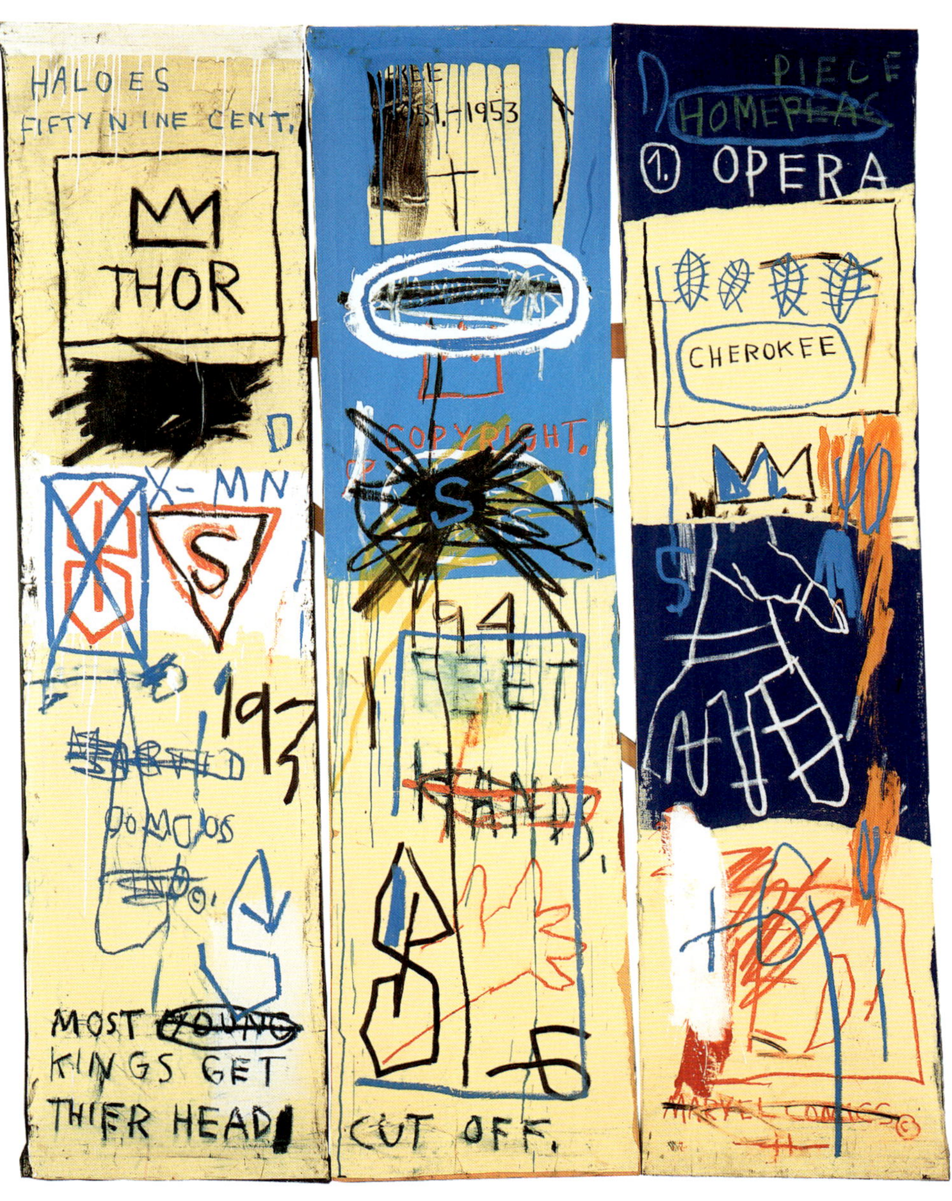

PLATE 6

Jean-Michel Basquiat

Charles the First, 1982

Acrylic and oil stick on canvas, three panels

78 × 65 inches (198.1 × 165.1 cm) overall

Estate of Jean-Michel Basquiat

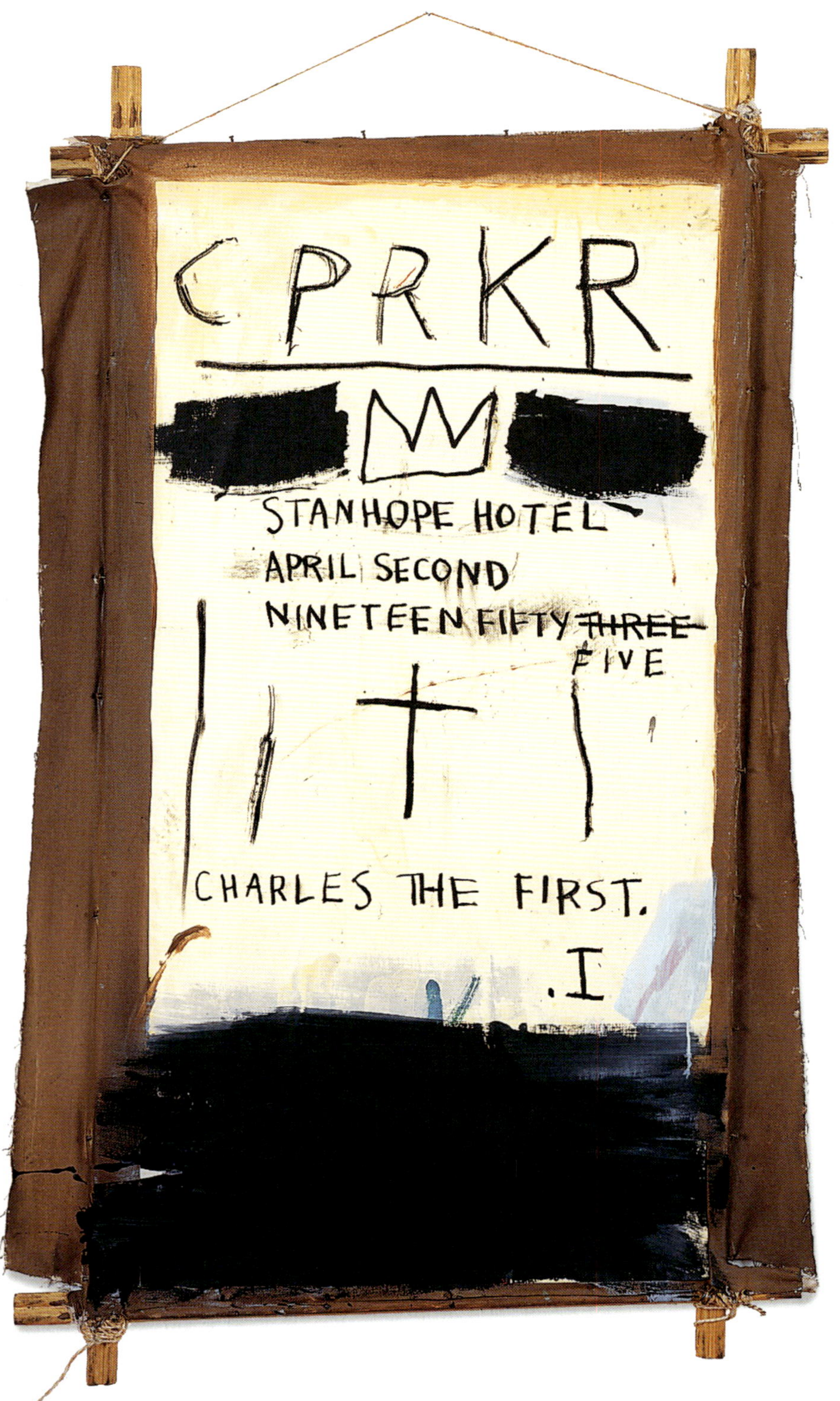
CPRKR
STANHOPE HOTEL
APRIL SECOND
NINETEEN FIFTY THREE
FIVE
CHARLES THE FIRST.
.I

does not necessarily connote a lack of majesty in Basquiat's oeuvre; *CPRKR*, *St. Joe Louis Surrounded by Snakes* (1982), and *Sugar Ray Robinson* (1982) are all works that explore majesty while also employing material roughness as an aesthetic.[44] They become majestic through their compositions and their visions of achievement. In *Defacement*, however, neither the painting's materiality nor its depiction of Stewart's blackness conveys majesty, and its gilded frame, added posthumously, becomes a bitter irony. *Defacement*'s material urgency is a complement to the unfiltered, devastated stream of consciousness that Basquiat allowed himself to record on canvas.

While Basquiat's strategy of majesty may have in effect provided entrée into the art galleries, it seems to have done little for his inner peace. In the same 1983 interview by Henry Geldzahler noted earlier, Basquiat announced that his work was 80 percent anger,[45] and in 1985 he confirmed it as an ongoing and primary source of his work.[46] What was he so angry about? Basquiat never said much, not on the record, anyway. When asked by his interviewer in 1985, "What are you angry about?" Basquiat declines to answer. He refused to answer—"I don't remember"—with a coy smile. It seems one part protective, one part middle finger, and a mischievous yet clear refusal from Basquiat to do the exhausting, deleterious emotional and psychic labor of *explaining*. Explaining to an audience—in this case, the interviewer and presumably his viewers—the multitudes, minutiae, and millennia of blackness that the said audience, historically speaking, seemed to only see—if not understand—via economic exploitation, consumption, or riots. In short, through the very lens of violence that Basquiat ran to, and from, in his work. To appropriately answer the question, Basquiat would have had to first explain to the interviewer just exactly who *he* is. To an unknowing audience Basquiat seems difficult. To the audience that knows the deck of cards and the score, it is understood. The access into his intimate interior was unwelcomed, as that space was for him, and him alone. It is why *Defacement* remains a multitasking outlier, a diary and forensic evidence, and a necessary yet voyeuristic look into Basquiat's peace and his terrordome. We don't actually know if Basquiat or Haring were still here, if we'd have ever been welcome into it. Fittingly, what Basquiat was really thinking is all hearsay, secondary sources, and posthumous psychoanalysis at this point. The artist's experience of quotidian life, whether in the largely white art world or the black and multiracial world of his Brooklyn origins, is rarely

PLATE 7
Jean-Michel Basquiat
CPRKR, 1982
Acrylic, oil stick, and paper collage on canvas, mounted on tied-wood support
60 × 40 inches (152.4 × 101.6 cm)
Private collection

documented or explored on canvas. Their themes, yes, their histories, without question—he packed the history of five thousand years of art into roughly two thousand works—but not the mundane and unremarkable intimacies that make a life—he took that with him. Or perhaps *Defacement* is what Basquiat thinks of the quotidian, unremarkable life—life between the contrastive worlds that he straddled, life beyond the rhetoric of optimistic, de-segregating activism and the apolitical, of spiritually repatriating colonized lands and outlandish, superhuman achievement, and the idea that any modern capitalistic society can move beyond the fatalism of its founding. Which is to say, can any modern society—America in particular—move beyond what it fundamentally is? And if that society doesn't know who they are, who will tell them? Maybe all one can hope for is just to survive, which is more than what Michael Stewart was allowed, Basquiat reminds us. Maybe *Defacement* is what Basquiat thinks about how much anyone invested in white supremacy or the hallucinogen that is the American dream can comprehend of the reality of American life, and what a black man can reasonably expect with regard to his inner peace. Maybe the copyright symbol, a sign of protection, represents the patented lies that we tell ourselves about ourselves—mainly about the inhumanity that defines us. "A liar always knows he is lying," James Baldwin writes, "and that is why liars travel in packs. . . . They have a tacit agreement to guard each other's secrets."[47] The terror of history doesn't keep most of us awake at night, nor does joy cometh in the morning. From behind the gilded frame, it all looks so awfully bleak; and that may just be the point.

NOTES

I'd like to thank a number of people and institutions that were instrumental in the creation and success of my initial research and its first iterations. It has taken fifteen years of research, four specifically on *Defacement*, to reach this moment. Thank you to the Williams College Museum of Art and the people that I worked with closely for our show there: Sonnet Coggins, Lisa Dorin, Nina Pelaez, Brooks Foehl, and Sharifa Wright. Thank you: Joseph A. Hutchinson III, for a beautiful alcove in London; Tom Dunning, for your immeasurable support; Melissa Russell Paige; Kate Robards; Victor Littlejohn; Eric Justin Johnson; the Los Angeles/UCLA crew, C. Samala, Joshua Owens, Lisa Winston-Hicks, the Claytons, the Culbersons; my former Williams professors, Chris Waters, Gretchen Long, Liza Johnson, and Andy Jaffe; Franklin Sirmans and the Hermitage Artist Retreat; my beloved grandmother, Viola, and my parents, for introducing me to Basquiat; the Black family, I. Thompson-Fowler, M. Mims, and to the Taylor-Browns for their steadfast love and support. To Josh Baer: I can't thank you enough. To Janie Cohen, Brynn Hatton, and Magdalyn Asimakis: you were essential to the creation of this essay. To the interviewees who spoke honestly, candidly, and beautifully: our catalogue would not be complete without your voices. Thank you to the collectors who believed in our vision and generously lent their works, and to Michael Warren, Peter Noel, Carlo McCormick, Luc Sante, Jeffrey Deitch, Fab, and the Estate of David Wojnarowicz, for their tremendous support. A heartfelt thank-you to the Basquiat family, the Stewart family, and the Clemente family for their blessing, support, and their trust. Thank you to Nancy Spector for seeing what this could be back in 2017, and to Joan Young for her curatorial guidance. To Marcella Lowery and Andrea Whittington: New York became a home and this could not have happened without you and your sacrifices. And a final thank-you to Clinton Roébexar Allen, who remains my audience of one.

1

Ben Jonson, *The Devil Is an Ass*, act 1, scene 2, line 43.

2

Derek Walcott, "Ruins of a Great House," in *In a Green Night: Poems, 1948–1960* (London: Jonathan Cape, 1962), p. 20.

3

Jean-Michel Basquiat embraced a very expansive practice that included, early on with Al Diaz, tagging the city's streets as SAMO©. In one of his last interviews, he stated, "My work has nothing to do with graffiti. It's painting, it always has been." Démosthènes Davvetas, "Jean-Michel Basquiat," *New Art International* (October–November 1988), pp. 10–15.

4

Michael Small, "When Graffiti Paintings Sell for Thousands, the Art World Sees the Writing on the Wall," *People*, August 22, 1983, https://people.com/archive/when-graffiti-paintings-sell-for-thousands-the-art-world-sees-the-writing-on-the-wall-vol-20-no-8/.

5

Patrick Fox; see p. 115 in this volume.

6

Patrick Fox, interview by author, New York, October 31, 2018.

7

Interview by author, New York, November 5, 2018. The interviewee's name is withheld by request.

8

George Condo; see p. 109 in this volume.

9

Patricia Pesce, interview by author, New York, December 19, 2018.

10

Pesce; see p. 116 in this volume.

11

Kostick, quoted in M. A. Farber, "Officer Swore Police Did Not Abuse Stewart," *New York Times*, September 7, 1985, https://www.nytimes.com/1985/09/07/nyregion/officer-swore-police-did-not-abuse-stewart.html.

12

Farber, "Officer Swore."

13

Jane Gross, "Witness Says Stewart Was Calm After Arrest," *New York Times*, July 26, 1985, https://www.nytimes.com/1985/07/26/nyregion/witness-says-stewart-was-calm-after-arrest.html.

14

Rodriquez, quoted in Marcia Chambers, "Witness Tells Stewart Jury He Saw Assaults by Police," *New York Times*, July 30, 1985, https://www.nytimes.com/1985/07/30/nyregion/witness-tells-stewart-jury-hew-saw-assaults-by-police.html.

15

Kostick, quoted in Farber, "Officer Swore."

16

Reiss, quoted in M. A. Farber, "Student Recalls She Saw Police Beating Stewart," *New York Times*, July 23, 1985, https://www.nytimes.com/1985/07/23/nyregion/student-recalls-she-saw-police-beating-stewart.html.

17

Carrie Stewart; see pp. 152–53 in this volume.

18

See recollections by George Condo, Fred Brathwaite, and Patrick Fox in this volume.

19

Culminating two years of my research to establish the work's authorship, the yellow poster by David Wojnarowicz was officially recognized as a work by the artist in March 2019 by the Wojnarowicz estate, courtesy of PPOW Gallery. The writer and curator Carlo McCormick and his partner, Tessa Hughes-Freeland, recalled being given a copy of the poster by Wojnarowicz. James Romberger, a former gallerist, writer, and coauthor of the artist's comic book *7 Miles a Second*, recalled Wojnarowicz's distress about what happened to Stewart. Another contemporary, identified as

E.G.B., recalled in a January 2019 interview with the author walking into the room as Wojnarowicz finished the original poster, which has not yet been found.

20
Eric Drooker, interview by author, New York, November 3, 2018. See also pp. 131–33 in this volume.

21
Kenny Scharf, interview by author, New York, January 9, 2019.

22
Keith Haring, "The Death of Michael Stewart," in Jeffrey Deitch, Suzanne Geiss, and Julia Gruen, *Keith Haring* (New York: Rizzoli, 2008), p. 352.

23
Pesce; see p. 116 in this volume.

24
Haring, quoted in Anthony Haden-Guest, "Burning Out," *Vanity Fair*, November 1988, https://www.vanityfair.com/news/1988/11/jean-michel-basquiat.

25
Diego Cortez, interview by author, New York, February 2019.

26
Dates verified by author based on Haring's passport, accessed at the Keith Haring Foundation, New York, December 6, 2018.

27
On Thursday, October 6, 1983 in Milan, Warhol writes, "Got home. Jean Michel came by and said he was depressed and was going to kill himself and I laughed and said it was just because he hadn't slept in four days, and then after a while of that he went back to his room." *The Andy Warhol Diaries*, ed. Pat Hackett (New York: Warner Books, 1991), p. 532.

28
See recollections by Fred Brathwaite, George Condo, and Jeffrey Deitch in this volume.

29
Sam Havadtoy, interview by author, New York, December 20, 2018.

30
The death of the actor brought international attention to the issue of police brutality in Brazil, where many killed by the police are disproportionately residents of the favelas and of African descent. Da Silva was best-known for playing the titular role in *Pixote* (1981), a critically acclaimed film that was popular in New York art house cinema circles and among aficionados.

31
My research on the trilogy series was conducted prior to and in conjunction with the exhibition but was not included in the essay. It will appear in a forthcoming publication.

32
Jean-Michel Basquiat, "From the Subways to SoHo," interview by Henry Geldzahler, *Interview*, January 1983, https://www.interviewmagazine.com/art/jean-michel-basquiat-henry-geldzahler.

33
Huey Copeland, "Untitled (Jackpot!)," in *Glenn Ligon—Some Changes*, exh. cat. (Toronto: Power Plant, 2005), p. 124.

34
"Black-Atlantic" is a term coined by Paul Gilroy and first published in his 1993 book, *The Black Atlantic: Modernity and Double Consciousness* (Cambridge, Mass.: Harvard University Press, 1993).

35
Describing the '80s art world, in the 2010 documentary *Radiant Child*, Diego Cortez said, "I was just tired of seeing white walls with white people and white wine, you know?" In 2013 Patti Astor made the same observation: "It was white wine, white walls, white people; the art world was closed off and boring." Patti Astor, interview by Richard J. Goldstein, *Bomb*, February 27, 2013, https://bombmagazine.org/articles/patti-astor.

36
State of the Art: Ideas and Images in the 1980s, "Jean-Michel Basquiat and Andy Warhol," directed by Geoff Dunlop (London: Illuminations Media, 1987), accessed on YouTube, https://www.youtube.com/watch?v=foerFJqupYM.

37
Fred Hoffman, interview by author, Los Angeles, August 2018.

38
King Charles I of England and Scotland was the son of King James VI, Queen Elizabeth's successor. As the son of Mary, Queen of Scots, James VI joined the Scottish and English monarchies under one crown—the union of crowns—which was considered to be a dynastic union. The Union Jack flag was designed in 1606 by order of James, "which bore the combined crosses of St. George and of St. Andrew, patron saints of England and Scotland, respectively.

39
"It is true that Thor is now-a-days thought of merely as the god of thunder, but that he . . . really was a sun god, we gather partly from the fact that he was called upon . . . when famine was threatening,—(it belonged to the sun god to grand a good harvest)." Oscar Montelius, "The Sun-God's Axe and Thor's Hammer," *Folklore* 21, no. 1 (March 1910), p. 74, https://www.jstor.org/stable/1253798. Returning to a classical Indo-European mythology framework, the sun deity is usually regarded as the most powerful god or goddess among deities due to its overriding control of the seasons and fertility, and thus the cycle of all life. It is for this primacy and other metaphors that the eighteenth-century French King, Louis XIV, named himself the Sun King.

40
The themes of family, dynasty, and serialization were woven throughout Superman, on-and-off screen. The *S* was cinematically established as shorthand for the noble House of El dynasty in the 1978 *Superman* movie. Superman's father, Jor-El, played by actor Marlon Brando, appears in the first scene of the movie with a white *S* on his chest. Baby Kal-El appears later in a red, blue, and yellow swaddling blanket, foreshadowing his own donning

of the House of El family insignia, thus continuing the dynastic lineage. This connection would have been further strengthened for the audience, as Brando was not far removed from playing another dynastic head-of-clan role: he portrayed the Don of the Corleone family, Vito, in Francis Ford Coppola's mafia epic *The Godfather* (1972). Mario Puzo, the author of the novel on which the film was based, is also credited with story and a co-screenwriting credit in *Superman*. On devoted fan wiki sites, the family tree of the El family is well documented and maintained. "House of El," DC Database, accessed December 4, 2018, https://dc.fandom.com/wiki/House_of_El. The online El family tree is compiled from the tree first published in November 1981. Online lists have been updated to include post-Crisis family members. "The Race to Overtake the Past," *Krypton Chronicles* 1, no. 3 (November 1981).

41

Saggese, *Reading Basquiat*, p. 94.

42

There is much scholarship that points to Charlie Parker's contrafact recording "Ko-Ko" as a seminal moment in jazz history for its announcement of Parker's, and the retrospective understanding of the record as one of the first recordings of what became bebop. In *Charlie Parker: His Music and Life*, Carl Woideck writes, "This solo, more than any other . . . announced Parker's brilliance . . . as a musical mind to the world." Carl Woideck, *Charlie Parker: His Music and Life* (Ann Arbor: University of Michigan Press, 1996), p. 115. "['Ko-Ko"s] harmonic complexity, rhythmic drive, and above all the improvisational gestures . . . built on Parker's mastery of the blues. . . . In the space of a few moments, Parker's group grasped the difference between swing and bop, creating a new form of American jazz." Peter Rutkoff and William Scott, "Bebop: Modern New York Jazz," *Kenyon Review* 18, no. 2 (1996), pp. 91–92, http://www.jstor.org/stable/4337359.

43

Vanessa Corby expands upon Freud's theory of trauma by explaining the protective shield as a "crust" that is meant to protect against harmful "stimuli" that adversely impact the psyche. She relates this to "its implications for [Eva] Hesse's practice." Vanessa Corby, *Eva Hesse: Longing, Belonging and Displacement* (London: I. B. Tauris, 2010), pp. 70–71.

44

"The rough-hewn frames [made by Stephen Torton] are still singled out as one of Basquiat's original innovations." Phoebe Hoban, *Basquiat: A Quick Killing in Art* (New York: Penguin Books, 2004), p. 102.

45

Geldzahler, "From the Subways to SoHo."

46

State of the Art, "Jean-Michel Basquiat."

47

James Baldwin, "No Name in the Street," in *Baldwin: Collected Essays* (New York: Literary Classics of the United States, 1998), p. 468.

THE DEATH OF MICHAEL STEWART IS A HAUNTING, THE SPECTER OF WHICH IS MANIFEST

TO THIS DAY IN MULTIPLE CREATIVE WORKS THAT CONTINUE TO TELL HIS UNFINISHED STORY,

NANCY SPECTOR

THE MAN NOBODY KILLED

The death in 1983 of aspiring artist Michael Stewart at the hands of New York City Transit Police officers was just one in a long continuum of murders of unarmed black men in this country. With the litany of names we recite today in an unrelenting chorus of recent loss—Trayvon Martin, Eric Garner, Michael Brown, Tamir Rice, Philando Castile—it is easy to lose sight of the fact that this steady beat of violence has had a sustained and resilient history on U.S. soil.[1] Ironically, at the time of Stewart's death, congressional hearings were being held in Harlem to investigate long-standing complaints of police brutality against people of color in New York City.[2] The decade leading up to Stewart's demise was marked by numerous other police killings, all treated with impunity: Randolph Evans was only fifteen years old in 1976 when he was shot in his housing complex following a false report of a gun-wielding man; businessman Arthur Miller was thirty when he was strangled in 1978 during an attempted arrest by a squad of sixteen officers; and Luis Baez was twenty-nine when he was shot twenty-one times for brandishing a pair of scissors in 1979.[3] But it was Stewart, a shy, unassuming, twenty-five-year-old black artist and model in one of the social circles radiating outward from the ever-charismatic Jean-Michel Basquiat, whose death galvanized the

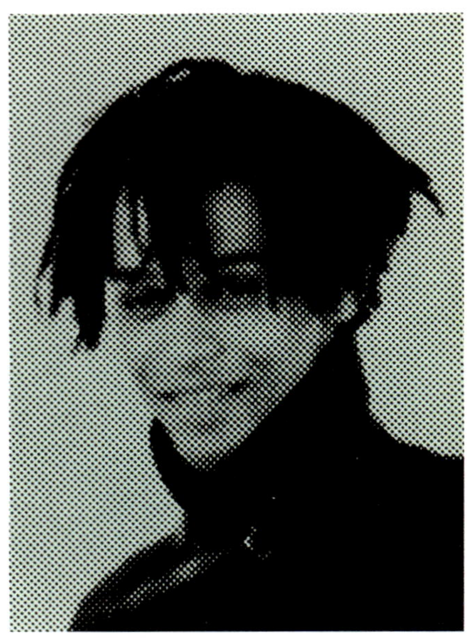

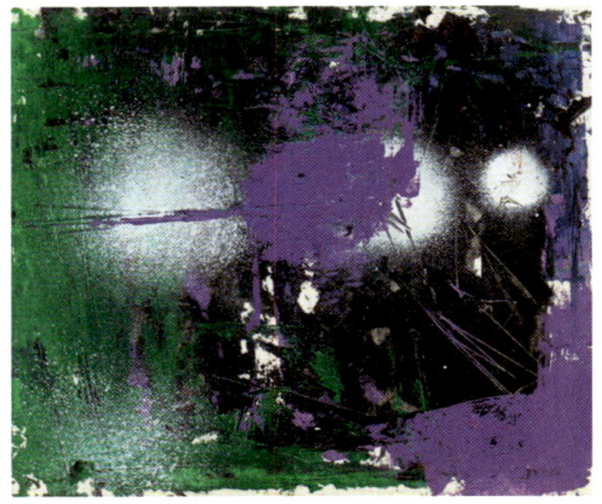

FIGURE 1
Portrait of Michael Stewart, from card for benefit at Danceteria, July 7, 1984. Collection of Patricia Pesce, New York

FIGURE 2
Untitled artwork by Michael Stewart, n.d. Collection of the Stewart Family

creative community on Manhattan's Lower East Side **[FIGS. 1, 2]**. From the beginning, Stewart's arrest at 2:50 a.m. on September 15, 1983, was racially coded: he was allegedly caught tagging a wall in the L train station at First Avenue, where he was violently accosted, then transported to Union Square, where the brutal beating continued. Once he slipped into a coma, he was tossed hog-tied into a police van and driven to Bellevue Hospital, where he died thirteen days later. Considered by authorities an urban blight—a criminal desecration of property—graffiti was defined as the province of black and Latinx street culture. The police cited the never-witnessed tag by an artist who never tagged as the excuse for assailing their unarmed victim.[4]

The criminality of Stewart's death was exacerbated by a subsequent police cover-up, complete with a misleading coroner's report; two grand-jury investigations; a five-month criminal trial that acquitted six white officers of any offense; and two further inquiries conducted by the Metropolitan Transit Authority. The media's coverage during this protracted process reflected the inherent values of each particular platform. To name a few, the *East Village Eye* (1979–87) dug deep, determined to uncover the truth behind the death of one of its own. The *New York Amsterdam News*, one of the oldest African American newspapers in the country (founded in 1909), was relentless in its exposure of the racist underpinnings of the city's investigation, and the *New York Times* presented a "balanced," if not anemic, accounting of the trials.[5] On television, WABC's news reporter Lou Young devoted over sixty reports to Stewart's death and the cover-up, and black newscaster John Johnson of WCBS was considered, in his coverage of the trials, a true conduit to the community.[6] Even with the settlement achieved between the city, the Transit Authority, and Stewart's family in 1990,[7] Michael Stewart's unresolved death has triggered the imagination of artists over the years, sparking, in addition to street protests, graphic poster campaigns, creative fund-raisers, feature and documentary films, ballads, and searing artworks that commemorate and excoriate the utterly unfathomable death of this innocent young man, who was, by all accounts, on the verge of his prime.[8]

At the close of the criminal trial in 1986 in which the police officers were exonerated by an almost all-white jury, the *East Village Eye* published an illustrated editorial titled "The Man Nobody Killed" **[FIG. 3]**. In it they registered a lament by Stewart family attorney Louis Clayton Jones, who stated that the verdict was a "forgone conclusion" given the extent of the cover-up, and they offered condolences—"sympathy, outrage, and sorrow"—to all those in the community who continued to stand with the young artist.[9] It was the title of the text, however, that provocatively evoked the true horror of the crime. An unsolved

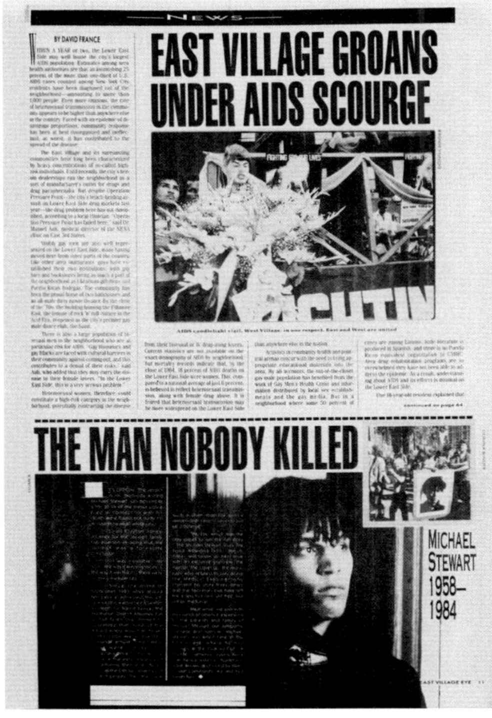
NEWS

BY DAVID FRANCE

EAST VILLAGE GROANS UNDER AIDS SCOURGE

AIDS candlelight vigil, West Village: in one respect, East and West are united

continued on page 44

THE MAN NOBODY KILLED

MICHAEL STEWART 1958–1984

FIGURE 3
"The Man Nobody Killed," *East Village Eye*, December/January 1986, page 11. Courtesy *East Village Eye*

murder, an inexplicable death, and a total lack of accountability do not allow for proper mourning or any kind of emotional or psychological closure. The death of Michael Stewart is a haunting, the specter of which is manifest to this day in multiple creative works that continue to tell his unfinished story. Artist David Hammons, whose conceptual practice is rich with ironic takes on cultural mythologies of blackness, responded directly to the *East Village Eye* story in a series of prints created for *Eye* magazine, a limited-edition art publication, in 1986. Using individual sheets of cardboard cut from packing boxes, he stenciled the image of Stewart from the newspaper, complete with his signature dreadlocks, along with the title "The Man Nobody Killed" in bright red letters **[PL. 8]**. He then glued a small rectangular portion of the actual newspaper page with the epitaph "Michael Stewart 1958–1984 [*sic*]" on the front. Created in an edition of approximately 150, each print is unique; the exercise of its making, an assembly line of outrage, a ritual of grief.[10]

In 1984 or '85 singer-songwriter Michelle Shocked composed "Graffiti Limbo" to voice her indignation over the killing and evident corruption designed to circumvent the multiple cases brought against the police in its aftermath. Poetically referencing the debunked idea that Stewart was writing on the subway station walls when apprehended, she wrote an ode to artistic freedom:

Lay down your burdens
Lay down your cares
The Holy Virgin, she's gonna greet you up there
With a big can of spray paint, yeah

And a big blank wall
And I can guaran-damn-tee you
There ain't no cops around at all[11]

In the middle of the song, she interrupts the lyrics to explain how the coroner in Stewart's case (Dr. Elliot M. Gross) had "lost the evidence," referring to the fact that the victim's eyes were removed and soaked in a bleaching solution, an unauthorized act that, according to the family's lawyers, erased evidence of the hemorrhaging that would have proven death by strangulation.[12] Gross, the city's chief medical examiner, actually supplied three contradictory autopsy reports over a period of months, the first claiming that Stewart had died from excessive drinking, which had led to a coma and eventual heart attack.[13]

The bruises and abrasions all over his body were excused as collateral damage inflicted when he allegedly tried to fight off the police in a violent rage—a claim rejected by the numerous eyewitnesses who recalled seeing and hearing the excessive beating of the victim on the sidewalk outside the Union Square Transit Police station, where Stewart was taken following his arrest on First Avenue.[14] For Stewart, in addition to not being killed by anyone, there was no discernible cause of death.

In a similar vein of artistic protest, rock musician Lou Reed invoked Stewart's name in his song "Hold On" from the album *New York* (1989), in which he tears into the rising tide of racism in the city, with a specific evocation of the Lower East Side as a site for activism:

There's blacks with knives and whites with guns
fighting in Howard Beach
There's no such thing as human rights
when you walk the N.Y. streets
A cop was shot in the head by a ten-year-old kid
named Buddha in
Central Park last week
The fathers are lined up by
the coffins by the Statue of Bigotry
You better hold on something's happening here
You better hold on—meet you in Tompkins Square
The dopers sent a message to the cops last weekend
They shot him in the car where he sat
And Eleanor Bumpurs and Michael Stewart must have
appreciated that . . .[15]

In the same year, filmmaker Spike Lee released his inimitable comedic drama *Do the Right Thing*, which foregrounds seething racial tensions in the Brooklyn neighborhood of Bedford-Stuyvesant. The character of Radio Raheem, an affable, boom-box-carrying local, was modeled loosely on Michael Stewart in that he is strangled by the police in the movie's climactic scene, during a pizza parlor brawl. One bystander even notes, "They did it again. Just like Michael Stewart." Before the credits roll at the end of the film, Lee includes a dedication to the "families of Eleanor Bumpurs, Michael Griffith, Arthur Miller, Edmund Perry, Yvonne Smallwood and Michael Stewart," all black New Yorkers who had been killed by the police in the few years prior to the film's making.[16]

PLATE 8
David Hammons
The Man Nobody Killed, from *Eye* magazine, no. 14, "Cobalt Myth Mechanics," 1986
Stenciled paint on commercially printed cardboard with cut-and-taped photocopy, from a spiral-bound periodical with works by various artists
Composition (irreg.): 10 5/8 × 8 1/16 inches (27 × 20.5 cm); sheet: 11 1/8 × 8 9/16 inches (28.2 × 21.7 cm)
Publisher: Eye Publications, New York
Printer: the artist, New York
Edition: 200 announced, approx. 150 printed
The Museum of Modern Art, New York. Henry Church Fund (by exchange), 2015

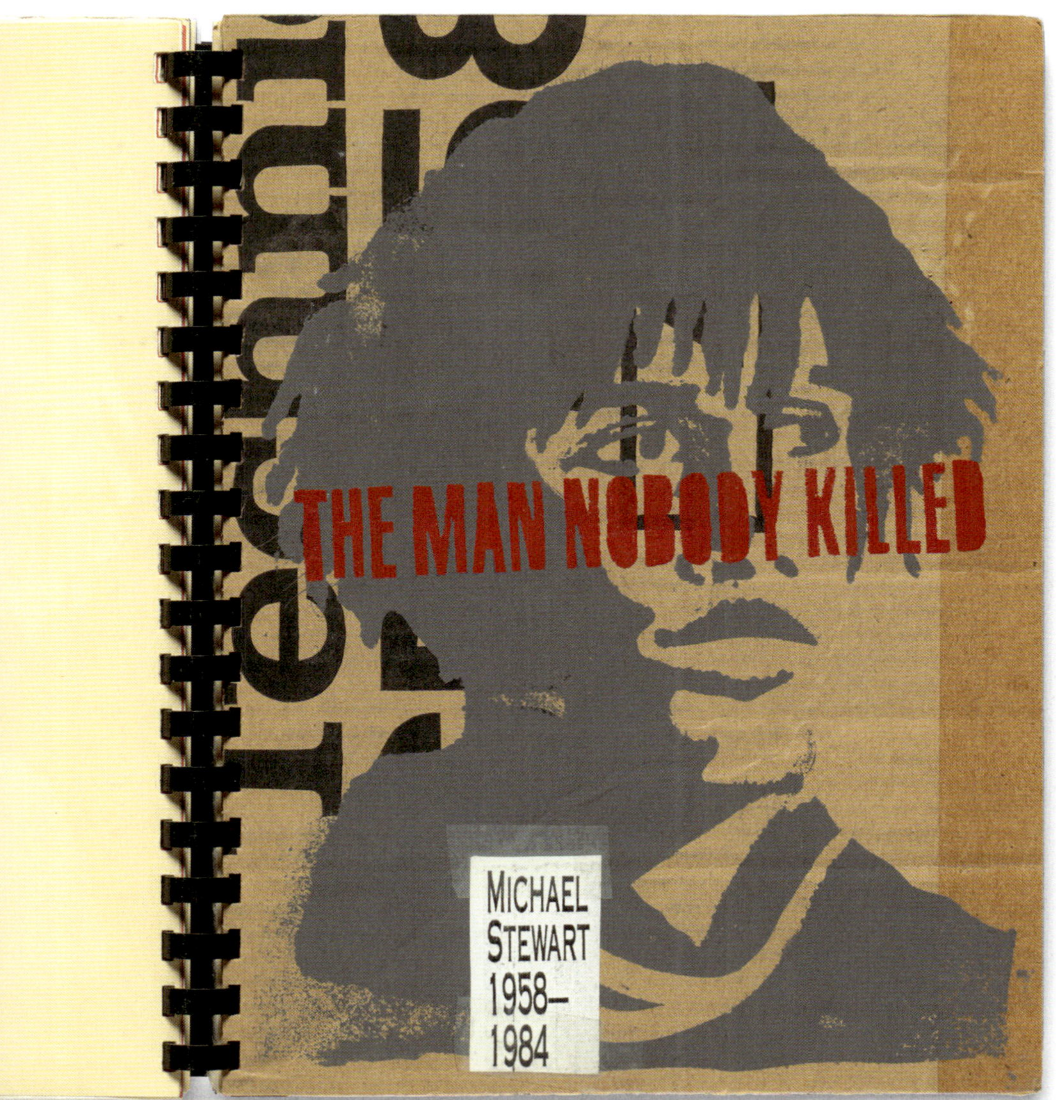
THE MAN NOBODY KILLED
MICHAEL STEWART 1958–1984

Perhaps the most immediate and deeply metaphorical response to Stewart's death is the painting *Defacement (The Death of Michael Stewart)* **[P. 17, PL. 1]**, created by Jean-Michel Basquiat directly on the wall of Keith Haring's studio in the Cable Building in 1983 **[FIG. 4]**. Poet and critic Rene Ricard recalled that it was painted "right after the murder," during "a moment of true terror for many artists."[17] Executed quickly over a surface of residual brushstrokes and spray-paint mist, all overspills from the edges of Haring's tacked-up canvases and tarps,[18] the composition comprises three figures: two colorful, cartoonish policemen wielding their batons over a barely articulated person between them, rendered entirely in black paint. The word "¿DEFACEMENT©?" hovers above the trio in the upper register, posing a question about defilement: can the (alleged) desecration of property ever be an excuse for erasing the life of an individual? Assuming that Basquiat had heard the graffiti alibi used by the cops, this painting creates a through line from his own early history on the street tagging as SAMO© to Keith Haring, whose own illicit chalk line-drawings in the subway were already legendary, to the fate of Michael Stewart.[19] This was conceived as an insiders' painting, to be seen only in situ by the friends and artists who frequented the studio.[20] And because of this, the painting can be understood as one of Basquiat's most intimate and probing meditations on blackness and the profoundly entrenched experience of violence associated with it, what African American poet Claudia Rankine has referred to as the "rope inside us, the tree inside us," from which "we are all caught hanging."[21] Or, put more directly by cultural essayist Greg Tate as it applies to the artist's production, "[T]here's no way you can look at Basquiat's work and not get beat up by his obsession with the black male body's history as property, pulverized meat and popular entertainment. No way not to be reminded that lynchings and minstrelsy still vie in the white supremacist imagination for the black male body's proper place."[22]

Unlike the majority of Basquiat's paintings in which bodies are depicted as the loose accumulation of anatomical parts—bones and organs float in proximity to signify a sentient being[23]—in *Defacement*, the figure of Michael Stewart is a solid black form, a negative space amid the floating patches of color, a vortex of vulnerability. A single black line emanating from his head loops and swerves to form a crown of dreadlocks, a hip-hop halo. Stewart is martyred for a crime he did not commit, for inhabiting a black body, and for being in the wrong place at the wrong time. "[B]lackness" in Basquiat's art, writes Tate, "is rendered as something holy, esoteric, and visceral." It is not the "blackness of the cultural nationalists, though it has their intensity and anger . . . but a blackness that demands hermeneutic intervention, ardor, and respect."[24] Basquiat was famously distraught over the killing of Michael Stewart, as was Haring. In his diary (on Thursday, September 29, 1983), mega-artist Andy Warhol, a friend of Basquiat and Haring, recounted that

> Keith was ranting and raving about this black graffiti artist that's in the papers now because the police killed him — Michael Stewart. And Keith said that he's been arrested by the police four times, but because he looks normal they just sort of call him a fairy and let him go. But this kid that was just killed, he had the Jean Michel look — dreadlocks.[25]

On the bigotry scale in 1983 New York, it was apparently less of a crime to be queer and white than to be black. Basquiat knew this intrinsically; he lived it daily. Haring observed, "One thing that affected Jean-Michel greatly was the Michael Stewart story."[26] It is unclear how well, if at all, Basquiat knew Stewart, but they were romantically involved with the same woman, Suzanne Mallouk.[27] And another of the artist's girlfriends—Madonna—included Stewart in one of her early music videos as a dancer.[28] According to Haring, Basquiat was "completely freaked out" the night he learned of Stewart's death. "It was like it could have been him. It showed him how vulnerable he was."[29] Basquiat's identification with the killing ran deep, as *Defacement* reveals, relentlessly, to this day. Granted, he was engaged throughout his work with what late curator and museum director Okwui Enwezor termed "Afro-Atlantic imagery," in which he freely drew from and hybridized African, African American, and Caribbean sources, from his superheroes—black athletes and jazz musicians—to depictions of the slave trade.[30] Whereas during the early 1980s Basquiat's paintings initially fulfilled a hunger in the market for a return to figuration as part of what was dubbed the Neo-Expressionist moment for its near-mythic themes and grandiose scale, in reality, he delivered a scorching indictment against the exclusionary tactics of the very (white) world that embraced him. But, as Enwezor points out in reference to the turbulent times in which the artist lived and worked—defined by the AIDS crisis, but also rampant racism and poverty—Basquiat "chose processes of personal mourning against the overt strategies of public commemoration of mourning."[31] *Defacement* was a private lamentation in paint and, perhaps, a talisman to ward off a similar fate from happening to him.

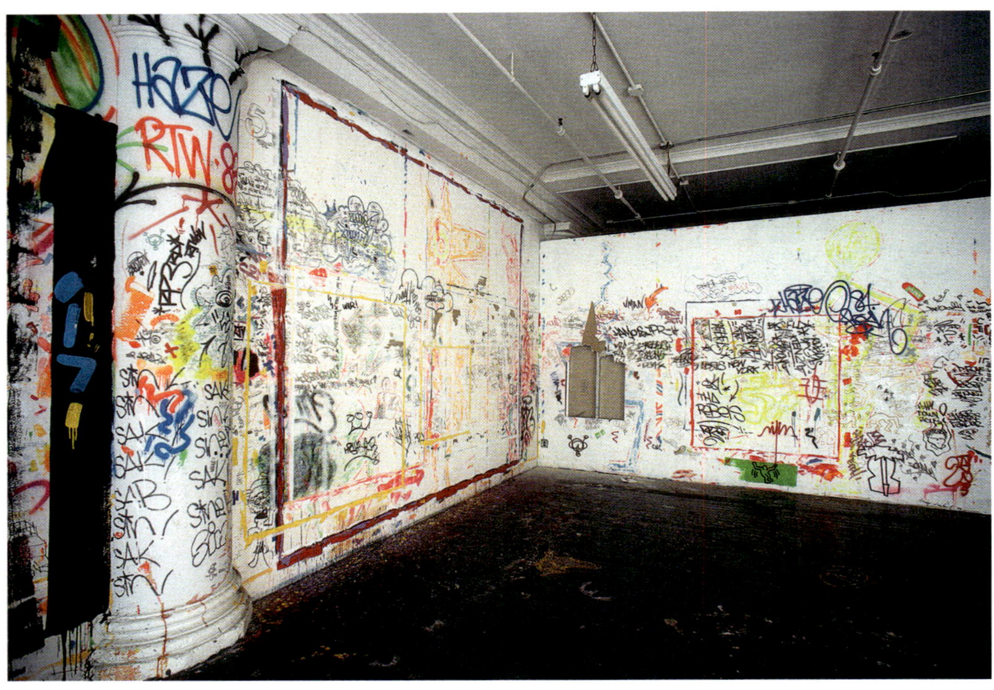

FIGURE 4
Keith Haring's studio after *The Death of Michael Stewart* was cut from the wall, Cable Building, New York, ca. 1985

The story on the street about Stewart's fatal beating was that he was not actually arrested for tagging but, rather, because the police witnessed him kissing a white woman before descending the subway stairs on his way home to his parents' house in Clinton Hill, Brooklyn.[32] If this is true, Stewart's death is tethered across history even more tightly to that of the young Emmett Till, whose horrific lynching in Mississippi in 1955 for allegedly flirting with a white woman helped spur the civil rights movement. As poet and author Elizabeth Alexander has argued, "black bodies in pain for public consumption have been an American national spectacle for centuries."[33] And it is the internalization of this bitter truth, the unspeakable collective trauma of this reality, that makes deaths like Stewart's so instantly legible to those historically governed under its regime. In reference to the brutal police beating of Rodney King in Los Angeles captured on video in 1991 and the subsequent acquittal of its perpetrators, Alexander notes how the entire tragic scenario "called upon a constructed national historical memory, a code in which African Americans are . . . perfectly literate."[34] That code informs the very DNA of Basquiat's *Defacement*, rendering it at once deeply personal and extraordinarily public.[35]

NOTES

This essay has benefited from ongoing conversations with Chaédria LaBouvier, who has shared her research on Basquiat's *Defacement* with me over the past three years.

1

In 2016, for instance, Castile was one of 233 African Americans shot and killed by police, a shocking statistic when demographics are taken into account. African Americans comprised 13 percent of the U.S. population but 24 percent of all people killed by police that year. See Katie Nodjimbadem, "The Long, Painful History of Police Brutality in the U.S.," *Smithsonian*, July 27, 2017, https://www.smithsonianmag.com/smithsonian-institution/long-painful-history-police-brutality-in-the-us-180964098/.

2

Convened by John Conyers, a Michigan Democrat and chairman of the House Subcommittee on Criminal Justice, at the behest of Reverend Calvin Butts, executive minister of the Abyssinian Baptist Church in Harlem (who would play a role in the protests against Stewart's death), the hearings took place on July 18 and September 20, 1983, to investigate allegations of systemic police brutality against black and Hispanic New Yorkers. While inconclusive, the hearings as well as the press they engendered shed light on the Koch administration's resistance to any such inquiry. See Sam Roberts, "Police Brutality Charged at Forum," *New York Times*, September 20, 1983, https://www.nytimes.com/1983/09/20/nyregion/police-brutality-charged-at-forum.html.

3

For Evans, see Max H. Siegel, "Boy, 15, Shot to Death Point Blank; Officer Arrested in East New York," *New York Times*, November 27, 1976, https://www.nytimes.com/1976/11/27/archives/boy-15-shot-to-death-pointblank-officer-arrested-in-east-new-york.html; for Miller, see Joseph B. Treaster, "Brooklyn Businessman Strangled in Struggle with Police Officers, *New York Times*, June 17, 1978, https://www.nytimes.com/1978/06/17/archives/brooklyn-businessman-strangled-in-a-struggle-with-police-officers-2.html; for Baez, see Joseph P. Fried, "Police Ruled Not Liable in Killing," *New York Times*, November 21, 1979, https://www.nytimes.com/1979/11/21/archives/police-ruled-not-liable-in-killing.html. These three names were cited by Reverend Herbert Daughtry, the third national presiding minister of the House of the Lord Churches in Brooklyn, in an interview on November 8, 2018, about the scourge of police violence in New York City prior to Michael Stewart's death and the role he played in organizing support for the Stewart family. See p. 138 in this volume.

4

According to visual artist and hip-hop pioneer Fred Brathwaite (a.k.a. Fab 5 Freddy), Michael Stewart was not a graffiti artist. He never traveled with spray paint, the go-to medium for any artist involved with tagging. Interview by the author, Chaédria LaBouvier, and Joan Young on June 14, 2018.

5

In addition to the cited coverage, Gabe Pressman of WNBC devoted much airtime to covering the labyrinthine twists and turns of the Stewart case.

6

See the recollection by journalist Peter Noel in this volume, pp. 149–51.

7

See an article on the settlement that summarizes the legal ordeal faced by the Stewart family. William G. Blair, "Family Gets $1.7 Million for Stewart's Death," *New York Times*, August 29, 1990, https://www.nytimes.com/1990/08/29/nyregion/family-gets-1.7-million-for-stewart-s-death.html. In a statement issued by Mayor David Dinkins's office, it was said that the settlement "does not constitute any admission of wrongdoing," even though paid by the Transit Authority. See also pp. 96–153 in this volume for accounts from a number of individuals who either covered or protested the murder and subsequent trials.

8

The young artist's brief bio is included in a press release announcing a benefit concert for the Michael J. Stewart Legal Defense Fund on October 26, 1983. In addition to being an artist and model, he worked as a production assistant and sound and lighting technician for the Richard Allen Cultural Center, the Black Arts Festival at Lincoln Center, and the Henry Street Settlement. Stewart also worked for WOR-TV Channel 9 at Shea Stadium as a production assistant during baseball seasons. In 1978 and 1979 he worked at Pratt Institute, operating 16 mm and video cameras as well as sound and lighting equipment. In addition, a flyer announcing the *Y.E.T.P. Art Exhibit* at Pratt Institute (January 31–February 14, 1979) includes Stewart's name among twenty-one other artists. Both documents were shared with us by the Stewart family.

9

"The Man Nobody Killed," editorial, *East Village Eye*, December/January 1986, p. 11.

10

This issue of *Eye* magazine was edited by Paul Hasegawa-Overacker. From Hasegawa-Overacker's (now defunct) website regarding this issue of *Eye*: it was "published in 1986 with a lot of help from Cynthia Kuebel, Dona Ann McAdams and the East Village Lesbians (a loose gang). The publishing party was held at the Baskerville and Watson Gallery in 1986. The first customers I see in the ledger are Sherrie Levine, Joy Silverman (Director L.A.C.E), and artist Nancy Evans. The first copies sold for $25. . . . They were so labor intensive each copy averaged over two hours after collating so I produced the copies in small batches, and in fact I never finished more than about 150." Quoted from the files of the Museum of Modern Art, New York. A copy of *Eye* no. 14 resides in the museum's Department of Drawings and Prints.

11

Michelle Shocked, "Graffiti Limbo," track 5 on *Short Sharp Shocked*, Mercury Records, 1988.

12

For the complete lyrics and breakout explanation, see http://michelleshocked.com/ears/lyrics/graffiti-limbo/, accessed December 6, 2018. And see pp. 120–21 in this volume for an account from Shocked about the song and her reaction to Stewart's death. For a newspaper report of what was described as a "surreptitious autopsy" by

Dr. Gross, who removed the victim's eyes after the official postmortem exam, which was observed by a doctor appointed by the Stewart family, see Peter Noel, "Docs: Where Are the Victim's Eyes," *New York Amsterdam News*, October 15, 1983, p. 8.

13

Lindsey Gruson, "Injuries of a Police Prisoner Did Not Kill, Autopsy Finds," *New York Times*, September 30, 1983, https://www.nytimes.com/1983/09/30/nyregion/injuries-of-a-police-prisoner-did-not-kill-autopsy-finds.html. Three people who were with Stewart the night of his arrest claimed that he was not drunk or on drugs. See M. A. Faber, "3 Witnesses Say Stewart Appeared Sober on the Night He Was Arrested," *New York Times*, July 24, 1985, https://www.nytimes.com/1985/07/24/nyregion/3-witnesses-say-stewart-appeared-sober-on-the-night-he-was-arrested.html.

14

During the criminal trial in 1985, twenty-seven students were called who claimed to have witnessed the beating from their Parsons School of Design dormitory windows at 31 Union Square West, at East Sixteenth Street. Rebecca Reiss was quoted in a *New York Times* article as saying that "[o]ne of the officers was kicking the man, and the other officers were hitting the man," who was yelling, "Oh, my God, someone help me, someone help me." See M. A. Farber, "Student Recalls She Saw Police Beating Stewart," *New York Times*, July 23, 1985, https://www.nytimes.com/1985/07/23/nyregion/student-recalls-she-saw-police-beating-stewart.html.

15

Lou Reed, "Hold On," track 10 on *New York*, Sire Records, 1989. Eleanor Bumpurs's name is often invoked with Stewart's in that she was shot to death by a police officer in a botched attempt to evict her from her apartment for unpaid rent on October 29, 1984. She was a sixty-seven-year-old African American woman with an alleged history of mental instability. See Leonard Buder, "Police Kill Woman Being Evicted; Officers Say She Wielded a Knife," *New York Times*, October 30, 1984, https://www.nytimes.com/1984/10/30/nyregion/police-kill-woman-being-evicted-officers-say-she-wielded-a-knife.html.

16

Do the Right Thing, directed by Spike Lee (1989; Universal City, Calif.: Universal Studios, 2001), film. Spike Lee's choice of a pizza parlor as the setting for the murder of Raheem directly referred to the incident in Howard Beach also invoked by Lou Reed—a horrifying instance of racial violence in 1986, when twenty-three-year-old Trinidadian immigrant Michael Griffith was chased onto a highway by a group of white youths and killed by an oncoming car driven by the son of a police officer, who faced no criminal charges. In his production journal, Lee recorded, "I'm making an allusion to the Howard Beach incident by using a pizza parlor" as a key location in the story. "If a riot is the climax of the film, what will cause the riot?" he wrote in 1987. "Take your pick: an unarmed black child shot, the cops say he was reaching for a gun; a grandmother shot to death by cops with a shotgun; a young woman, charged with nothing but a parking violation, dies in police custody; a male chased by a white mob onto a freeway is hit by a car." Quoted in Elahe Izadi, "What Inspired 'Do the Right Thing' Character Radio Raheem, and Why He's Still Relevant Today," *Washington Post*, September 26, 2016, https://www.washingtonpost.com/news/arts-and-entertainment/wp/2016/09/26/what-inspired-do-the-right-thing-character-radio-raheem-and-why-hes-still-relevant-today.

17

Rene Ricard, "World Crown©: Bodhisattva with Clenched Mudra," in Richard Marshall, *Jean-Michel Basquiat*, exh. cat. (New York: Whitney Museum of American Art, 1992), p. 49.

18

I want to thank guest curator Chaédria LaBouvier and Joan Young for this observation, which is based on their visit to the Keith Haring Foundation and meeting with Anna Gurton-Wachter, its archivist, who unearthed the photo showing the wall from which the painting was eventually removed. *Defacement* was painted over an area of the wall that Haring would later use to pin up fabric for a group of painted banners for an event at the Palladium nightclub, in 1985, some of which he collaborated on with graffiti artist LA II. Bleed-through from one of the Palladium banners is visible on *Defacement*, layered on top of Basquiat's painted surfaces.

19

The word *defacement* is used in vexillology (the study of flags) to refer to the addition of a symbol or design element to another flag, often signaling the annexation of another country or the overthrow of a colonial power. Basquiat's use of the word makes a compelling commentary on both the abuses of power and the notion of decolonization as liberation.

20

The painting has never been on the market. When he moved studios, Haring had it cut from the wall and eventually placed in the gilded, baroque frame it lives in today and hung it above the bed in his bedroom. At the time of his death, Haring bequeathed the painting to Nina Clemente, daughter of artist Francesco Clemente and Alba Clemente, who generously lent it to Chaédria LaBouvier for her study of Basquiat's *Defacement* at Williams College in the fall of 2016.

21

Claudia Rankine, *Citizen: An American Lyric* (Minneapolis: Graywolf Press, 2014), p. 90.

22

Greg Tate, "Nobody Loves a Genius Child: Jean-Michel Basquiat, Lonesome Flyboy in the '80s Art Boom Buttermilk," *Village Voice*, November 14, 1989, p. 33. To this day, Tate has written some of the most incisive and searing texts on Basquiat and race.

23

Art historians have convincingly made the case that this compositional strategy and the artist's keen interest in human anatomy date to the time that Basquiat was hospitalized after being hit by a car at age seven and his mother gave him a copy of the book *Gray's Anatomy* to occupy his mind and to give him visual references to the parts of his body that sustained injuries. Apparently, for instance, his spleen was removed. Olivier Berggruen, "The Prints of Jean-Michel Basquiat," *Print Quarterly* 26, no. 1 (March 2009), p. 28. Nathan Brown writes about "the disintegration of the body into anatomical components" in Basquiat's art. See Nathan Brown, "The Irony of

Anatomy: Basquiat's Poetics of Black Positionality," *Radical Philosophy*, no. 195 (January/February 2016), p. 16.

24

Greg Tate, "Black like B.," in Marshall, *Jean-Michel Basquiat*, p. 58. See the reprint of this essay in the present volume, pp. 89–94.

25

The Andy Warhol Diaries, ed. Pat Hackett (New York: Twelve, 2014), p. 542.

26

Haring, quoted in Anthony Haden-Guest, "Burning Out," *Vanity Fair*, November 1988, https://www.vanityfair.com/news/1988/11/jean-michel-basquiat.

27

Suzanne Mallouk's story is memorialized in Jennifer Clement's *Widow Basquiat* (Edinburgh: Payback Press, 2000). Her involvement with Stewart is recounted on pp. 117–32.

28

Madonna is interviewed about Stewart in Franck Lazare Goldberg's documentary film *Lynch: Who Killed Michael Stewart* (1984), which includes a brief excerpt of Stewart dancing; https://vimeo.com/103611383, accessed December 9, 2018.

29

Haring, quoted in Haden-Guest, "Burning Out."

30

See Okwui Enwezor, "El Gran Espectáculo: Jean Michel Basquiat, Modernity, Modernism," in *Jean-Michel Basquiat*, ed. Dieter Buchhart and Anna Karina Hofbauer, exh. cat. (Paris: Fondation Louis Vuitton and Éditions Gallimard, 2018), p. 46.

31

Enwezor, p. 42.

32

This account was published in the detailed article by Terry Bison, "The Murder of Michael Stewart," that was commissioned by the *Village Voice* but published by the *East Village Eye* (March 1985, pp. 7, 54). A recollection by Patricia Pesce, who was with Stewart the night he was assaulted, is included in this volume on pp. 116–17.

33

Elizabeth Alexander, "Can You Be Black and Look at This?: Reading the Rodney King Video(s)," in *The Black Interior* (Saint Paul, Minn.: Graywolf Press, 2004), p. 177. First published in Thelma Golden, *Black Male: Representations of Masculinity in Contemporary American Art*, exh. cat. (New York: Whitney Museum of American Art, 1994).

34

Alexander, p. 178.

35

Chaédria LaBouvier makes the argument about how *Defacement* is Basquiat's most private and personal painting in her essay in this volume. See pp. 13–37.

STEWART BELONGED TO THE DOWNTOWN SCENE, BUT HIS HUMANITY WOULD BE CLAIMED CITYWIDE. AS GRAFFITEROS WOULD SAY, STEWART'S SPIRIT WENT

ALL CITY.

J. FAITH ALMIRON

THE ART OF BASQUIAT BELONGS TO THE PEOPLE

OPEN THE WAY, A LIBATION

May all the holy ancestor spirits of all times and all places bless this meditation on the young humanity stolen, and destroyed by state violence. Our children deserve a better world. We must fight for it—together, today.[1]

GUNS, GOONS, AND GHOSTS

Guns. So primitive.
OKOYE, *BLACK PANTHER* [2]

The bullets were premonitions, ghosts from dreams of a hard, fast future. The bullets moved on after moving through us, became the promise of what was to come, the speed and the killing, the hard, fast lines of borders and buildings. They took everything and ground it down to dust as fine as gunpowder, they fired their guns into the air in victory, and the strays flew out into the nothingness of histories written wrong and meant to be forgotten. Stray bullets and consequences are landing on our unsuspecting bodies even now.
TOMMY ORANGE, *THERE THERE* [3]

Even as a third grader, Jean-Michel Basquiat recognized the *omnipotence paradox* of the police state. In response to a potential buyer's request, Basquiat composed a curriculum vitae (CV) document outlining his educational journey **[PL. 9]**.[4] Toward the bottom of the page, the text reads: "(A.) SENT A DRAWING OF A GUN TO J. EDGAR HOOVER IN 3RD THIRD GRADE. (NO REPLY)." In sending a gun in the mail—even if it was merely an illustration—Basquiat turned the gun's aim toward Hoover.

Basquiat knew intuitively how to undermine power structures, because he did not believe in them. Looking back as an adult, Lisane Basquiat described how her brother "pulled the art from [within] himself."[5] To manifest this formidable destiny, Jean-Michel had to reject any entity that would limit himself or his conception of the world, including the value systems of Western Eurocentrism and antiblack white supremacy. In the same CV, Basquiat indicates that his "early themes" included "NIXON . . . WARS . . . WEAPONS."

Basquiat's CV further articulates his cultural identity and transnational origins through migration, generation, and education. He describes his mother as "PUERTO RICAN (FIRST GENERATION)" and his father as "PORT AU PRINCE, HAITI." In a list of schools attended, between P.S. (Public School) 45 and I.S. (Intermediary School) 293, Basquiat inserts "(SOME CATHOLIC SCHOOL DURING YEAR + ½ IN PUERTO RICO ________)," marking an impactful detour from his New York City public schooling in 1974 when his father, Gerard, followed a job promotion to Santurce, in San Juan. Thus Basquiat encountered two divergent yet intrinsically linked examples of American education—a postcolonial territory in the Caribbean and a cosmopolitan enclave with intensifying integration anxiety. With the advent of the Immigration and Nationality Act of 1965, the demographics of New York City's middle class turned a darker hue. The policy broadly abolished existing quotas on the entry of West Indians and other nonwhite groups into the country. The growing presence of a new black, brown, and Asian labor force pushed up against white sovereignty in America's urban neighborhoods. Contrary to the popularized notion of white flight, many white people stayed in the 'hood. They fiercely guarded their property and all that came with it, including the taxes to influence school districting. This racially charged battle over fundamental resources meant an increase of police presence and thus violence against new Americans of color.[6]

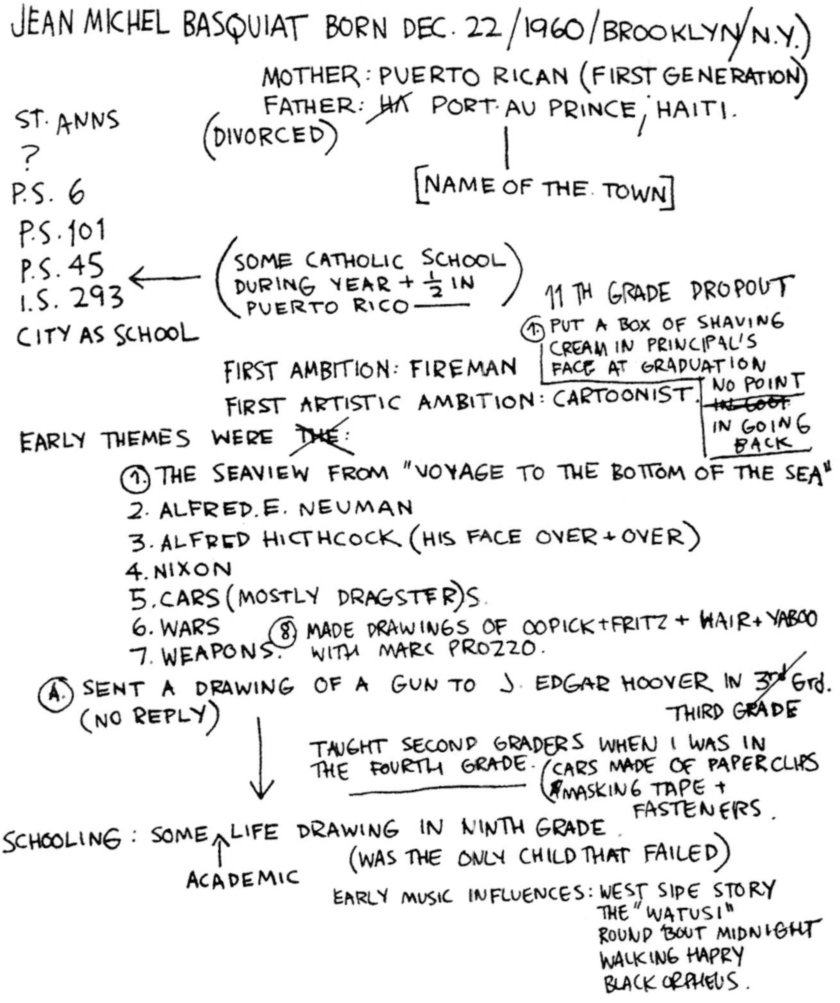

JEAN MICHEL BASQUIAT BORN DEC. 22/1960/BROOKLYN/N.Y.)

MOTHER: PUERTO RICAN (FIRST GENERATION)
FATHER: ~~HA~~ PORT-AU PRINCE, HAITI.
(DIVORCED)
[NAME OF THE TOWN]

ST. ANNS
?
P.S. 6
P.S. 101
P.S. 45 ← (SOME CATHOLIC SCHOOL DURING YEAR + ½ IN PUERTO RICO)
I.S. 293
CITY AS SCHOOL

11 TH GRADE DROPOUT
(1) PUT A BOX OF SHAVING CREAM IN PRINCIPAL'S FACE AT GRADUATION
NO POINT ~~IN GOOT~~ IN GOING BACK

FIRST AMBITION: FIREMAN
FIRST ARTISTIC AMBITION: CARTOONIST.

EARLY THEMES WERE ~~THE~~:

(1) THE SEAVIEW FROM "VOYAGE TO THE BOTTOM OF THE SEA"
2. ALFRED. E. NEUMAN
3. ALFRED HICTHCOCK (HIS FACE OVER + OVER)
4. NIXON
5. CARS (MOSTLY DRAGSTER)S.
6. WARS (8) MADE DRAWINGS OF OOPICK + FRITZ + HAIR + YABOO WITH MARC PROZZO.
7. WEAPONS.

(A.) SENT A DRAWING OF A GUN TO J. EDGAR HOOVER IN ~~3rd~~ Grd. THIRD GRADE
(NO REPLY)

TAUGHT SECOND GRADERS WHEN I WAS IN THE FOURTH GRADE. (CARS MADE OF PAPER CLIPS + MASKING TAPE + FASTENERS.

SCHOOLING: SOME ACADEMIC LIFE DRAWING IN NINTH GRADE.
(WAS THE ONLY CHILD THAT FAILED)

EARLY MUSIC INFLUENCES: WEST SIDE STORY
THE "WATUSI"
ROUND 'BOUT MIDNIGHT
WALKING HAPPY
BLACK ORPHEUS.

PLATE 9

Jean-Michel Basquiat

Untitled (Biography), 1983

Graphite on paper

No longer extant

In a lesser-known interview published in the July 1984 issue of Andy Warhol's *Interview* magazine, Basquiat speaks with filmmaker Emile de Antonio, who is introduced as an "anarchist, ex-professor, author, and the only filmmaker on Richard Nixon's enemies list" **[FIG. 1]**.[7] They rap about Nixon's FBI director, J. Edgar Hoover, "40 years the no. 1 policeman."[8]

BASQUIAT: Talk more about J. Edgar Hoover. I think he's interesting.

DE ANTONIO: J. Edgar Hoover was born January 1, 1895. His father was a bureaucrat in Washington. His grandfather was a bureaucrat. He became head of FBI in 1924, and he was still the head of it in 1972 when he died. He was in the saddle 48 years. Nowhere, not in Russia, not in Nazi Germany, not in the history of the world has one guy run the secret police for 48 years . . . The minute he died everybody in the FBI was ready to pounce on his files because his files were all about John F. Kennedy and who he was sleeping with, it was about what Nixon *really* did, it was about what LBJ *really* did . . .

BASQUIAT: That would make the great American novel.

DE ANTONIO: That's the truth; he had it on everybody. His files, one at a time, would expose everybody in political life. He wouldn't care about de Kooning or Pollock, and he wouldn't care about baseball players unless they said something. If Babe Ruth got up and said the FBI was full of crooks, then they would have had a file on him, too . . . I don't know what J. Edgar Hoover knew about painters; I'm sure he knew nothing about painting . . . Picasso was a Communist, that he knew. Picasso was a member of the communist party of France. He did the peace dove. The hardline communists hated his paintings. They thought he did decadent, bourgeois painting. What those people have to say is economically not incorrect; it's artistically incorrect. They say art should belong to the people, whatever that means.

BASQUIAT: It does, though.

Basquiat interjects to distinguish his own belief that, indeed, *art belongs to the people*. De Antonio goes on to theorize about how the police at the federal level monitor artists and the propagation of culture, and claims that Hoover would generally overlook artists and

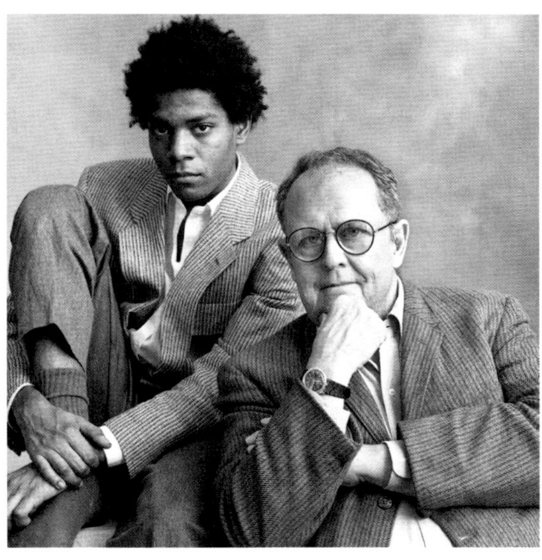

FIGURE 1
Jean-Michel Basquiat and Emile de Antonio, 1984. Photograph by Gordon Munro for *Interview* magazine, July 1984

entertainers unless they exhibited subversive thought or articulated forceful social statements. According to the extensive research of historian William J. Maxwell, the FBI did in fact recognize the critical role that art and cultural production played in catalyzing social movement and uprising, and conducted in-depth surveillance of black bookstores, arts and literature organizations, artists, and intellectual leaders dating back to the beginning of the Harlem Renaissance in 1919.[9]

Not by coincidence, 1919 was also Hoover's first year at the bureau. Hoover was preoccupied with the emergence and expression of black consciousness since its earliest iterations in the diaspora. For example, he targeted Pan-Africanist revolutionary leader Marcus Garvey and his Universal Negro Improvement Association. Garvey's Pan-Africanist philosophy laid the foundation for international movements of Black Power that persist today.

Through the Freedom of Information Act, historian Maxwell was able to solicit thousands of FBI files on artists, intellectuals, and their affiliated cultural institutions, such as James Baldwin, the Black Arts Repertory Theater/School in Harlem, W.E.B. Du Bois, *Ebony* magazine, and many more. According to former FBI agent Tyrone Powers, the FBI's aim was "to weaken and unlink the unified chain" between Black Consciousness movements, from generation to generation. The surveillance program existed for five decades and only expired when Hoover did too, in 1972. As was widely discussed with the release of Clint Eastwood's biographical film on Hoover in 2011, Hoover's ancestry can apparently be traced to African Americans in McComb, Mississippi.[10] Oh, the *Irony of a Negro Policeman*!

As de Antonio and Basquiat continue to discuss the impact of and intrigue around Hoover, Basquiat confirms the information written in his CV sketch.

BASQUIAT: I wrote to J. Edgar Hoover as a kid, did you know that?

DE ANTONIO: No.

BASQUIAT: I sent him a drawing.

DE ANTONIO: That's wonderful, and you got a letter?

BASQUIAT: I didn't get any letter back. It was one of the first art things I did. I must have been eight or nine.

DE ANTONIO: He answered practically everything unless he thought it was insulting.

BASQUIAT: I got no letter back. It was a design for a gun.

DE ANTONIO: *That* he might not have answered.

BASQUIAT: It was by a child, though. The bullets were really, really big . . .

Born in 1960, Basquiat would have been in the third grade right at the swell of social tumult, both nationally and abroad, between 1968 and 1969. This period likewise reflects dramatic shifts in his private world. In an interview with Becky Johnston, Basquiat shares that his most vivid childhood memory was of getting hit by a car while playing in the street: "I remember it just being very dreamlike, and seeing the car sort of coming at me and then just seeing everything through sort of a red filter."[11] He would spend a month in Kings County Hospital, in Brooklyn, where his mother, Matilde Basquiat, gave him a copy of *Gray's Anatomy*—key source material that he would eventually draw great influence from. That year would also mark the separation of Jean-Michel's parents.[12]

In the essay "Black Liberation and 1968," Donna Murch explains:

> In reassessing 1968 from a half-century of hindsight, what is most striking is how definitive the year was for the criminalization of radical black protest, ranging from the punitive attack on urban rebellions that swept the country after King's assassination to the targeted assaults on the segment of the black liberation movement that confronted domestic racial violence through the lens of state socialism and anticolonial struggle.[13]

Empowered by President Nixon's campaign promise in the election of 1968 to dispose of "troublemakers," Hoover declared militant black nationalist organizations—namely, the Republic of New Africa, the National Committee to Combat Fascism, the Black Liberation Front, and the Black Panther Party—"the greatest threat to the internal security of this country."[14] Hoover's singular goal was to infiltrate and dismantle revolutionary organizations through intensive counterintelligence programs, more commonly known as COINTELPRO. Murch further describes how Hoover's "virulent campaign" to destroy the Black Panther Party was unleashed at the very moment the party was initiating strident community survival programs for working poor communities, such as free medical clinics, community ambulance services, legal clinics, and children's services like the free book and breakfast programs.[15]

In 1969, the year third grader Basquiat sent his mailer to Hoover, the police arrested 749 Black Panthers, and twenty-seven Panthers died. Two historical flash points of that traumatic moment include a deadly shootout on UCLA's campus and predawn police raids in Chicago. Alprentice "Bunchy" Carter and John Huggins were slain in the school's Campbell Hall by a leader of a rival black organization under precarious circumstances that many Panthers believe were influenced by COINTELPRO.[16] In Chicago, the police raided the homes of party leaders Fred Hampton and Mark Clark and killed them.[17] All four of these casualties were in their twenties. Had they lived, both Carter and Hampton would have become young fathers in the coming months. Fifty years later, in 2018, certain members of the administration employed eerily similar rhetoric to criminalize dissent and social protest. Using the problematic category "Black Identity Extremists," this campaign traps and targets poor and working-class black and brown youth for speaking out against police abuse and brutality.[18]

A primary example of how this policy has manifested can be found in Ferguson, Missouri, after the impactful death of Michael Brown. A string of nefarious deaths have occurred since the decision not to indict white officer Darren Wilson, including those of the following leaders in the Movement for Black Lives: Edward Crawford, Darren Seals, Deandre Joshua, Shawn Gray, and Danye Jones, who was found hanging from a tree in his mother's yard.[19] Jones's mother, Melissa McKinnies, has rejected the police characterization of his death as a suicide. In a heartbreaking Facebook post featuring a photo of her son wearing a suit and corsage, she wrote, "They lynched my baby."[20] Much like the slain Panthers, all five of these men were in their twenties.

In her book *In the Wake: On Blackness and Being*, cultural studies scholar Christina Sharpe explains, "That these and other Black deaths are produced as normative still leaves gaps and unanswered questions for those of us in the wake of those specific and cumulative deaths." She continues, "In the wake, the past that is not past reappears, always, to rupture the present."[21] Basquiat's artwork illuminates this historical yet ongoing cultural crisis to inspire new social transformation. In honoring Basquiat's belief that art belongs to the people, then We-the-People must retrieve and reclaim its life force from the thin rarified air of exclusionary spaces and ground it back to what Hawaiians call the *'āina*, or the land, planet Earth.[22] In multiple works across the stretch of his oeuvre, Basquiat visualized the savagery of antiblack police terror in contemporary America and beyond.

BEATING HEARTS AND LA HARA

In many of his paintings, including *Irony of a Negro Policeman* (1981) **[PL. 10]**, *La Hara* (1981) **[PL. 11]**, *Untitled (Sheriff)* (1981) **[PL. 12]**, and *Defacement (The Death of Michael Stewart)* (1983) **[P. 17, PL. 1]**, Basquiat portrays law enforcement officers as terrifying monsters. These depictions of the police, all produced during the early 1980s in New York City, aid our contemporary understanding of how race and state power function through the visual. For example, in *Defacement* and *Sheriff*, the cops appear racialized as white with pinkish shrimp-scampi skin tones. In *Irony of a Negro Policeman*, Basquiat renders a lone officer as a darkened figure. The striking subtext of the title is that the "negro" policeman foolishly identifies as white. Basquiat's use of the term *negro* should be interpreted within the context of his cultural background as Puerto Rican and Haitian, his early educational

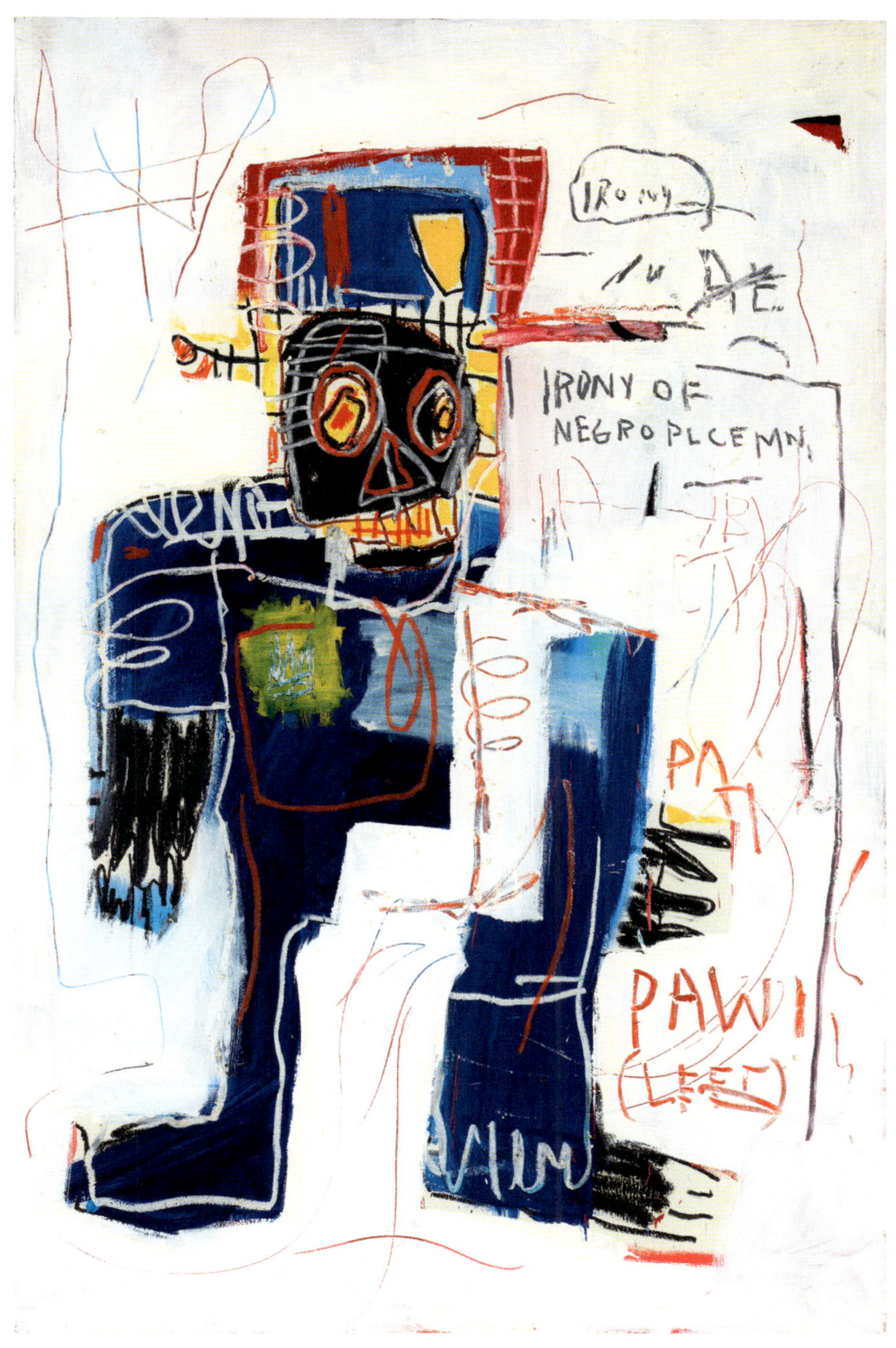

PLATE 10
Jean-Michel Basquiat
Irony of a Negro Policeman, 1981
Acrylic and oil stick on wood panel
72 × 48 inches (182.9 × 121.9 cm)
AMA Collection

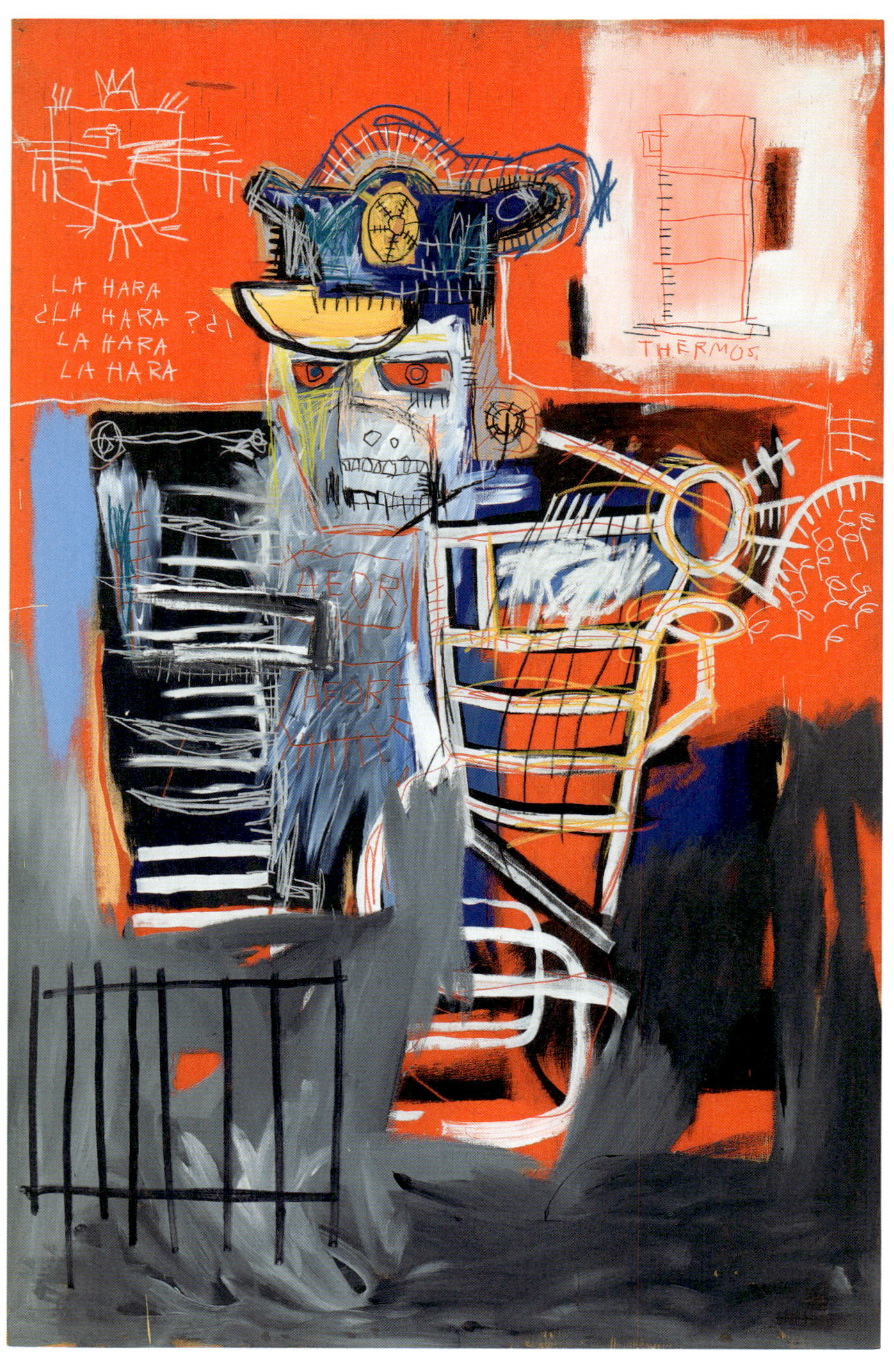

PLATE 11
Jean-Michel Basquiat
La Hara, 1981
Acrylic and oil stick on wood panel
72 × 48 inches (182.9 × 121.9 cm)
Arora Collection

experiences in the Caribbean, and also the etymological shifts in racial terminology during the periods of his formative years.[23] If we take a cue from the language slippage between *negro* in Spanish and Portuguese, or *nègre* in French, and its direct translation as *black*, then Basquiat is signifying the coded layers and linguistics of black subjectivity from Puerto Rico to Port-au-Prince to Brooklyn.

If *Defacement* and *Sheriff* illustrate the projection of white power and its gaze, and *Irony of a Negro Policeman* depicts the incongruity of black authority and internalization of self-hatred, then *La Hara* represents both dynamics. *La Hara*'s central subject is less identifiably black or white and appears like a ghost with white bones and an opaque shadow. This critical ambivalence conjures *abstraction*—a key strategy in racial ideology. *La Hara*'s countenance frightens with its translucent mutability. The powder-white skin loosely covers bloodshot eyes, with the jaw open just enough to conjure a felt yet muffled scream, hiss, or grunt.

La Hara commands a large presence. Unlike in *Defacement* and *Irony of a Negro Policeman*, the background is not a spare white negative space or white wash of paint, but is drenched in fire-engine red. Basquiat includes the words "LA HARA," repeated four times, the second in question form, "¿LA HARA ?¿!" The title *La Hara* derives from a Nuyorican/Boricua slang term for a policeman, which came into use between the 1940s and 1970s and was based on the name O'Hara, since the majority of New York policemen at the time were Irish. In the Spanish language, the *j* has an *h* sound, so the popular spelling is *jara*, with the common phrases "Cuidado ahi viene la jara," or "La jara! La jara!" meaning "Be careful, the police are coming" or "The police!"[24] Evoking a Spanglish sensibility, Basquiat stylizes the spelling to match its sound.

At the bottom of *La Hara*, Basquiat fills the canvas with a gray expanse of paint that spreads like smog across the foreground. A black gate, like a grid, separates the viewer and *la hara*, a phantom prison. On the opposite, bleached corner, the word "THERMOS" appears scratched underneath a rectangular shape that resembles the kind of canister a beat cop might carry coffee in on nightly rounds. In the matter of death, the thermos could signify a morgue for frozen bodies, a vessel for cremation, or an urn. Alternatively, it could represent the "Afro-Atlantic cool" that Robert Farris Thompson described as a requisite for survival.[25]

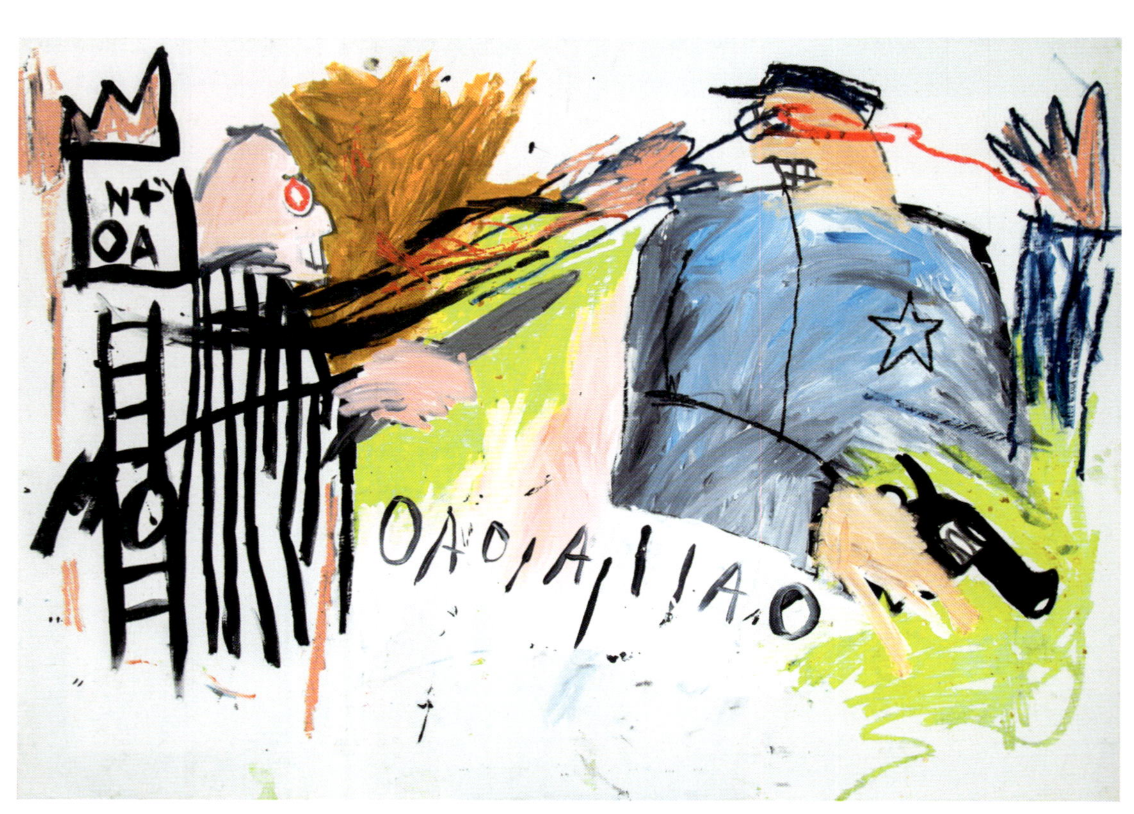

PLATE 12

Jean-Michel Basquiat

Untitled (Sheriff), 1981

Acrylic and oil stick on canvas

51½ × 74 inches (130.8 × 188 cm)

Carl Hirschmann Collection

La hara acts as a grim reaper flanked by two possible outcomes—incarceration or death by fire or ice. In faith systems such as Christianity, gates symbolize the entry to heaven or hell, enacting *la hara* as the gatekeeper.[26] The figure's body has no flesh, only bones and breath, as in many paintings by Basquiat where the rib cage and chest are exposed, including *Flexible* and *Gold Griot* (both 1984). The rib cage protects the lungs, the breathing mechanism. The center of *la hara*'s chest is a blur of whitish grays, like a puff of air or smoke, and contains a red-outlined circle twice inscribed with "AEOR." Did Basquiat replace *aero* for the Latin root word for air, in the same way he revised *la jara* as *la hara*? The letters "AEOR" may also represent the different chambers of the heart—the aorta, artery, and ventricle.

So what of the heart? Why does it stop or start beating? The deaths of Eric Garner in 2014 and artist Michael Jerome Stewart in 1983 catalyzed a collective consciousness around police brutality and corruption in American cities. Both deaths were first reported by authorities as being the result of cardiac arrest. However, before the heart went, first went the breath—by force, by chokehold.[27] To obfuscate a death by sustained strangulation by labeling it cardiac arrest is to naturalize death from murder to objective scientific fact.

DON'T HOLD YOUR BREATH: POLICE TERROR AND SAVING FACE

Racizm in the air. Don't breathe.

GRAFFITI BY GOD ON THE CHAZEN MUSEUM AT THE UNIVERSITY OF WISCONSIN AT MADISON IN APRIL 2016 [28]

Breath is the bridge, which connects life to consciousness, which unites your body to your thoughts. Whenever your mind becomes scattered, use your breath as the means to retake hold of your mind.

THICH N. HANH, *THE MIRACLE OF MINDFULNESS* [29]

In the ancient medical treatise on traditional Chinese medicine the *Huangdi Neijing*, written by the Chinese emperor Huangdi about 2600 BCE, the lung organ is a bridge between heaven and earth, and the initial vessel to receive pure energy, or *qi*: "When the lung is cold, then both outside and inside [transmission] have come together. Subsequently, the [two cold] evils settle in the [lung]. This, then, causes lung cough."[30] And the breath negotiates the external and internal cycles of life. Grief therefore manifests as an imbalance in the lungs. In 2017 Erica Garner named her newborn son after her slain father, Eric Garner. Only four months after giving birth to her son, Erica experienced an asthma attack that led to cardiac arrest, coma, and then death at the age of twenty-seven. After witnessing her father's unjust death via news footage and citizen journalism, she seized upon the liberty torch and transformed his pleas for his life into protest chant—*I can't breathe, I can't breathe, I can't breathe*. Eric Garner uttered this phrase eleven times when his asthma met the outsize stress of police ambush.[31] As Paul Butler explains in *Chokehold: Policing Black Men*, Daniel Pantaleo, one of Garner's arresting officers, used a chokehold even though the NYPD banned this excessive and lethal practice nearly thirty years ago.[32]

In 1983 on the Left Coast, Adolph Lyons, a twenty-four-year-old black man, sued the Los Angeles Police Department for placing him in a chokehold, in *City of Los Angeles v. Lyons*. Although the Supreme Court denied Lyons's claim, the case created a legal precedent and discourse on chokehold practices in law enforcement. Thurgood Marshall, the first African American Supreme Court justice, wrote in dissent, "It is undisputed that chokeholds pose a high and unpredictable risk of serious injury or death. Chokeholds are intended to bring a subject under control by causing pain and rendering him unconscious. . . . The result may be death caused by cardiac arrest or asphyxiation."[33]

In the same year of 1983, Michael Stewart, a twenty-five-year-old black man in New York City, died of the hypothetical yet "undisputed" sequence noted by Justice Marshall—police chokehold, asphyxiation, cardiac arrest, coma, and then death. Thirty years and eleven mercy pleas later, Eric Garner suffered the same fate. In 2014 Broken Windows policing killed Eric Garner.[34] Zoom back to the future in 1983, when transit officers beat Michael Stewart over his entire body of a mere 140 pounds.[35] According to Jennifer Clement's *Widow Basquiat*, based on Suzanne Mallouk's account of her relationship with Basquiat, "[Stewart's] face is covered in small cuts and bits of glass are visible in his flesh."[36] The city's chief medical examiner, Dr. Elliot M. Gross, first reported to the press that the cause of Stewart's death was cardiac arrest, with no evidence of beating.[37] Forensic pathologists that worked on behalf of the Stewart family found the final cause of death to be strangulation by an illegal chokehold with a nightstick, and a massive brain hemorrhage. To bleach evidence of the blood veins in the eyeballs indicative of hemorrhage, Gross removed them and placed them in a formalin solution so they might become as blindingly white as the lies that construct and reproduce white supremacy.[38]

Stewart belonged to the downtown scene, but his humanity would be claimed citywide. As *graffiteros* would say, Stewart's spirit went ALL CITY.[39] His death catalyzed a civic moral reckoning against the drumbeats of Reagan's moralistic culture wars.[40] Graffiti became the cipher for straw-man arguments used to justify police violence. In response to the tragedy, Keith Haring created a large mural titled *Michael Stewart—USA for Africa* (1985) **[PL. 13]**. Haring's imagery connects the police strangulation of Stewart to the violence of South Africa's apartheid regime. The anti-apartheid struggle had become a site of burgeoning Afro-diasporic internationalism and global protest through a disinvestment movement.[41] Unlike Basquiat's ghostly figures, Haring's extremely graphic depiction features Stewart's naked black body with a neck stretched by the nightstick chokehold of two enormous peach-toned fists. Haring realized the scene as a large mural, nearly 10 feet in height by 12 feet wide, that reenacts the violation against Stewart on a spectacular scale.[42]

On the wall of Haring's studio in the Cable Building two years earlier, in 1983, Basquiat created his own tribute to Stewart, the diminutive *Defacement (The Death of Michael Stewart)*.[43] The distinction between their responses reveals the underlying racial divide that existed among white and black participants in graffiti and art society. According to scholar Frances Negrón-Muntaner, "The Haring-Basquiat counterpoint enables an analysis of the role racialization plays in the making of commercially viable artists."[44] With regard to physical safety and personal security when doing graffiti, Negrón-Muntaner continues, "Haring broke the law and risked being caught by drawing along the subway stops, yet once he was arrested the artist received lenient treatment."[45] Basquiat knew the risk for him was perilous, even fatal.

The word "¿DEFACEMENT©?" hangs over the violent scene depicted in Basquiat's painting, but with its legibility complicated: the central *E* has been marked over.[46] The stain in the middle of the word bifurcates it; the word itself becomes broken. *Defacement* can evoke multiple meanings. The primary connotation signifies vandalizing property with any foreign material applied to a surface, disrupting its original appearance. In the seminal graffiti documentary *Style Wars*, also from 1983, graffiti writer IZ describes the antagonism between writers and the train, stating, "This is the transit system. They don't like it to be defaced."[47] In a *High Times* feature by Glenn O'Brien titled "Graffiti '80," graffiti legend and subculture hero Lee Quiñones reacted to the term:

> "I hate that word defacing; it's a sinful word to me," says Lee. "People say, 'It's not yours, Lee. It's not yours.' I say, '*I don't care!*' I just want to make it nice. Wake you up in the morning when you're seeing the train. . . . People see my pictures, (he says) and say, 'Wow, it's really beautiful, but you're defacing and destroying property.' I say, 'Then what the fuck are you saying it's beautiful for?'"[48]

Burning an entire car earned the respect of other graffiti writers throughout the city. The train was the most coveted surface because of its mobility and size and the risk associated with producing on it. Using a similar definition of *defacement*, Basquiat once described his collaborative style with Warhol: "Andy would start most of the paintings. He would start one and put something very recognizable on it, or a product and I would sort of deface it."[49]

An alternative reading of the term *defacement* could refer to Michael Stewart's figurative decapitation by strangulation, the disconnection between his face and body, or a reference to the bleaching of Stewart's eyes, removed from his body in the morgue as part of the city authority's attempt to "save face" with a massive cover-up.[50] Basquiat applies Spanish punctuation, framing the word with the double question mark, posing defacement as a question or an exclamatory statement, a statement of outraged disbelief. Does writing your name on the subway platform justify physical abuse and death? Creating spectacle as a disciplinary gaze is a key dialectical strategy in maintaining the performance of race.

Historian Robin Kelley explains how lynching reflects the "history and character of police violence in the America of the twenty-first century precisely because it reveals the sexual and gendered dimensions of maintaining the color line and disciplining black bodies."[51] Kelley notes, "Even though only about one fourth of the lynchings from 1880 to 1930 were prompted by accusations of rape, and though a significant number of lynch victims were political activists, labor organizers, or Black men and women deemed 'insolent' or 'uppity' toward Whites, the most sensationalized and highly publicized lynching involved a Black man accused of raping a White woman: hence the genital mutilation. . . . More than anything else, lynching was a means of protecting the purity of White womanhood from Black male rapists."[52] While the press described the catalyst behind the brutality against Stewart as a display of antigraffiti policing, artist Lyle Ashton Harris discussed an alternative history to explain the backstory of his photograph titled *Saint Michael Stewart* (1994) **[P. 128, PL. 18]**. Harris, a native of New York, had befriended Basquiat at the nightclub Area in 1985, where Basquiat was a regular; such downtown clubs and dive bars mapped fertile ground for creativity and community. Musician and downtown hero Felice Rosser recalled how Stewart would frequent the Second Avenue dive bar where she worked after he finished his shift at the nearby Pyramid Club, a job that connoted a certain status in the downtown scene.[53] On the fateful night of his attack, Stewart had been socializing at the Pyramid on a night off; his coworkers would become primary witnesses for the case, attesting to his sober state.[54]

Describing the inspiration behind his photographic portrait, Harris shared one rumor that had been circulating: that the police victimized Stewart because he was found kissing a white woman outside the train station.[55] Whether or not this has been confirmed as true, Harris's version reflects the local community's cognizance of how the NYPD helped enforce social divisions of race, class, and sexuality. Stewart's killing symbolized how the growing practice of racial profiling created a visual death warrant against the bodies of young black and brown males. In an interview from 2017, Harris explains further, "But I think Michael Stewart, in a way, spoke to . . . the mythological saint, or the possibility of transcendence. Or the possibility of the spirit that cannot be destroyed, and that was the ghost that somehow ran through all of us."[56]

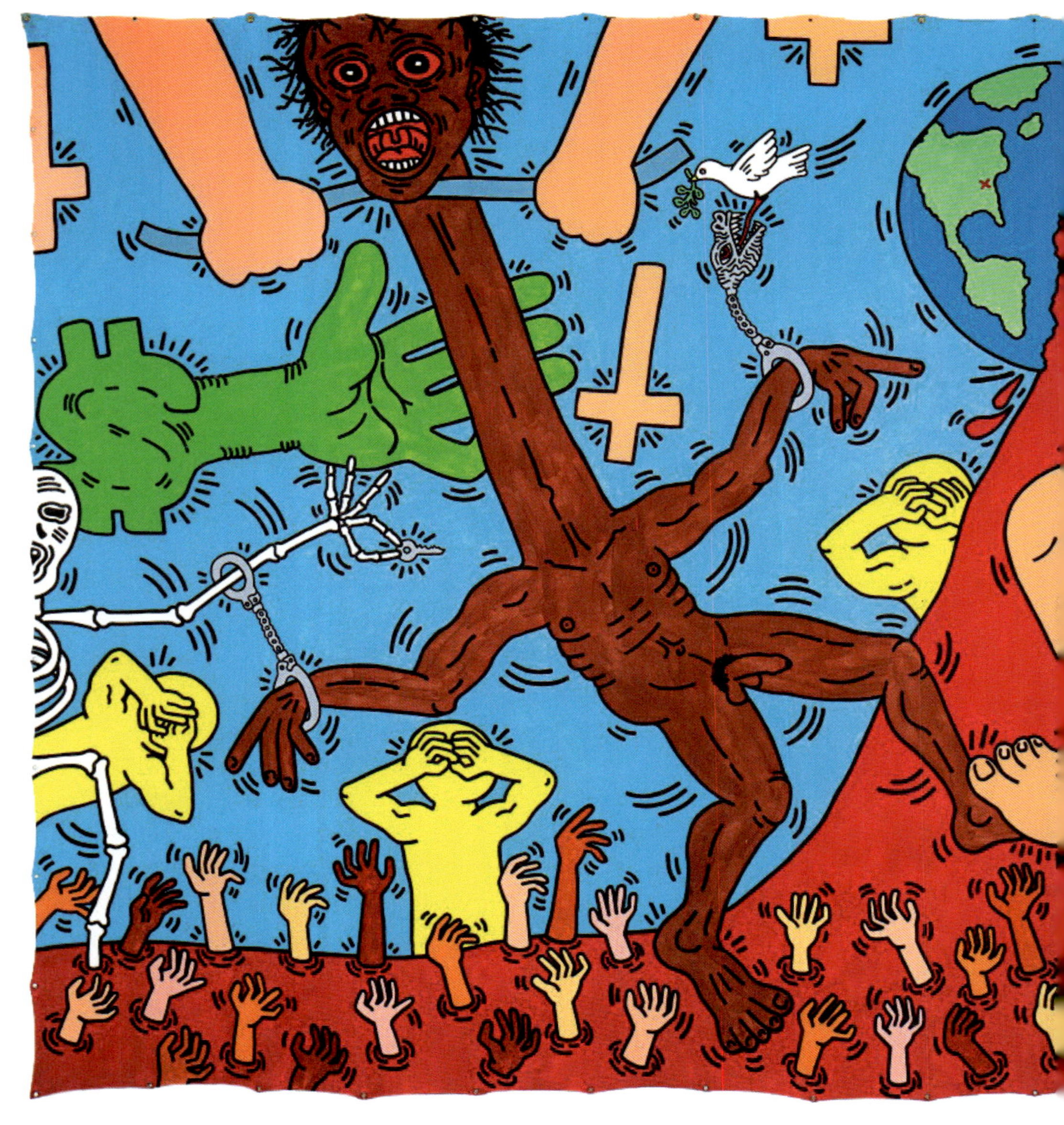

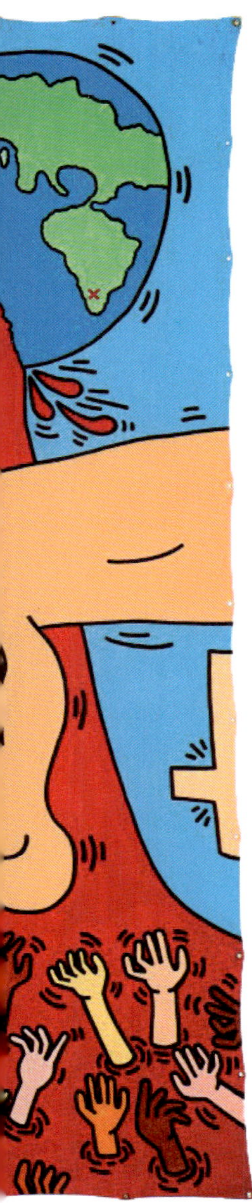

PLATE 13

Keith Haring

Michael Stewart—USA for Africa, 1985

Enamel and acrylic on canvas

116 × 144 inches (294.6 × 365.8 cm)

Collection of Monique and Ziad Ghandour

This ghost appears in many of Basquiat's pieces and engenders a particular violence against black lives that is at once structural, historical, ongoing, and futuristic. "Gothic violence remains a part of everyday black life," notes literary scholar Sheri-Marie Harrison in her essay "New Black Gothic."[57] In countless other works, Basquiat isolates body parts portraying the depersonalization and commodification of blackness. However, in his tribute piece to Stewart, Basquiat does not focus on black anatomy. Instead, the subjects are otherworldly. The face of the central, monochromatic figure that represents Stewart is blotted out. Facial features are obscured. Caribbean studies scholar Jana Evans Braziel describes how the "black sarcophagus figure evokes entombment, a catacomb, a 'defaced' or violently erased human life."[58] Like the children's game where one must catch another's shadow, the stain reflects disembodiment, a falling apart.

Many graffiti writers frequented Haring's art studio and marked up the wall surrounding Basquiat's piece. For example, graffiti legend Zephyr wrote his graffiti tag on the bottom-right corner of the painting, next to an unshapely dark spot. Basquiat's portrait obscures any specific facial features or recognizable body parts except for the head and shoulders, creating a black abstraction mimicking the very lack of distinction at the heart of racial profiling. Scholar and poet Elizabeth Alexander describes the conundrum of articulating race at the moment of unspeakable acts of violence in response to what pioneering scholar of black Marxism and racial capitalism Cedric Robinson called "the pavement lynching of Rodney King," twenty-six-years-old in 1991:[59]

> What do black people say to each other to describe their relationship to their racial group when that relationship is crucially forged by incidents of physical and psychic violence which boil down to the "fact" of abject blackness? Put another way, how does an incident like King's beating consolidate group affiliations by making blackness an unavoidable, irreducible sign which, despite its abjection, leaves creative space for group self-definition and self-knowledge?[60]

Although race is a social construct, racial profiling relies on visual identification, or what postcolonial philosopher Frantz Fanon calls "the facts of blackness."[61] Devoid of any specific features, Basquiat's figure of Stewart becomes a black everyman.

THE SPECTACULAR POLICE MOB THEATER

You were put here to protect us
But whc protects us from you?
KRS-ONE, "WHO PROTECTS US FROM YOU?"[62]

Beat me, hate me
You can never break me
Will me, thrill me
You can never kill me
MICHAEL JACKSON, "THEY DON'T REALLY CARE ABOUT US"[63]

In *Loaded: A Disarming History of the Second Amendment*, scholar Roxanne Dunbar-Ortiz states, "Following the Rodney King riots in Los Angeles and the development of Cop Watch groups in cities around the United States, along with the widespread incarceration of black men in the 1990s, what had long been known by scholars, but rarely acknowledged in media or history texts, became increasingly clear on a national level: The origins of policing in the United States were rooted in slave patrols."[64] These patrols were in charge of tracking and capturing runaway enslaved persons, or, put another way, black people already free.

Framing the black figure in *Defacement*, Basquiat casts two police figures with pink faces with large oblong eyes and fangs for teeth, wearing gold stars and badges in NYPD blue. The porcine faces of the police reference the characterization of the policeman as "pigs," a derogatory term for the London police force coined in the early nineteenth century. There is speculation that the phrase "fascist pig" emerged during the 1960s in reference to the gas masks worn by American police subduing civil rights protestors, or to the pigs in George Orwell's 1945 novel *Animal Farm*.[65]

In a poetry collection based on Basquiat's works, titled *To Repel Ghosts* (2005), Kevin Young responds to *Defacement*: "Give those men a PABST BLUE RIBBON, a slap on the wrist a meddle of honor."[66] Young's wordplay on *Pabst Blue Ribbon* and *meddle of honor* suggests another interpretation of what happened that fateful evening. Perhaps the policemen's pink skin is the result of rosacea caused by alcohol intake, a can of Pabst Blue Ribbon beer causing them to "meddle" or interfere with Michael Stewart unnecessarily. *Meddle* further connotes a culture of gossip and proliferation of unreliable information, as in, "Stop meddling in your neighbor's affairs." Or it might reference the state *meddling* with evidence and the truth. Although there was an abundance of witnesses to Stewart's assault, the city's attempt to cover up police misconduct corrupted the truth of Stewart's death. *Meddle* puns on *medal of honor*, as in, the award given for outstanding service. Alternatively, Young could be playing on the word *cop*, which originated from *copper*, or "one who cops or catches or arrests a criminal," and its link to the metal. According to *The Merriam-Webster New Book of Word Histories*, the term *cop* first appeared in print in 1864: "The connection with the metal copper must have been almost at once in the popular mind, for a British newspaper reported in 1864 that 'as they pass a policeman they will . . . exhibit a copper coin, which is equivalent to calling the officer copper.'"[67]

Defacement's police duo appear to hold coral-brown phallic sticks in midstrike against the black statuesque void that hangs amid a frenzy of motion in blue and brown swirls. Basquiat creates a scene like a witness's testimony, evoking the live footage of the killing of Oscar Grant captured on a cell phone in Oakland in 2008, or the video of Rodney King in 1991 or Philando Castile in 2016, and on and on.[68] The police figures in Basquiat's *Defacement* are faded in motion, the bottom half of their bodies blending into the negative white space. They do not have legs, but their arms wield weapons. The police figure on the right projects a steely gaze. An upside-down triangle hangs in the center of one officer's uniform like a badge, yet the figure is mute, with no mouth. The artist portrays the other cop in profile with one evil eye and a set of vampire fangs out to suck blood.

Basquiat's painting offers a black-authored "national narrative" in which racist cops are exposed as vicious monsters, and Michael Stewart symbolizes innumerable black victims from the present, past, and future. Responding to the 1943 antipolice uprisings in Harlem, William H. Johnson offered another version of this story in the painting *Moon over Harlem* (ca. 1943–44) **[FIG. 2]**. According to the Schomburg Center for Research in Black Culture, "The Harlem Riots of 1943, which took place on August 1–2, began with a white policeman's attempt to arrest a black woman for disorderly conduct, and his shooting of an interceding black soldier, Private Robert Bandy."[69] The riots brought about the death of six people, over a thousand arrests, and property damages estimated at five million

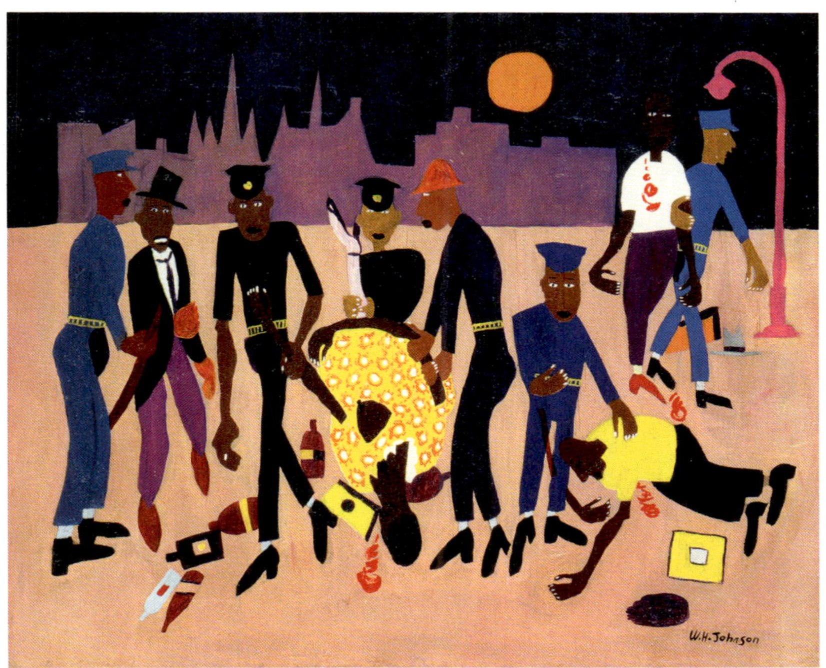

FIGURE 2
William H. Johnson
Moon over Harlem, ca. 1943–44
Oil on plywood
28½ × 35¾ inches (72.5 × 90.8 cm)
Smithsonian American Art Museum, Gift of the Harmon Foundation, 1967

dollars. The Schomburg cites racial discrimination in the armed forces and police brutality against black people as the root cause of the conflict, as well as the broader discriminatory policies and practices perpetuated by whites in general.

Akin to Basquiat's *Irony of a Negro Policeman* portrait, Johnson's black police officers personify the frustrating reality of social and economic inequality for black veterans despite their patriotic service, including that of Private Bandy. Johnson's isolation of body parts creates a "still life" effect, evoking James Baldwin's description of the event in "Notes of a Native Son": "All of Harlem indeed seemed to be infected by waiting. I had never before known it to be so violently still."[70] In Basquiat's *Defacement* the policemen's limbs are fragmented but connected by violent motion. In Johnson's painting, bottles resemble the shape of the officers' shoes and the limbs of the citizens that clutter the ground. Amid the fury of police batons, Basquiat etches a massive five-point star that matches the stars on the cop hats and a smaller one that floats like an asterisk, creating the cartoon illusion of being dizzy. Johnson likewise creates a Harlem moon that looms above the shadowed city skyline, like a solitary witness to history.

HALOS, HOODIES, AND (RE)COVERING THE HEAD

And these children that you spit on
As they try to change their worlds
Are immune to your consultations
They're quite aware of what they're going through
DAVID BOWIE, "CHANGES"[71]

I want you to know we will support your two children in a way that you will not.
EMMA GONZALES, PARKLAND STUDENT AND SURVIVOR ADDRESSING DANA LOESCH, NATIONAL RIFLE ASSOCIATION SPOKESWOMAN, AT A TOWN HALL MEETING IN SUNRISE, FLORIDA, FEBRUARY 2018[72]

In *Defacement* the oblique dark figure has three round peaks and a fourth, larger ring atop the head. The shortly rounded shapes could signify Stewart's dreadlocks or perhaps a damaged halo or wreath of thorns, wrought like a wire hanger.[73] Crowns and halos are iconic Basquiat motifs. In this instance, by placing a halo, Basquiat transforms a mutilated head with celestial orbs, creating what the Yoruba call *ori*, the crowned divinity. In painting a new crown and halo, Basquiat restores humanity to a mutilated face. Jana Evans Braziel interprets Basquiat's "aura" theme as a "reversal of light and dark, white and black."[74] Seen through Braziel's interpretation, Basquiat redefines dark radiant energy as brighter than whiteness.

In the current historical moment, a halo becomes a hoodie. In 2012 George Zimmerman, a neighborhood watchman, shot to death Trayvon Martin, a seventeen-year-old African American boy in Tampa, Florida. As in the Stewart case, media imagery has played a pivotal role in constructing contrary narratives. After the wide circulation of a black-and-white photograph of Trayvon in a hooded sweatshirt, commonly called a "hoodie," community activists mobilized the hoodie's visual symbolism through virtual protests and in-person demonstrations such as the Million Hoodie March in New York on March 21, 2012. The march's organizers called upon individuals to wear a hoodie in solidarity and to post portraits online.[75]

Like Basquiat's conferral of the halo, wearing a hoodie has become a way to reclaim power through reclaiming the head. Beyond its subversive political significance, the hoodie functions to cover the head. This simple practice is a common religious custom, present in

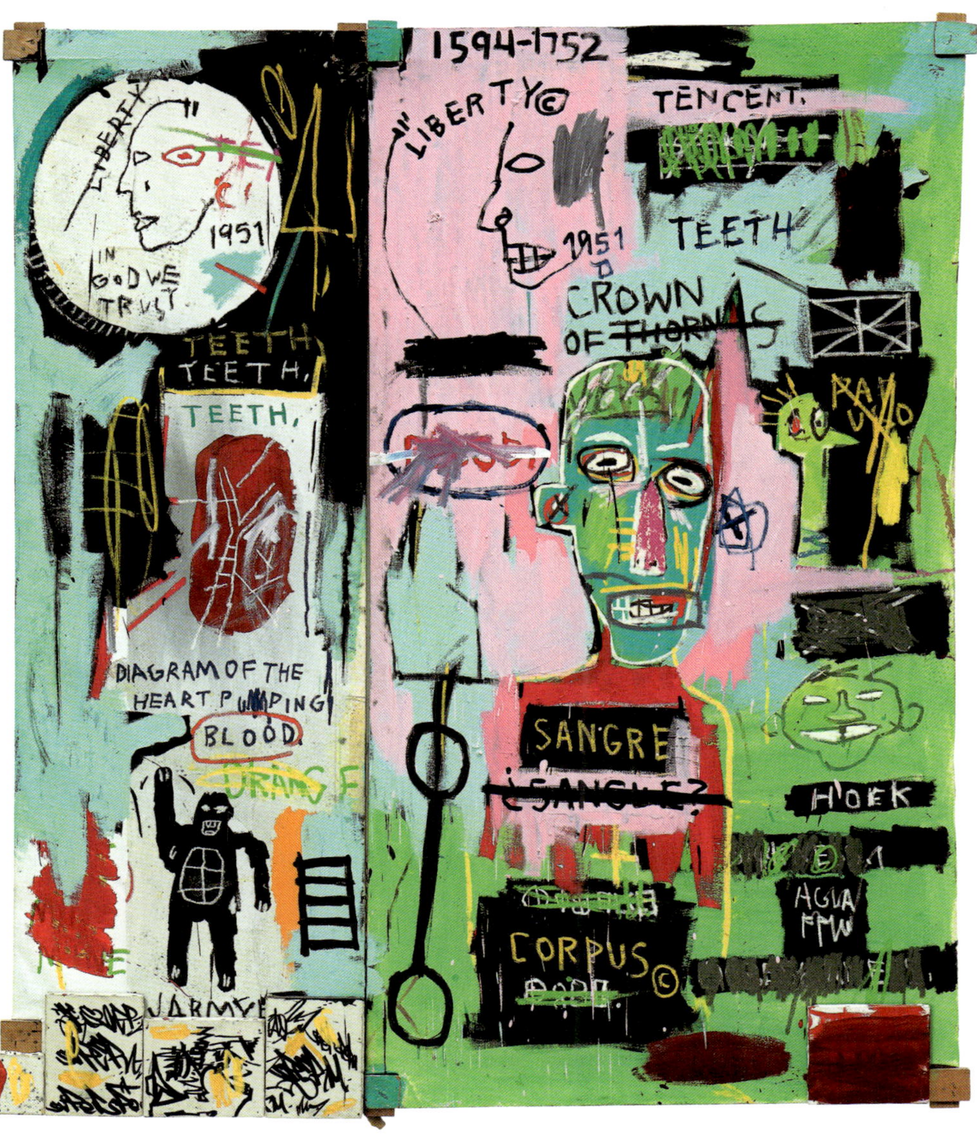

PLATE 14
Jean-Michel Basquiat
In Italian, 1983
Acrylic, oil stick, and ink marker on canvas
with wood supports, two panels
88½ × 80 inches (224.8 × 203.2 cm) overall
Courtesy The Brant Foundation,
Greenwich, Connecticut

Judaism with a *kippah* or yarmulke, Hinduism with turbans or *ghoonghat*, Islam with hijabs, and Rastafarian Nyabinghi and Boboshanti customs, among other faith systems.[76] In adorning the sacred head, these symbolic amulets mark and protect where the spirit resides in the human body. Or as Basquiat has written in paintings, talismans help "to repel ghosts."[77] Ritual intention and its costume then become armor for bodies vulnerable to guns, chokeholds, and bloodletting.

Cultural critic Greg Tate has emphasized how Basquiat transformed the criminality of blackness into "something holy, esoteric and visceral . . . [if not] deeply cerebral, meditative and unfixed to the purgatorial fantasy landscapes it has been consigned to."[78] In Tate's interpretation, Basquiat's portrait of Stewart shifts the physical violence toward a spiritual, contemplative plane that transcends the space and context of the crucible of antiblack racism in New York City, 1983.

Throughout contemporary history, the state has reproduced these "purgatorial fantasy landscapes" again and again. But not without families, communities, and artists who are pushing back with courage and resolve. Performance scholar and poet Fred Moten notes about building a social movement across difference, "The coalition emerges out of your recognition that it's fucked up for you, in the same way that we've already recognized that it's fucked up for us. I don't need your help. I just need you to recognize that this shit is killing you, too, however much more softly, you stupid motherfucker, you know?"[79]

Monsters, vampires, and zombies may be having a moment right now, occupying the highest offices in the homeland and beyond. But daybreak is coming with the relentless fury of the sun. Scholars Damien Sojoyner and Shana Redmond explain, "We say 'rebellion'; they say 'riot.' We say 'uprising'; they say, yet again, 'riot.' The narrative power of this difference is steeped in historical precedent."[80] From 1968 to 2019—rebel, rebel, toil and trouble.

Basquiat's artwork forebodes a warning to future devils and demons: recognize and defend the humanity of the most vulnerable among us or lose your very own.

NOTES

I conducted most of my research on *Defacement* and Basquiat's police portraits under snow embankments at the University of Rochester during my 2009–10 tenure as the predoctoral fellow at the Frederick Douglass Institute of African and African-American Studies (FDI). And I delivered my first lecture on it, titled "Basquiat's Babylon: Portraits of Police Brutality in the Age of Graffiti," during FDI's Speakers Series on December 1, 2009. Special thank-you to FDI's former director Jeffrey A. Tucker for his constant engagement and guidance of my journey as a scholar, as well as to Ghislaine Radegonde-Eison, GerShun Avilez, and the Visual and Cultural Studies community. Greg Tate planted the seed for this study on the impact of Michael Stewart. We met uptown on May 7, 2008, of the "slowdown protests" for Sean Bell, led by the Reverend Al Sharpton and the National Action Network. That moment initiated our dynamic exchange on Basquiat, and I am grateful that it continues to this day. At the University of Wisconsin at Madison, I acknowledge the critical support of the Nellie McKay Fellowship, Vilas Life Cycle Professorship of the Women in Science and Engineering Leadership Institute, and the Department of Afro-American Studies. I offer my deep gratitude and respect to the Basquiat family, especially Hervey and Jeanine Heriveaux. *Mojuba* to my godsister Rashida Bumbray for always helping the stars align and to Nancy Spector for her vision to recognize it as such. *Agyaman nak unay Nanangko ken Tatangko*, Dr. Sylvester Jr. and Mrs. Virginia; Jennifer and Christian Almiron; Frances and Sylvestre Acuña-Almiron; Rick, Leonardo, and Everisto Ziegler; and Bernice and Ervin (RIP) Everett. *Àse. Mabuhay* to J. Lorenzo Perillo, Christine Duque, Lindsay Dunn, Cindy Bello, Richard M. Naples, Vina Orden, and Simone Leigh. Lastly, I dedicate this essay to my tribe with every beat of my heart—Anthony, Sekou, and Noa Almiron-Johnson.

1

My invocation is inspired by the Afro-Atlantic libation ritual to honor the dead, which African art historian Robert Farris Thompson describes in his essay "An Aesthetic of the Cool": "It is going to seek the water. . . . Because water has the power of sustaining, within itself, the spirits of the dead and dominating them. Water attracts the souls of the dead; its coolness clarifies them, lends them tranquility. . . . 'The spirit of the departed brother is [thus] dispatched to the mystic river . . . the priest . . . lights the gunpowder sprinkled over the chalked representation of an arrow leading from a circle drawn around the base of the drum within the secret chamber to a point beyond the door. The gunpowder is ignited. It burns immediately along the length of the drawing, expelling, in this way the soul of the dead man [from the drum to the water] . . . the carrier of the vessel of water then chants: May your soul arrive cool at the sacred river, cool as it once existed in union with our sacred drum.'" Robert Farris Thompson, "An Aesthetic of the Cool," *African Arts* 7, no. 1 (Autumn 1973), p. 64. Basquiat and Thompson shared a simpatico connection; Basquiat cited Thompson's seminal work *Flash of the Spirit* (1983) as one of his favorite books and invited Thompson to write for the catalogue of his second solo show at Mary Boone Gallery, in 1985. According to curator Franklin Sirmans, it was the first time that Basquiat's art had been discussed "in terms of an Afro-Atlantic tradition." Franklin Sirmans, chronology, in Richard Marshall, *Jean-Michel Basquiat*, exh. cat. (New York: Whitney Museum of American Art, 1992), p. 246. See Robert Farris Thompson, "Activating Heaven: The Incantatory Art of Jean-Michel Basquiat," in *Jean-Michel Basquiat*, exh. cat. (New York: Mary Boone Gallery and Michael Werner Gallery, 1985), n.p.

2

Black Panther, directed by Ryan Coogler (Burbank, Calif.: Walt Disney Studios Motion Pictures, 2018), film. The character Okoye is the general of the Dora Milaje army of Wakanda. In breaking down a fight scene, director Ryan Coogler explains, "Okoye is a traditionalist, so she fights with a traditional weapon, the African spear, even though it's made out of vibranium, and she fights in a very traditionalist style. It almost looks like dancing when she fights. . . . You never see Okoye pick a gun up." "Black Panther's Director Ryan Coogler Breaks Down a Fight Scene," "Vanity Fair Videos," *Vanity Fair*, February 17, 2018, https://video.vanityfair.com/watch/black-panther-s-director-ryan-coogler-breaks-down-a-fight-scene. See also Sean P. Means, "How to Remove Movies from the Gun Debate: Follow the Lead of 'Black Panther,'" *Salt Lake Tribune*, February 21, 2018, https://www.sltrib.com/artsliving/movies/2018/02/21/how-to-remove-movies-from-the-gun-debate-follow-the-lead-of-black-panther/.

3

Tommy Orange, *There There* (London: Harvill Secker, 2018), p. 10. Orange's novel corrects the Thanksgiving narrative with devastating measure, linking the genocidal history of Native Americans to urban experiences in contemporaneity. In tribute to the host culture of the Lenape Nation, this passage serves to remind readers that the hyperviolence in New York City is part of an ongoing historical continuum tracing back to when Manhattan was called Manahatta, and begins in the mid-1600s with the Lenape Nation's encounter with European settlers. See Elizabeth De La Garza, *Manahatta to Manhattan: Native Americans in Lower Manhattan*, comp. Johanna Gorelick, ed. Alexandra Harris (New York: Smithsonian National Museum of the American Indian, 2010), http://www.k12.wa.us/IndianEd/TribalSovereignty/Elementary/USElementary/USElementary-Unit1/Level2-Materials/Manahatta_to_Manhattan.pdf.

4

On the official website of the Basquiat estate, the CV is featured alongside a chronology composed by Franklin Sirmans, which draws upon an interview that Sirmans conducted with Jean-Michel's father, Gerard Basquiat, on February 4, 1992. Gerard recalls, "He was always so bright, absolutely an unbelievable mind. . . . He drew and painted all of his life from the time he was three or four years old." Quoted in Franklin Sirmans, 1968 chronology entry, "The Artist" section, Basquiat estate website, accessed November 9, 2018, http://www.basquiat.com/artist.htm. First published in Marshall, *Jean-Michel Basquiat*.

5

Lisane Basquiat, quoted from a public discussion following the U.S. premiere of the documentary *Basquiat: Rage to Riches* (BBC Studios, 2018) at the Brooklyn Museum on August 30, 2018. Also participating were Jean-Michel's younger sister, Jeanine Basquiat, director David Shulman, and producer Janet Lee.

6

T. J. English, *The Savage City: Race, Murder, and a Generation on the Edge* (New York: William Morrow, 2011), p. xiv.

7

Jean-Michel Basquiat, "Emilio de Antonio with Jean-Michel Basquiat," *Interview*, July 1984; quoted from the online reprint, Basquiat, "New Again: Emilio de Antonio," *Interview*, May 6, 2015, https://www.interviewmagazine.com/culture/new-again-emilio-de-antonio; *J. Edgar*, directed by Clint Eastwood (Burbank, Calif.: Warner Brothers Pictures, 2011), film.

8

Homer Bigart, "J. Edgar Hoover: 40 Years the No. 1 Policeman," *New York Times*, May 10, 1964, https://www.nytimes.com/1964/05/10/archives/jedgar-hoover-40-years-the-no-1-policeman.html.

9

Maxwell describes, "Worth noting here is the case that the majority of the files devoted to Harlem Renaissance figures reveal anxieties over cosmopolitan fickleness and inadequate patriotism." William J. Maxwell, *F. B. Eyes: How J. Edgar Hoover's Ghostreaders Framed African American Literature* (Princeton, N.J.: Princeton University Press, 2017), p. 67. See also Maxwell, "F. B. Eyes Digital Archive: FBI Files on African American Authors and Literary Institutions Obtained through the U.S. Freedom of Information Act (FOIA)," Washington University Digital Gateway, accessed November 1, 2018, http://digital.wustl.edu/fbeyes/; Joshua Clark Davis, "The FBI's War on Black-Owned Bookstores," *The Atlantic*, February 19, 2018, https://www.theatlantic.com/politics/archive/2018/02/fbi-black-bookstores/553598/; and Sameer Rao, "How Hoover's FBI Targeted Black-Owned Bookstores," *Colorlines*, February 21, 2018, https://www.colorlines.com/articles/read-how-hoovers-fbi-targeted-black-owned-bookstores.

10

Educator Millie McGhee asserts this claim by tracing Hoover's black ancestry to her own family in McComb, Mississippi, in her book *Secrets Uncovered: J. Edgar Hoover—Passing for White?* (Rancho Cucamonga, Calif.: Allen-Morris, 2000).

11

Jean-Michel Basquiat: The Radiant Child, directed by Tamra Davis (New York: Arthouse Films, 2010), film.

12

Sirmans, chronology, in Marshall, *Jean-Michel Basquiat*, p. 233.

13

Donna Murch, "Black Liberation and 1968," *American Historical Review* 123, no. 3 (2018), p. 719, https://doi.org/10.1093/ahr/123.3.717.

14

Hoover, quoted in Murch, p. 720.

15

Murch, p. 720; and Erin Blakemore, "How the Black Panthers' Breakfast Program Both Inspired and Threatened the Government," History channel website, February 6, 2018, https://www.history.com/news/free-school-breakfast-black-panther-party. See also Ruth-Marion Baruch and Pirkle Jones, "The Black Panthers: Revolutionaries, Free Breakfast Pioneers," *National Geographic*, January 23, 2018, https://www.nationalgeographic.com/people-and-culture/food/the-plate/2015/11/04/the-black-panthers-revolutionaries-free-breakfast-pioneers/.

16

See, for example, a speech by Elaine Brown, a former Panther and witness to the shootings, at a 2010 launch event for the Memory Project commemorating the deaths of Carter and Huggins, "Elaine Brown Shares Context behind Events Surrounding Huggins and Carter Deaths," *Daily Bruin* (UCLA) on YouTube, December 28, 2012, https://www.youtube.com/watch?v=w4FpEEgAAME. See also Andra Lim, "The Memory Project Memorializes, Remembers Black Panthers Killed in Campbell Hall 41 Years Ago," *Daily Bruin*, May 25, 2010, https://dailybruin.com/2010/05/25/memory-project-memorializes-remembers-black-panthe/.

For the broader history of the Los Angeles Black Panthers, the emergence of the Black Studies department at UCLA, and the fatalities of Carter and Higgins, see Scot Ngozi-Brown, "The US Organization, Maulana Karenga, and Conflict with the Black Panther Party: A Critique of Sectarian Influences on Historical Discourse," *Journal of Black Studies* 28, no. 2 (November 1997), pp. 157–70, https://doi.org/10.1177/002193479702800202; Devon McReynolds and Ariel Smith, "Another Side of the Sixties: Black Panthers at UCLA," *Huffington Post*, May 25, 2011, https://www.huffingtonpost.com/devon-mcreynolds/another-side-of-the-sixti_b_589322.html; "Black History at UCLA: Bunchy Carter and the Black Panthers," produced by Dean Hughes, Victor Rocha, and Iris Less, *Daily Bruin* (UCLA) on YouTube, February 27, 2017, https://www.youtube.com/watch?v=JDS7urXsbsE; and *41st and Central: The Untold Story of the L.A. Black Panthers*, directed by Gregory Everett (Ultra Wave Vision / Film Revolution 2027, 2010), film.

17
Murch, "Black Liberation," p. 720. For more on the Black Panther Party, see Murch, *Revolution in Our Lifetime: A Short History of the Black Panther Party* (London: Verso, 2017); *The Black Panthers: Vanguard of the Revolution*, directed by Stanley Nelson (Arlington, Va.: PBS Distribution, 2015), film; and Alondra Nelson, *Body and Soul: The Black Panther Party and the Fight against Medical Discrimination* (Minneapolis: University of Minnesota Press, 2013).

18
At the House Judiciary Committee hearing that would eventually confirm Attorney General Jeff Sessions, Representative Karen Bass directly asked Sessions, "Could you name an African-American organization that has committed violence against police officers? Can you name one today that has targeted police officers in a violent manner?" Sessions could not. Quoted in Khaled A. Beydoun and Justin Hansford, "The F.B.I.'s Dangerous Crackdown on 'Black Identity Extremists,'" *New York Times*, January 20, 2018, https://www.nytimes.com/2017/11/15/opinion/black-identity-extremism-fbi-trump.html. See also Murch, "Black Liberation," p. 720.

19
See Jason Johnson, "Ferguson, Mo., Activists Are Dying, and It's Time to Ask Questions," *The Root*, last modified May 5, 2017, https://www.theroot.com/ferguson-activists-are-dying-and-it-s-time-to-ask-quest-1794955900. On Crawford's death in particular, see Kirsten West Savali, "Edward Crawford: Ferguson, Mo., Activist in Iconic Photo Found Dead from Gunshot Wound," *The Root*, last modified May 5, 2017, https://www.theroot.com/edward-crawford-ferguson-activist-in-iconic-photo-foun-1794950790; and Howard Johnson, "What Happened to Edward Crawford after This Photo?," BBC News, May 14, 2017, https://www.bbc.com/news/av/world-us-canada-39785768/what-happened-to-edward-crawford-after-this-photo.

20
McKinnies, quoted in "Mom of Man Found Hanging from Tree Says Anyone Involved 'Better Start Turning In on Your Folks,'" CBS News, November 2, 2018, https://www.cbsnews.com/news/danye-jones-death-melissa-mckinnies-tells-anyone-involved-to-start-turning-in-on-your-folks/. For more information on the organizing in Ferguson, see *Whose Streets?*, directed by Sabaah Folayan and Damon Davis (New York: Magnolia Pictures, 2018), film. For broader research on the Movement for Black Lives, an essential gathering of sources is Frank Leon Roberts's *Black Lives Matter Syllabus*, "'We Could Be Free': (Fall 2017 Course Version)," New York University, Black Lives Matter Syllabus website, accessed November 12, 2018, http://www.blacklivesmattersyllabus.com/. See also Keeanga-Yamahtta Taylor, *From #BlackLivesMatter to Black Liberation* (Chicago: Haymarket Books, 2016); and Jordan T. Camp and Christina Heatherton, eds., *Policing the Planet: Why the Policing Crisis Led to Black Lives Matter* (London: Verso, 2016).

21
Christina Sharpe, *In the Wake: On Blackness and Being* (Durham, N.C.: Duke University Press, 2016), pp. 7, 9.

22
Native Hawaiian scholar-revolutionary Haunani-Kay Trask describes *mālama 'āina* or *aloha 'āina* as "care and love of the land. . . . *'Āina*, one of the words for 'land,' means 'that which feeds.'" Haunani-Kay Trask, *From a Native Daughter: Colonialism and Sovereignty in Hawai'i* (Honolulu: University of Hawai'i Press, 2005), p. 141. Basquiat developed a special relationship to Hawai'i and frequently traveled to Hana, Maui. For Basquiat's experience in Hawai'i, see Susan Ryan, "Basquiat on the Beach," *Observer*, March 28, 2005, https://observer.com/2005/03/basquiat-on-the-beach/; and Cathay Che, "Polaroids from Paradise: Basquiat's Time in Hawaii," *Amuse*, August 14, 2015, https://amuse.vice.com/en_us/article/438d7w/polaroids-basquiat-hawaii.

23
The word *negro* may be outdated, but it continues to circulate. In the new Netflix comedy series *Patriot Act*, comedian Hasan Minhaj criticized the U.S. military for using the term in the context of a welcome packet used to orient service members to Saudi Arabia. Updated June 2018, it stated, "The population of the [Kingdom of Saudi Arabia] is mainly composed of descendants of indigenous tribes that have inhabited the peninsula since prehistoric times with some later mixture of Negro blood from slaves imported from Africa." See Thomas Gibbons-Neff, "American Military Apologizes for Booklet with Racially Offensive Language," *New York Times*, November 2, 2018, https://www.nytimes.com/2018/11/01/world/middleeast/american-military-racist-language.html. On the evolving history of racial terminology, see Key Malesky, "The Journey from 'Colored' to 'Minorities' to 'People of Color,'" *Code Switch*, NPR, March 30, 2014, https://www.npr.org/sections/codeswitch/2014/03/30/295931070/the-journey-from-colored-to-minorities-to-people-of-color.

24
On their self-titled album of 1998, the eclectic hip-hop, Latin rock band Ozomatli begins the song "Chota" by invoking *la jara* in the chorus: "Cuidado, ahi viene la placa, la jara / Cuidado, ahi viene, cubrete lacara." Translated: "Be careful, here comes the badge, the cops / Be careful, here they come, cover your face." The rap verse by emcee Chali 2na (Charles Stewart) describes a fatal interaction with the police: "He caught a nightstick lick to the brain piece." Charles Stewart, "Chota," track 10 on Ozomatli, *Ozomatli*, Almo Music, 1998.

25
In "An Aesthetic of the Cool," Thompson describes the Afro-Atlantic conception of cool: "According to these sources, coolness is achieved where one person restores another to serenity ('cools his heart'), where group calms group, or where an entire nation has been set in order ('this land is cool'). The phrase, 'this country is cool' (di konde koto) is used with the same valence and the same suggestiveness by the descendants of runaway African slaves on the

Piki Lio in the interior of Suriname, in northern South America. Idioms of cool heart and cool territory do not, to my knowledge, communicate in Western languages the same sorts of meanings of composure and social stability unless the phrasing is used by or has been influenced by the presence of black people of African heritage. I think that the African definition of metaphorical or mystical coolness is more complicated, more variously expressed than Western notions of *sang-froid*, cooling off, or even icy determination. It is a special kind of cool." Robert Farris Thompson, "An Aesthetic of the Cool," *African Arts* 7, no. 1 (Autumn 1973), p. 41.

26
"Gates Christian Symbol," Catholic Saints, accessed April 29, 2013, http://www.catholic-saints.info/catholic-symbols/gates-christian-symbol.htm.

27
According to an article from the Associated Press, "Dr. Elliot Gross, the city's chief medical examiner, performed the autopsy on Stewart. He first listed the cause of death as 'cardiac arrest pending further study,' adding, 'There Was No Evidence of Physical Injury Resulting or Contributing to Death.'" Samuel Maull, "Six Cops Indicted in Connection With the Death of Graffiti Artist." *AP News*, Associated Press, February 21, 1985, https://www.apnews.com/1ee169f691f2dda0f4af7d6477e7d343. An article in the *New York Times* stated: "Much of the controversy in the case had centered on Dr. Gross, who initially attributed Mr. Stewart's death to cardiac arrest and ruled out physical injury as a factor." Isabel Wilkerson, "Jury Acquits All Transit Officers in 1983 Death of Michael Stewart," *New York Times*, November 25, 1985, https://www.nytimes.com/1985/11/25/nyregion/jury-acquits-all-transit-officers-in-1983-death-of-michael-stewart.html.

In the media coverage of Eric Garner's death, one headline reports, "Man Dies after Suffering Heart Attack during Arrest." C. J. Sullivan, *New York Post*, July 18, 2014, https://nypost.com/2014/07/18/man-dies-after-suffering-heart-attack-during-arrest/. A time line published by the *New York Times* indicates that medical workers reported that Mr. Garner was in cardiac arrest in the ambulance. Ford Fessenden, "New Perspective on Eric Garner's Death," *New York Times*, last modified June 13, 2015, https://www.nytimes.com/interactive/2014/12/03/us/2014-12-03-garner-video.html. Another article notes, "The first official police report on his death failed to note the key detail that vaulted the fatal arrest into the national consciousness: that a police officer had wrapped his arm around Mr. Garner's neck." Al Baker, J. Goodman, and Benjamin Mueller, "Beyond the Chokehold: The Path to Eric Garner's Death," *New York Times*, June 13, 2015, https://www.nytimes.com/2015/06/14/nyregion/eric-garner-police-chokehold-staten-island.html. According to a Staten Island news source, "Police originally said he died from cardiac arrest but cell phone video taken by a bystander shows an officer, identified as Daniel Pantaleo, place Garner in a chokehold and drag the heavyset man to the ground with the help of other officers, as he gasped, 'I can't breathe! I can't breathe!'" Zak Koeske, "Eric Garner's Death Caused by Chokehold, Ruled a Homicide, Medical Examiner Says," *Staten Island Live*, accessed January 28, 2019, https://www.silive.com/news/2014/08/chokehold_caused_eric_garners.html#incart_big-photo.

28
On April 14, 2016, during a session of my undergraduate course Black Visual Culture at the University of Wisconsin–Madison, two white police officers arrested one of my students, Denzel McDonald, for writing graffiti on a campus building. As he would later share, McDonald had created pieces to voice resistance against multiple racist incidents on campus and to expose the university's inadequate response. McDonald drew inspiration from Basquiat's SAMO© street texts and in these pieces had adopted Basquiat's signature style of drawing the letter *E* with three detached horizontal lines. Immediately following the arrest, Professor Karma Chavez and I organized a press release and petition to support McDonald and to hold the university accountable. Then Chavez and I collaborated with student organizers—namely, Bianca Gomez, Michael Davis, Nyesha Brown, Eric J. Newble, Hannah Frank, William Mensah, Mara Horowitz, and Oliver Whiting—and the local grassroots community organization Freedom Inc. to lead a campus-wide protest and a subsequent creative response at the Chazen Museum with faculty artists Emily Arthur, John Hitchcock, and #TheRealUW. As of November 2018—more than two years after the arrest—the official UWPD website continues to publish videos of the arrest despite my formal requests to remove them. Owing to its ongoing publication, I continue to receive hate mail including death threats for supporting and defending my student. See Jack New, "Race, Graffiti and an Arrest," *Inside Higher Ed*, April 18, 2016, https://www.insidehighered.com/news/2016/04/18/u-wisconsin-student-pulled-class-arrested-anti-racist-graffiti. For further information on contemporary student movements toward social justice and racial equality, see Roderick A. Ferguson, *We Demand: The University and Student Protests* (Oakland: University of California Press, 2017).

29
Thich Nhat Hanh, *The Miracle of Mindfulness: An Introduction to the Practice of Meditation* (Boston: Beacon Press, 2016), p. 15.

30
Huang Di nei jinj Su wen, trans. Paul U. Unschuld and Hermann Tessenow with Zheng Jinsheng (Berkeley: University of California Press, 2011), p. 575.

31
In 1989 Spike Lee made a crucial contribution to the historical memory of Michael Stewart with his seminal film *Do the Right Thing*, through the martyrdom of the iconic character Radio Raheem. Unlike Basquiat's portrait of Michael Stewart as a slender shadow, Radio Raheem embodies the militancy of hip-hop, blasting Public Enemy's anthem "Fight the Power" on his boom box, larger than life. The police kill him by chokehold, lifting his large body off

the ground, the shot framing his feet dangling in the air. On July 21, 2014, Lee connected the chokehold police killings of Eric Garner and Michael Stewart, posting a chilling video titled "Radio Raheem and the Gentle Giant," in which he'd edited together the mob scene of Radio Raheem from *Do the Right Thing* and video footage of the police killing of Eric Garner. In the spirit of citizen journalism, a bystander named Ramsey Orta took and released the footage of Garner. Orta believed that he subsequently faced persistent police retaliation as a result, including eight arrests over the next two years and eventually prison. For more on the cultural significance and relevance of the iconic character Radio Raheem, see Elahe Izadi, "What Inspired 'Do the Right Thing' Character Radio Raheem, and Why He's Still Relevant Today," *Washington Post*, September 26, 2016, https://www.washingtonpost.com/news/arts-and-entertainment/wp/2016/09/26/what-inspired-do-the-right-thing-character-radio-raheem-and-why-hes-still-relevant-today/; Jelani Cobb, "Doing the Right Thing for Eric Garner," *New Yorker*, July 17, 2018, https://www.newyorker.com/news/news-desk/doing-the-right-thing-eric-garner; and Anealla Safdar, "NY Man Who Filmed Eric Garner's Death Heading to Jail," Al Jazeera, October 1, 2016, https://www.aljazeera.com/indepth/features/2016/10/ny-man-filmed-eric-garner-death-heading-jail-161001074627241.html.

32
Paul Butler, *Chokehold: Policing Black Men* (New York: New Press, 2018), p. 3.

33
City of Los Angeles v. Lyons, 461 U.S. 95 (1983); quoted in Butler, pp. 4–5.

34
For an analysis of the intrinsic relationship between Broken Windows policing and the victimization of Eric Garner, see Molly Crabapple, "How 'Broken Windows' Policing Harms People of Color," *Fusion* on YouTube, February 3, 2015, https://www.youtube.com/watch?v=iXl1QJRqPD8; and "Museum of Broken Windows," New York Civil Liberties Union website, September 26, 2018, https://www.nyclu.org/en/mobw.

35
Hip-hop historian Jeff Chang explains, "The public would learn that eleven transit cops had been involved with Stewart's arrest. But it was a mystery why so many were needed to subdue a 140-pound man." Jeff Chang, *Can't Stop Won't Stop: A History of the Hip-Hop Generation* (New York: Picador, 2005), p. 195.

36
Jennifer Clement, *Widow Basquiat* (New York: Broadway Books, 2014), p. 118.

37
Wayne Dawkins, *City Son: Andrew W. Cooper's Impact on Modern-Day Brooklyn* (Jackson: University Press of Mississippi, 2012), p. 130.

38
Dawkins, p. 130.

39
In the classic graffiti film *Style Wars* (1983), writer Zeb Roc Ski explains the expression: "It's called *going all city*—people see your tags in Queens, uptown, downtown, all over." *Style Wars*, directed by Tony Silver (New York: Public Art Films, 1983), film. In *Subway Art*, edited by Martha Cooper and Henry Chalfant: "A crew, according to T-Kid, 'is a unit of dudes who work together to achieve a goal: to get up and to go all city.'" Cooper and Chalfant presented their combined photo archives of graffiti in the exhibition *Moving Murals: Henry Chalfant & Martha Cooper's All City Graffiti Archive* at City Lore Gallery in New York in 2014. For a detailed historiography of the idiom *all city*, see Barry Popik, "'Going All City' (Graffiti Slang)," *Big Apple*, July 3, 2004, https://www.barrypopik.com/index.php/new_york_city/entry/going_all_city_graffiti_slang/.

40
In the seminal hip-hop film *Wild Style* (1983), Lee Quiñones, a bona fide graffiti legend, plays the protagonist who transitions from graffiti artist outlaw to darling studio artist. In the popular film *Beat Street* (1984), the protagonist is also a graffiti artist, who tragically dies on the third rail of the subway in pursuit of painting, or "bombing," a train. Both fictional stories reflect this particular moment of social anxiety and dilemma around inclusion, creativity, and the mainstreaming of marginalized voices. *Wild Style*, directed by Charlie Ahearn (New York: Submarine Entertainment, 1983), film; and *Beat Street*, directed by Stan Lathan (Los Angeles: Orion Pictures, 1984), film.

41
As historian Peniel Joseph explains, "America's civil rights struggles helped to inspire South Africa's anti-apartheid movement, and the Sharpeville Massacre, reverberating around the world in 1960 after South African police killed 69 peaceful demonstrators, became a clarion call for civil rights activists in the U.S." Joseph further asserts that the Black Consciousness movement in South Africa drew inspiration from the Black Power movement in the 1960s and 1970s in the U.S. Peniel E. Joseph, "South Africans and African Americans Bound by Struggle," *The Root*, January 12, 2017, https://www.theroot.com/south-africans-and-african-americans-bound-by-struggle-1790899235. As the reciprocity between both places and cultures endures, geography and urban anthropology scholars such as Anthony Johnson have noted how mayoral politicians such as Parks Tau and Amos Masondo drew inspiration from New York City as a blueprint for implementing conservative policy as well as policing in postapartheid inner-city Johannesburg. See Anthony Johnson, "Post-Apartheid Citizenship and the Politics of Evictions in Inner City Johannesburg," CUNY Academic Works, September 2016, https://academicworks.cuny.edu/gc_etds/1566/. Amos Masondo consults Mayor Rudy Giuliani in Bill Corcoran's "Johannesburg Turns a Corner," *Real Deal New York*, November 4, 2009, https://therealdeal.com/issues_articles/johannesburg-turns-a-corner/.

42

Haring reflected on painting *Michael Stewart—USA for Africa* (1985) in John Gruen, *Keith Haring: The Authorized Biography* (New York: Prentice Hall Press, 1991), p. 132.

43

Eric Fretz, *Jean-Michel Basquiat: A Biography* (Santa Barbara, Calif.: Greenwood, 2010), pp. 112–14; and Franklin Sirmans, chronology, in Marshall, *Jean-Michel Basquiat*, p. 243.

44

Frances Negrón-Muntaner, "The Writing on the Wall: The Life and Passion of Jean-Michel Basquiat," in *Boricua Pop: Puerto Ricans and the Latinization of American Culture* (New York: New York University Press, 2004), p. 127.

45

Negrón-Muntaner, p. 128.

46

Basquiat used the copyright symbol throughout his artwork beginning in 1977 with his collaborative conceptual project with classmate Al Diaz from City-As-School known as SAMO©. Basquiat's application of the symbol brings forth his preoccupation with property, ownership, and race within the historical context of the transatlantic slavery economy. The definitive text on the SAMO© phenomenon is *SAMO© . . . Since 1978: SAMO© . . . Writings, 1978–2018*, authored and illustrated by Al Diaz, edited by Mariah Fox (Santa Fe, N.M.: Irie Books, 2018).

47

Style Wars, directed by Tony Silver (New York: Public Art Films, Plexifilm, 1983), film; and *Style Wars* blog, accessed April 29, 2013, http://www.stylewars.com.

48

Quiñones, quoted in Glenn O'Brien, "Graffiti '80: The State of the Outlaw Art," *High Times*, June/July 1980, p. 54.

49

Basquiat, quoted in Negrón-Muntaner, p. 142.

50

In the *New York Times* Philip Shenon reported, "According to Dr. Grauerholz [Stewart family doctor], Dr. Gross placed the eyes in a container of Formalin, a solution that preserves tissue but tends to wash out any trace of blood. 'It bleaches out the red cells,' Dr. Grauerholz said." Another doctor authorized by the Stewart family, Dr. Wolf, states, "The removal of the eyes was superfluous. . . . At a minimum it was irreverent. At a maximum it may have been illegal." Philip Shenon, "Family of Victim Levels Charges of Deceit in Autopsy Conclusion," *New York Times*, January 28, 1985, https://www.nytimes.com/1985/01/28/nyregion/family-of-victim-levels-charges-of-deceit-in-autopsy-conclusion.html.

51

Robin D. Kelley, "'Slangin' Rocks . . . Palestinian Style': Dispatches from the Occupied Zones of North America," in *Police Brutality: An Anthology*, ed. Jill Nelson (New York: W. W. Norton, 2002), p. 27. Like the mother of Emmett Till almost thirty years earlier, Michael Stewart's parents, Carrie and Millard Stewart, chose to publicly release an image of their battered son; a surreptitiously taken photograph of Michael Stewart lying comatose in a hospital bed at Bellevue was published in the *East Village Eye* (October 1983) and the *New York Amsterdam News* (May 12, 1984). In the Recollections section of this volume, Carrie Stewart describes their action as an attempt to force accountability for the brutality suffered by their son by making it visible (pp. 152–53). Her account echoes Mamie Till on her decision in 1955 to photograph and publish the image of her son's mutilated corpse in black publications such as *Jet* magazine and the *Chicago Defender*, which catalyzed national attention: "There was just no way I could describe what was in that box. No way. And I just wanted the world to see." Quoted in Henry Hampton and S. Fayer, *Voices of Freedom: An Oral History of the Civil Rights Movement from the 1950s through the 1980s* (New York: Bantam Books, 1990), p. 6. See also *The Murder of Emmett Till*, directed and produced by Stanley Nelson (New York: Firelight Production, 2003), *PBS American Experience blog*, http://www.pbs.org/wgbh/americanexperience/films/till/.

To galvanize public dissent, both mothers subverted the spectacle of their children's pain to push responsibility and blame back to the actual perpetrators of the violence. In shifting the gaze on the victim from the perspective of a white vigilante lynch mob to the point of view of a mother, Mamie Till and Carrie Stewart interrupt the visual white racist hegemonic narrative with an *oppositional gaze*. See bell hooks, "The Oppositional Gaze: Black Female Spectators," in *Black Looks: Race and Representation* (Boston: South End Press, 1992).

52

Kelley continues to describe the important work of Ida B. Wells, leader of the anti-lynching movement. According to Kelley, "At the same time, Ida B. Wells and others exposed the myth of the black male rapist. They demonstrated, among other things, that most interracial rape victims were black women who endured the assaults of white men for which they were never punished, and explained how these myths affected the lives of men and women on both sides of the color line." Kelley, "Slangin' Rocks," pp. 27–28.

53

Sarah Ferguson, "Community Vibe Is Alive at Annual Acker Awards," *The Villager*, February 16, 2017, http://thevillager.com/2017/02/16/community-vibe-is-alive-at-annual-acker-awards/.

54

M. A. Farber, "3 Witnesses Say Stewart Appeared Sober on the Night He Was Arrested," *New York Times*, July 24, 1985, https://www.nytimes.com/1985/07/24/nyregion/3-witnesses-say-stewart-appeared-sober-on-the-night-he-was-arrested.html.

55

Alex Fiahlo, oral history interview with Lyle Ashton Harris, March 27–29, 2017, Archives of American Art, Smithsonian Institution, https://www.aaa.si.edu/collections/interviews/oral-history-interview-lyle-ashton-harris-17456. See also Harris, *Lyle Ashton Harris: Blow Up* (New York: Gregory R. Miller, 2008), pp. 38–39; Harris, "Saint Michael Stewart," *Lyle Ashton Harris* blog, *The Good Life Series*

(1994), accessed April 28, 2013; and Anna Deavere Smith, *Lyle Ashton Harris* (New York: Gregory R. Miller, 2004).

Underground media such as the *East Village Eye* and *Workers Vanguard* also challenged the mainstream narrative. See Terry Bisson, "The Murder of Michael Stewart," *East Village Eye*, March 1985, p. 7. In a more recent editorial in the *Amsterdam News*, attorney Alton H. Maddox gives an account very similar to Harris's: "I best remember Michael Stewart for kissing a white girl before embarking on a subway train for Brooklyn. He never made it. This is reminiscent of Emmett Till. Eleven transit cops beat him into a coma in Manhattan. He died." Alton H. Maddox, "Orwell's '1984' and blacks in New York," *Amsterdam News*, April 12, 2011, http://amsterdamnews.com/news/2011/apr/12/orwells-1984-and-blacks-in-new-york.

56

Sedera Ranaivoarinosy, "Lyle Ashton Harris and Excessive Exposure," WNYU, April 14, 2011, https://citywidewnyu.wordpress.com/2011/04/14/lyle-ashton-harris-and-excessive-exposure/.

57

Sheri-Marie Harrison, "New Black Gothic," *Los Angeles Review of Books*, June 23, 2008, https://lareviewofbooks.org/article/new-black-gothic/.

58

Jana Evans Braziel, "Trans-American Art on the Streets: Jean-Michel Basquiat's Black Canvas Bodies and Urban Vodou-Art in Manhattan," in *Artists, Performers, and Black Masculinity in the Haitian Diaspora* (Bloomington: Indiana University Press, 2008), p. 199.

59

Cedric R. Robinson, "Race, Capitalism and the Antidemocracy," in Gooding-Williams, *Reading Rodney King*, p. 73. For more context on contemporary Los Angeles and the relationship between education, policing, and the incarceration state, see Damien Sojoyner, *First Strike: Educational Enclosures in Black Los Angeles* (Minneapolis: University of Minnesota Press, 2016).

60

Elizabeth Alexander, "'Can You Be Black and Look at This?': Reading the Rodney King Video(s)," in Thelma Golden, *Black Male: Representations of Masculinity in Contemporary American Art*, exh. cat. (New York: Whitney Museum of American Art, 1994), p. 91.

61

See Frantz Fanon, *Black Skins, White Masks*, trans. Richard Philcox (1952; New York: Grove Press, 2008).

62

Laurence "Kris" Parker, "Who Protects Us from You?," track 7 on KRS-One, *Ghetto Music: The Blueprint of Hip Hop*, Jive/RCA Records, 1989.

63

Michael Jackson, "They Don't Care About Us," track 2 on disc 2 of *HIStory: Past, Present, and Future, Book I*, Epic, 1995.

64

Roxanne Dunbar-Ortiz, *Loaded: A Disarming History of the Second Amendment* (San Francisco: City Lights Books, 2018), p. 59. See also Dunbar-Ortiz, "United States Policing and 'Gun Rights' Began with Slave Patrols," *Truthout*, May 14, 2018, https://truthout.org/articles/united-states-policing-and-gun-rights-began-with-slave-patrol/.

65

See Dex on The Straight Dope Science Advisory Board, "Why Are the Police Called Cops, Pigs, or the Fuzz?," *Straight Dope* blog, May 31, 2005, http://www.straightdope.com/columns/read/2209/why-are-the-police-called-cops-pigs-or-the-fuzz; and Ron Kurtus, "When Cops Were Pigs—1968," School for Champions by Ron Kurtus, December 3, 2012, https://www.school-for-champions.com/history/when_cops_were_pigs.htm. For more on the Yippie party and the Chicago Democratic Convention of 1967, see "Chicago 10: The Yippies," *Independent Lens*, PBS, accessed January 3, 2019, http://www.pbs.org/independentlens/chicago10/yippies.html.

66

Kevin Young, "Defacement," in *To Repel Ghosts: The Remix* (New York: Alfred A. Knopf, 2005), p. 29.

67

The Merriam-Webster New Book of Word Histories (1991), s.v. "cop."

68

For a response to the film *Fruitvale*, directed by Ryan Coogler, see Jack Bryson, "Oakland Father Reflects on 'Fruitvale Station,'" WBUR, July 25, 2013, http://www.wbur.org/hereandnow/2013/07/25/bryson-fruitvale-station.

69

Harlem riot of 1943 reports, Schomburg Center for Research in Black Culture, The New York Public Library, http://archives.nypl.org/scm/20584. For more historical context, see Nat Brandt, *Harlem at War: The Black Experience in WWII* (Syracuse, N.Y.: Syracuse University Press, 1996).

70

James Baldwin, "Notes of a Native Son" (1955), in *James Baldwin: Collected Essays*, ed. Toni Morrison (New York: Library of America, 1998), p. 73.

71

David Bowie, "Changes," track 1 on *Hunky Dory*, RCA Records, 1971.

72

"Stoneman Students' Questions at the CNN Town Hall" (transcript), CNN, February 22, 2018, https://www.cnn.com/2018/02/22/politics/cnn-town-hall-full-video-transcript/index.html.

73

Richard Marshall, "Repelling Ghosts," in Marshall, *Jean-Michel Basquiat*, pp. 16, 18.

74

Braziel, *Black Masculinity*, p. 189.

75

The symbolic power of Martin's hoodie helped mobilize broad social consciousness and political attention on the issue of racial profiling and racial violence. Politicians participated as well, including Representative Bobby

Rush, the Chicago Democrat who spoke on the floor of the House of Representatives on Capitol Hill wearing a hoodie, violating rules of decorum. See Ewen MacAskill, "Congressman Bobby Rush Escorted off House Floor for Wearing Hoodie," *The Guardian*, March 28, 2012, https://www.theguardian.com/world/2012/mar/28/congressman-bobby-rush-hoodie-trayvon-martin.

Scholar Nicole Fleetwood examines the visual culture of Trayvon Martin in the chapter "'I Am Trayvon Martin': The Boy Who Became an Icon," in *On Racial Icons: Blackness and the Public Imagination* (New Brunswick, N.J.: Rutgers University Press, 2015), pp. 13–31. Thousands of people responded to the call for action, from empathetic white families to members of the Miami Heat team (National Basketball Association) evoking the iconic moment when the runner John Carlos raised a fist in the 1968 Olympics, and football athlete extraordinaire Colin Kaepernick. Already iconic, since 2016 Kaepernick has led a kneeling protest tied to the national anthem in solidarity with victims of police brutality. For more on the history of protest and politics in the arena of professional sports, see Kat Chow, "A Brief History of Racial Protest in Sports," *Code Switch*, NPR, December 2, 2014, https://www.npr.org/sections/codeswitch/2014/12/02/367766230/a-brief-history-of-racial-protest-in-sports; Eric Reid, "Why Colin Kaepernick and I Decided to Take a Knee," *New York Times*, August 7, 2018, https://www.nytimes.com/2017/09/25/opinion/colin-kaepernick-football-protests.html; and David J. Leonard, *Playing While White: Privilege and Power on and off the Field* (Seattle: University of Washington Press, 2017).

76
Leah Mirakhor, "The Hoodie and the Hijab: Arabness, Blackness, and the Figure of Terror," *Los Angeles Review of Books*, June 6, 2015, https://lareviewofbooks.org/essay/the-hoodie-and-the-hijab-arabness-blackness-and-the-figure-of-terror-james-baldwin.

77
The phrase "To repel ghosts" appears in a Basquiat painting of the same title from 1986 (private collection). It has since inspired poet Kevin Young's book *To Repel Ghosts* (Knopf, 2005) and Philippe Lacôte's short film *To Repel Ghosts* (Banshee Films, 2013).

78
Greg Tate, "Black like B.," in Marshall, *Jean-Michel Basquiat*, p. 58. See the reprint of this essay in the present volume, pp. 89–94.

79
Fred Moten and Stefano Harney, *The Undercommons: Fugitive Planning & Black Study* (New York: Autonomedia, 2013), pp. 140–41.

80
Shana L. Redmond and Damien M. Sojoyner, "Keywords in Black Protest: A(n Anti-) Vocabulary," *Truthout*, May 29, 2015, https://truthout.org/articles/keywords-in-black-protest-a-n-anti-vocabulary/. For the black intellectual tradition, see Gaye Theresa Johnson and Alex Lubin, eds., *Futures of Black Radicalism* (London: Verso, 2017).

BASQUIAT REPRESENTS THE EXISTENTIAL LONELINESS OF BLACK MEN

TO SUCH A TRAGIC DEGREE AS TO SUGGEST THAT FRATERNITY CAN ONLY REALLY OCCUR IN THE ARTIST'S HAGIOGRAPHIES.

GREG TATE

BLACK LIKE B.

Consider our heroic tradition of painting, the last cargo cult in the Western world, a ritual grab bag of signs and strokes invested with the symbolic salvaging of the white man's soul. Contrary to popular belief, painting has never lost the redemptive aura it picked up during the Renaissance. Even after the subject matter evolved from priestly concerns to those of prostitutes to the nature of painting itself, the idea of a painting as a canonical article of faith has remained. As the language of the painting has grown more hermetic, specialized, and exclusive, painting has maintained its position in the art market by vaunting its exclusivity, rarity, purity, and, most of all, its investability. And the makers of these extraordinary things called high-art paintings become themselves a rarer breed too, thought to possess a deeper shade of soul.

In our video-literate world of digital paint boxes, flesh and blood painters are like scholar-priests with the key to a hazily remembered hieroglyphic system. Like most things in our culture that hold the power to confer cultural authority, privilege, and aristocratic access, and have been given the task of holding the line between the yahoos and the yacht-racing classes, the heroic tradition of painting is a wealthy white man's club. You don't have to be one to get into it, you just need one to escort you through the doors. You'll recall that Basquiat had to crawl before he walked: his first patrons entered using the servants' entrance, the basement of his first dealer, Annina Nosei.

Here they come again, those cornerstones of the American empire, racism and class struggle. Just as an exercise in self-denial I've wondered if I could talk about Basquiat's art without going ballistic on white people. I've decided that I can't. I find it impossible to discuss Basquiat's art without talking about white supremacy, and its victimization of him, even and especially after death. On the other hand, I also have to wonder if he doesn't partly appeal to me now because he seems less the young god I met at his loft surrounded by his court of downtown denizens. Maybe, like his detractors, I find him easier to handle now, just another dead black genius. When he was alive he was self-destructive; dead he's a signature, a self-invention, a figment of the pigment, and I'm not given to question anymore whether he's black enough for me.

The question of the hour is why do some people think Basquiat was a genius and others think he's a fraud? Why are major museums in Chicago, Los Angeles, and Washington, D.C., opposed to picking up the Whitney's Basquiat retrospective for a tour? If the criterion for entering the modern painting pantheon is an original voice, painterly sophistication, skills and ideas, then Basquiat more than made the grade. His paintings can't be confused with anyone else's anymore than Pollock's, Ernst's, or de Kooning's can, nor are they reducible to cartoon parody after the manner of Keith Haring and Kenny Scharf. The chaos theory that holds a Basquiat in architectonic balance departed with the builder's hands. (You don't know what bad painting is until you've seen an imitation Basquiat.)

If we want to compare him with anybody it's Thelonius Monk, who also devised a style of grand complexity out of seemingly infantile gestures. Bringing us to Basquiat the wild child, who will be remembered as an enigmatic junkie who pollocked Armani suits, but who his cataloguers know was productive if nothing else. From the documented evidence, doodling, drawing, image making, and writing turned up early as an obsessive reflex in Basquiat's nervous system. Apparently, Basquiat drew images as frequently as everybody else was drawing breaths.

If I want to prove Basquiat was a serious artist to an unbelieving world, talk of sheer productivity is not going to get it. Actually nothing is going to do it, they've decided he's worthless so why not say fuck 'em and be done with it. Okay, I'll try. So what is it that I respond to in his work? Why is it significant to me? Okay, some of his intellectual obsessions are my intellectual obsessions: ancestry and modernity, originality and the origins of knowledge, personhood and property, possession (in the religious sense) and slavery. Basquiat was also a populist postmodernist. He belongs to a black aesthetic tradition, well established by our musicians, of making work that is heady enough to confound academics and hip enough to capture the attention span of the hip-hop nation.

Talking about Basquiat is also talking about my generation. Born into a world of monster movies and science fiction, comic books and cultural nationalism, Parliament-Funkadelic, hip-hop, and punk rock. And if you're a young black person you're constantly trying to square the futurism of America with the barbarism of the place. So we live in a multiplicity of imaginative realms, the world of the technocrat and the world of the dixiecrat, savage Africa and Africa as paradise lost. We live in a world of signs and ciphers we manipulate to perform symbolic magic of our own devising. We ironically respond to language as a tool of oppression by disempowering it with crazed black wit. I call these linguistic safe houses home. I can't not respond to Basquiat any more than I can not respond to Chuck D and Public Enemy. It would be like brainwashing myself out of history and the call to action.

I tell myself that I will stop referring to Basquiat as a casualty of racism and stop blaming white folks for killing him with miscomprehension. On the other hand, I know that it is the inevitable curse of black genius to be tortured by white fools and that like The Honorable Elijah Muhammad I tend to blame all the world's evils on those grafted devils. But with Basquiat the artistic intelligence is always getting lost in somebody else's sauce or being used to grind axes against black people's right to exist in the art world. I can forgive myself for using him to lead the charge against the powers that be, only if I reiterate the milestone I consider his artistic contribution to have been.

There is a poster of Jimi Hendrix with wires tumbling out of his head snaking toward a flotilla of charged inputs. Basquiat's work evokes a similar image of an overloaded sensorium counterattacking the world via feedback loop. In it we find a maximalist consciousness that knows how to hit it and quit it like a cartoonist, while at the same time one that eschews maximalism not in favor of minimalism, but in favor of ellipsis, erasure, obscurantism, arcana—an art that finds its edge in describing the dazed state of semiconsciousness most of us filter our media-saturated urban wasteland through.

Among his multiple inheritances Basquiat is clearly heir to the Surrealists, but his surrealism is descriptive of New York in the day rather than Europe at night. Think of N.Y.C. as the ultimate action painting and Basquiat as the painter who didn't want to parody its chaos but pantomime it. So silhouettes, spirits, and spooks abound on his canvases, floating vessels of tarbrushed ectoplasm, dispossessed black spirits in a material world of tenement ruins, funny animals, flying saucers, consumer goods, and cryptograms. Sometimes these floating figures function like dark and innocent angels risen up from hell on earth to function as heaven's amanuensis, cub reporters on the spiritual condition of the world. Then again sometimes these figures are enshrouded and enshrined black saints, dead boxers, jazz musicians, freedom fighters, all of whom Basquiat eulogized as warrior-angels—ghostly figures upholding the magic scepter of black male athletic, musical, and intellectual prowess, even from beyond the grave.

Basquiat's art is an art of presences and resonances, acts and allusions. More often it is about the conflict and incomprehension that occur when a black subject enters the frame of Western history claiming special rights, special powers, requesting and requiring special acts of dispensation. The history of the African struggle for justice in the U.S.A. is the history of such declarations. The history of blacks in Western visual art is not. Or at least not on the level where the artist's arcane and signatory language itself speaks with the militance of Malcolm X and the subtlety of Miles Davis. In Basquiat's work blackness is rendered as something holy, esoteric, and visceral, when not as something deeply cerebral, meditative, and unfixed to the purgatorial fantasy landscapes it has been consigned to. Blackness in Basquiat's work is not the blackness of the cultural nationalists, though it has their intensity and anger—albeit as an emotional gateway through which to translate other passions—but a blackness that demands hermeneutic intervention, ardor, and respect. To make sense of Basquiat's language you have to first respect African people as language manipulators of the highest order, to respect the complexity of African cultures as series of overlapping texts, tongues, and dialects, ranging from the in-joke to the alienated, from the colloquial to the schizophrenic. In some respects the blackest thing about Basquiat's work is not his black figures but the work's verbal mastery and sheer verbosity. Words function in Basquiat's oeuvre like chants, spells, incantations, curses, cheers, raps, expletives—in other words like the normal flow of discourse heard in any urban American neighborhood on any given day or night. High mysticism shares these airwaves with gutter talk or gets flavored by it. Profundity and profanity are accepted as kissing cousins. In some instances the most profound thing that can be uttered is the most obscene thought one can think of, or the most violent.

Since slavery and oppression under white supremacy are visible subtexts in Basquiat's work, he is as close to a Goya as American painting has ever produced. The consequences of America's war on the black and poor are everywhere in evidence in Basquiat. The male spirits in his work are obviously homeless spirits, bereft of family, land, companionship, or clear connections to tradition, family, or the economy. They are adrift because they are strangers to the society that worships, fears, exploits, and abuses them, and even strangers to their own progeny. You have to search far and wide to find a female figure in Basquiat's output, and beyond his early cartoons it may be impossible to find a work that hints at male-female bonding on any level. Basquiat represents the existential loneliness of black men to such a tragic degree as to suggest that fraternity can only really occur in the artist's hagiographies.

Was it the sense that he only belonged among a hall of suicidal martyrs like Charlie Parker that pushed Basquiat into a coffin before we were ready for him to go? Sometimes my friend AJ and I are given to wonder how Basquiat would have responded to the explosive emergence of hip-hop as a redemptive and organizing force in the lives of young black men only a year after his death. Between 1988 and 1989 Public Enemy, Boogie Down Productions, Eric B & Rakim, Big Daddy Kane, and De La Soul manifested and injected a more politicized, cerebral, and literate edge into hip-hop and with it a new image of the black male's intellectual capacity and cultural sophistication and currency. In that short span of time hip-hop defined contemporaneity, modernity, the avant-garde in just about every arena of society imaginable. It did this not only with revolutionary formal content but with Basquiat's other stock in trade—verbal discourse. Just as Basquiat manipulated language in ways that were not supposed to be the province of young black males, so did the hip-hoppers. What would have been the effect on Basquiat of a hip-hop culture as polyglot as himself? What would have been his impact on hip-hop visually, socially? His one foray into hip-hop music production, "Beat Bop" with Rammellzee and K-Rob, yielded a prophetic classic—one that foretold the juxtaposition of raging meditative rapper and embattled backing track that Public Enemy would later refine to perfection. Would Basquiat have reconsidered music as an outlet for his expression in their wake and gone on to challenge and nudge hip-hop music into even more unhinged directions? Certainly the production work on "Beat Bop" invokes a Basquiat painting set to music and verse, with its things-that-go-bump-in-the-night sound effects, narcotized and downbeat tempo, and, through the frenetic ramblings of Rammellzee, cryptic and nightmarish lyric content.

Beyond hip-hop, Basquiat's bent for essaying black spirituality, identity, and oppression resonates in the work of other young artists who've emerged as significant figures since his death. Prominent among them are conceptual photographers Renée Cox and Lorna Simpson, painters Glenn Ligon and Kerry James Marshall, and Gary Simmons, who works in multimedia installations. By invoking their work here, I am taking an opportunity to offer a more fitting and responsible tribute to Basquiat than yet another eulogy or reappraisal. Certainly it does more to sustain the least recognized aspect of his contribution: a fight to the death against a white supremacist art world.

This essay was originally published in Richard Marshall, *Jean-Michel Basquiat*, exh. cat. (New York: Whitney Museum of American Art, 1992) and has been slightly revised for the present volume.

RECOLLECTIONS

LUC SANTE
JEFFREY DEITCH
FRED BRATHWAITE
ANNINA NOSEI
DIANNE BRILL
GEORGE CONDO
PATRICK FOX
PATRICIA PESCE
TONY SHAFRAZI
MICHELLE SHOCKED
SETH TOBOCMAN
CARLO McCORMICK

RECOLLECTIONS

FRANCK GOLDBERG
LYLE ASHTON HARRIS
ERIC DROOKER
KENNY SCHARF
LEONARD ABRAMS
REV. HERBERT DAUGHTRY
RONALD FIELDS
LOU YOUNG
MICHAEL WARREN
PETER NOEL
CARRIE STEWART

In an effort to capture the memories of individuals who either knew Michael Stewart or were directly involved in the response to his death—whether through artistic, journalistic, or legal means—interviews were conducted by Chaédria LaBouvier with the following people between November 2018 and March 2019. The interviews have been edited into concise statements that reflect the essence of each conversation and provide personal perspectives on the tragic events of 1983.

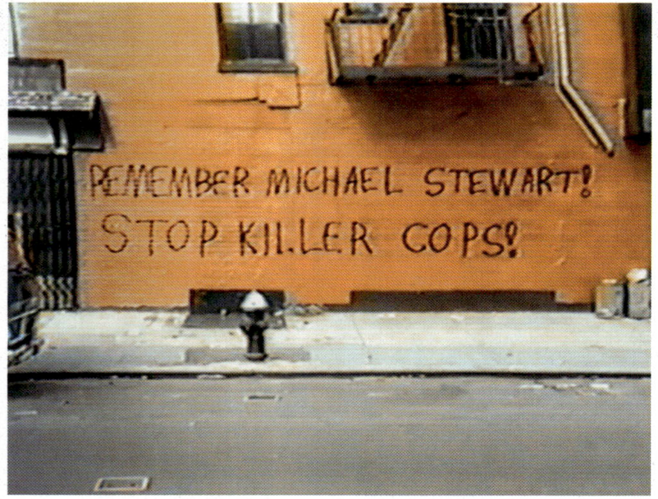

FIGURE 1
Graffiti on the Lower East Side, New York City, 1983, from video footage by Franck Goldberg

Luc Sante
WRITER

At the time, the Lower East Side was marked by an ever-increasing profusion of artist types from everywhere, with no political organization. It's not that people were apolitical, it's just there was nothing in particular to focus on. There was a kind of social consciousness, but it was pretty much palaver. There were no front lines at the time. It was just chaos. All of us had been teenagers during Vietnam, and so I went to a lot of demonstrations back then, but I was a kid. And then, after Nixon's resignation and the Paris Accord, there followed a long period where nothing much was happening politically. Everybody kind of had vague political sentiments and inclinations, but nobody was doing anything.

I had one friend, Philippe Bordaz, who made political posters. He was French. He came here in '76 because he had dual citizenship, and his initial purpose was to avoid the French draft. I remember he was disgusted by the apathy. He took it upon himself to become this one-man poster industry. He made a poster in collaboration with Robert Cooney, Jorge Mendez, and Tom Otterness that showed how to turn your gas meter around halfway through the month so it'd run backwards and cancel out the charges that had been racked up. He was a major educational force in my life, because I realized that we were content to be living on the margins of consumer society, and we were complacent in our marginality. In the early '80s a kind of social knowledge emerged around a series of events and places like the Fun Gallery in the East Village, the film *Wild Style* [1983], the bar Tin Pan Alley on Forty-Ninth Street, and Colab's shows—*The Real Estate Show* and the *Times Square Show* [both 1980]—which contributed to a major increase in consciousness. Philippe was affiliated with Colab, but in the Colab book, the works by him are all attributed to "anonymous."

By the late '70s, early '80s, for whatever reason, the cops had become almost invisible. This was the period where you could walk by a cop while smoking a joint, and they would just look the other way. This may not have been true in every neighborhood, mind you, but it was true in the East Village and in the larger Lower East Side. There was so much drug activity down there, and it was completely ignored by the cops. And that continued to be the case into the early '90s. I remember people hawking crack very loudly on Ludlow Street. We were always wary of the cops, and there was this uneasy feeling about not seeing much police activity. There was a lot of conspiracy talk about how they wanted us all to kill each other, how they wanted us all to die from overdoses. The cops were willing enough to let the Lower East Side destroy itself when property was worth a nickel, but when speculators starting coming in, suddenly there was something to protect. Nevertheless, the presence of police was like Chekhov's gun; it was just hanging above the mantelpiece, ready to eventually go off. I don't think that any of us could have marshaled an intellectual argument about any of this at the time, but there was a gestalt. There was this hovering feeling that there were powder kegs in this city, and they may not have been ready to go off then, but you know, they're still powder kegs, so they will go off at some point.

There was the sense in the late '70s and early '80s that the city was effectively abandoned by its former owners—that we had the place to ourselves, and we were going to take over and all that. But by '83 this was dissolved. And you know, the Empire strikes back. Nineteen eighty-three . . . that was a really dark year. The party was over in more than one way. A certain kind of downtown scene had just died, and the gallery scene was just starting. So it was this transition from a kind of noncommercial, seat-of-the-pants outlaw scene, led by Colab, to something commercial.

Police brutality happened all the time, but Michael Stewart's death seemed to come out of nowhere. I had a long conversation with [graffiti artist] Lee Quiñones a few weeks ago, and he was talking about how the cops were always after graffiti writers, and the artists got really good at running and figuring out escape plans and stuff like that. They knew the system; they knew all the tunnels, they knew where the tunnels went. But they weren't afraid of getting killed by the cops, they were afraid of being put in Spofford. It was the notoriously brutal juvenile facility at the time. But Stewart wasn't even a tagger; he certainly wasn't in that community, so what set this off? The graffiti thing was used as an excuse, and there was a way for the police to get the *New York Post* in their corner. It was an individual tragedy, and it was also this gigantic symbolic act, which made everybody shudder. It was something we'd all been expecting.

Jeffrey Deitch
GALLERIST AND ART ADVISOR

It was in the fall of 1980 when I first really got to know Jean-Michel, person-to-person. The first time I had seen him was when his band, Gray, performed in this club on the corner of Canal Street and West Broadway, and he was performing as a kind of beatbox. And someone said to me, "That's SAMO." Then, right after the *Times Square Show* [where Basquiat first exhibited under his own name] closed, Diego Cortez took me to this apartment on First Avenue and First Street where Jean-Michel was living with Suzanne Mallouk. I believe I'm the first person to ever have bought a Jean-Michel Basquiat artwork. I bought five drawings from him. There were drawings on typing paper strewn all over the floor, and I just went around the floor on my hands and knees and looked—"Oh, this is a really good one. How about this one?"—and we picked five of them. They were fifty dollars each.

I had been fascinated by graffiti since the mid-'70s. I would to go into the subway to see the invention of bubble letters. I followed all of that and met a number of the innovative graffiti artists, already some by the late '70s. I really got to know everybody in the scene around the time of the *Times Square Show*. Whether I met Fred Brathwaite [Fab 5 Freddy] before or after that, it's a little hard to differentiate because I was already part of that community. Fred was crucial because he was the link between the graffiti artists and the art world, because he was down with both. Fred was critical in connecting the graffiti artists with the hip-hop musicians. There was actually quite a bit of uptown-downtown dialogue. The two key points were Fashion Moda in the South Bronx and Fun Gallery on the Lower East Side. Fashion Moda was truly an amazing place; it showed graffiti by local people like Crash. And the openings there were fantastic. For Patti Astor's Fun Gallery, the uptown would come downtown and would very crucially mix with many kids from the projects on Avenue D, like LA II, who became Keith Haring's sidekick. It was a remarkable, fluid thing. And it all seemed like the art world was opening up to this.

There were various galleries in SoHo, like Jeanette Bonnier, who showed some of the graffiti artists. And early on, one of Barbara Gladstone's first exhibitions was Alan Suicide [Alan Vega]. She was involved at the beginning with this mixture of punk rock and graffiti. But then it was like a wall came down, and they stopped being invited. Diego Cortez once famously characterized the official art world as a place of "white walls with white people drinking white wine."

Michael Stewart was on the scene, but I did not know him well. He was not one of the central artists. I think what is important to understand is that this was a small, embracing community, where you would meet everybody right on the street. There was always a kind of star system. Like, from the minute Jean-Michel appeared, everyone knew this guy was a star. But everyone lived in the same situation. There wasn't much differentiation between how a curator, on a curator's salary, an art critic, or a famous artist lived. Everyone was at the same places and the same parties. But this incident electrified the scene, and people talked of nothing else for months. I remember Jean-Michel once saying to me, "It could have been me." The first person who told me the whole story was Kenny Scharf, and he described that he had an encounter with the same group of cops. Their turf was around the Fourteenth Street subway station, and he had some encounter where they chased him around Thirteenth Street. This is the first instance I can think of where this community came together around an issue. The group was certainly politically engaged and aware before that. They were living primarily in the Lower East Side, and others, like John Ahearn, were in the South Bronx, and they knew what it was like to be an underclass New Yorker. From the beginning, the work was politically engaged: whether it was Keith Haring's early works on lampposts, or SAMO© works, which were deliberately obscure but also had a strong political message. There was already a lot of political engagement and a feminist perspective in the work of Kiki Smith and her circle. With the Michael Stewart case, it became more overt, more public. In retrospect, it is amazing to see how politically engaged Jean-Michel's work is, through to the very end. His celebrity and style obscured that a little bit during his lifetime. But there's a searing history of fighting against oppression in the work; it's one of the most profound expressions of African American experience. But he was not someone who was ever out there hectoring. In a conversation, he wouldn't start with some political diatribe. But it was in the work.

Fred Brathwaite a.k.a. Fab 5 Freddy

ARTIST

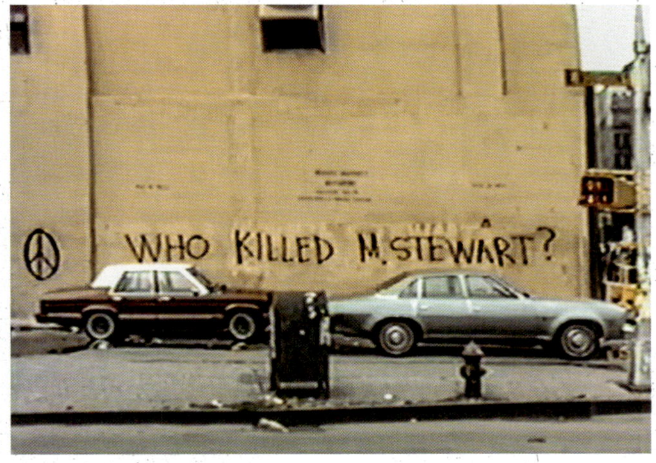

FIGURE 2
Graffiti on the Lower East Side, New York City, 1983, from video footage by Franck Goldberg

Tagging and bombing, for me and for many of the people in my immediate circle, had pretty much stopped by the early '80s, as we began to exhibit our work in galleries. Of course, you would put your name here and there occasionally, but it wasn't like we were going out to aggressively do graffiti. We were transitioning, for the most part. I was working with the Fun Gallery and doing some things with Holly Solomon's gallery uptown. So the work was getting out there. And I was involved in the making of the film *Wild Style* [1983], which was part of my ongoing assault on popular culture. So things were happening. People were getting the message, understanding what the various components of this culture were and how they interrelated.

I had been doing a series of still-life-in-space paintings and playing with imagery that wasn't what you would traditionally expect from a person who was a "graffiti artist." Those of us at the forefront now dealing with galleries, et cetera, were careful to not refer to ourselves as graffiti artists, because we knew that graffiti involved an act of vandalism on a wall, on somebody's property. I will admit that graffiti had been largely a scourge, but it was just our response to the bias—the inequity in the city against black and brown people. It was like a scream; it was a yell. But amidst all that, there was some creativity going down. Couldn't you discern a really interestingly created picture as opposed to somebody who was just defacing?

So, we were trying to be artists, expanding on the ways we could express ourselves. Nevertheless, as the work began to be written about in the press, we became known as "graffiti artists"—even people like Keith Haring and Kenny Scharf, who were sensitive about how they were portrayed, even though they did do work on the streets. We all worked interconnectedly, if you will, and we were all friends. The press began to simplify and label us all as such.

Very few of us had an art-historical background. That was why I made the Campbell's Soup Can train, the homage to Andy Warhol, so someone would stop and think about the fact that one or some of those kids, black or Latino, knows about art history, Pop art, and Warhol. I wanted those thoughts in the mix. My being that nerd who had spent time cutting school, going to museums, I specifically wanted to help stir this up. I wanted to put some fuel on this fire. When I connected with Jean-Michel that was one of the core tenets of our friendship. We were thinking similarly, yet coming from different places. We had similar goals and aspirations.

Michael Stewart was a new artist making moves on the scene and one of the few people of color in the mix downtown at that time. He came from an intellectual, educated family and wanted to find a place where he could express himself in a cool way around like-minded people. That's what downtown was at that point in time. When he was killed and the police claimed he was writing his name on the wall in the subway—which was surprising and seemed unlikely to us—the media jumped all over the idea that he was a graffiti artist; it was mentioned every time it was covered on the news. And every time you heard it, it was like a chill going through you, realizing that it could be me—it could be any of a number of people I knew. Even though we all knew that Michael Stewart was not the graffiti artist they were portraying him to be, it clearly could have been any person of color, particularly myself and the numerous others I knew who were making art and would maybe occasionally tag a wall, or had that background. That was frightening. There were clearly racial undertones. Jean-Michel, Keith, and I would talk about these things all the time. It was something that we all discussed, just in terms of how horrible, how sad, how sick that was. How we had all met him, you know? He was a new member of the community, moving around on the scene. I wasn't close with him, but I'd see him around and nod as an acknowledgment of each other, as we did. And I'm sure it was the same with Keith. It was an issue that touched us all deeply. I remember Jean-Michel saying, "Man, that's really horrible, man, can you believe that?" And we looked at each other, like, "Yo, that could be me. That could be me, too." Especially me and Jean-Michel, because we were both black and dealing with these issues on a regular basis—from not being picked up by cabs to people who didn't want to be in elevators with us. I can remember before I went to L.A., where I was working with Ace Gallery, Jean-Michel had had his shows there with Larry [Gagosian] and had gone back and forth a few times, and he said, "Man, you gotta be careful about the cops out there. Because in L.A. they will pull you over, and they like to put brothers on the street, and they lay you down, and they sit you on the ground, and they really put you through a lot. So if they pull you over in L.A., you want to be real careful." I took due note of that because just being black—driving while black, walking while black—could be problematic. As far as Michael Stewart, he was just waiting on the train, waiting for the train while black, you know?

Annina Nosei
GALLERIST

I included Jean-Michel Basquiat in a group show in my gallery called *Public Address* in 1981, after first seeing his work in the exhibition *New York / New Wave* at P.S.1 [Institute for Art and Urban Resources, Long Island City]. Initially I did not want to include him in the show, because what I had seen of his drawings and paintings seemed very personal and self-referential. The exhibition featured artists like Barbara Kruger and Jenny Holzer who were creating overtly political work. But Jean-Michel convinced me otherwise. He immediately said, "No, my work is about public address. And I want to be a part of that show. Yes, my work is political." Since he didn't have any paintings available at that moment, and he didn't have a studio, I set him up in a 3,000-square-foot basement space, with a skylight, below my gallery. Jean-Michel was very happy to be there, but people started to say, "Ah, he's in a space of a white woman," and then they said, "She is keeping him prisoner there." Others even said, "She gave him drugs, so he paints there." No. When Jean-Michel heard things like that, he said, "If I were white they would just say that I'm an artist in residence." And I had given other artists like Julio Galán and Helmut Middendorf spaces to work in, but nobody said that they were prisoners. Jean-Michel never did anything that he didn't want to. He made some beautiful, very interesting paintings there, and I said, "Okay, I'll show them." Immediately, it was a great success; I sold many of the works. From the very beginning, his work represented something completely new in the art history of the United States—or in the world—for the twentieth century. For the first time after Expressionism, or Minimalism, or Conceptual art, he created something entirely new. Every image he created had something to do with society and life and his connections to the reality of the moment. What I saw in Jean-Michel's work was an incredible strength in its direct relationship to his life, his person, and how he fit or didn't fit into society in the '80s as an African American artist. His work always had something to do with the problems that there are, or there were, in society. Jean-Michel was brilliant. He knew everything. He was nineteen, and he had read everything.

Dianne Brill
FASHION DESIGNER

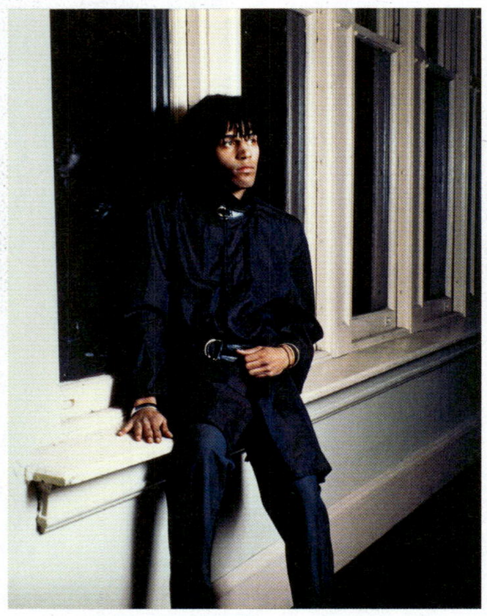

FIGURES 3, 4
Photos for Dianne Brill's menswear line, 1983, featuring Michael Stewart and, at right, Brill. Collection of the Stewart Family

There was this system called the Fab 500—like, "Fabulous 500." It evolved out of the guest list and mailing list from Danceteria, whose owner, the important nightclub king Rudolf Pieper, came up with the idea of a core group of five hundred people who would be invited to insider events. These were the conceptual movers and shakers of everything: music, fashion, art, et cetera, and I was lucky enough to be called the queen of that scene, which is something I'm still really happy about.

Out of that group came Marc Jacobs in fashion, Madonna, Jean-Michel Basquiat, Keith Haring—so many people. There were echoes of these people in the Mudd Club and Club 57, but Danceteria was where things came together in a broader way, with a bigger impact. And that's when Fab 5 Freddy started to bring hip-hop downtown. Michael Stewart was not yet part of the Fab 500. He was certainly there on the scene, but his voice wasn't formed yet as an artist. He was young, a baby. Everything was coming together, but he wasn't there yet. Michael was a really gentle kind of guy. Very beautiful to look at and easy to talk to. He had a very relaxed kind of personality, not aggressive or anything but chill, very chill. Now, Jean-Michel was already established as an artist, and Michael was just finding his way. He was playing and experimenting and learning his craft, and he was also in modeling to make money. He worked with me on an ad campaign for my company, Dianne Brill Menswear, in a shoot for Mexican *Vogue*.

One of my friends from the Fab 500 introduced me to him. I was looking for models for my clothing, which was quite unusual. We designed things for Prince, the Stones, and Duran Duran—different bands at the time. We dressed *Miami Vice*. So, we were looking for models who were super handsome and really tall, because the sample sizes were tall, and we needed someone who could work the look. When I met him, I thought, "Oh, he's perfect."

It was easy. He was so nice to work with; we just flowed and worked in Mexico and in New York and all over the place. And he always gave gorgeous faces—he was such a gorgeous person. I don't think I had one bad shot of him, honestly. If you were in the room with Michael Stewart, you would find yourself tilting your head, kind of looking at him dreamily, like we all did, because he just was light and lovely and easy and compelling, but quiet. At that time we were all blowing our horns. It was a time of self-promotion, but here was somebody who was not that but loved being part of everything. Michael was dreamier. Not angelic, but just a little dreamier. Honestly, he was the last person in the world you would ever imagine having this unfortunate legacy. The last person in the room, believe me, the last.

For Jean-Michel, after Michael died there must have been, in a weird way, a feeling of relatability—a "that could have been me" kind of feeling. Maybe it was all too much for him to deal with. Maybe he just said, "I don't want to deal with it." Or he decided to deal with it by creating something.

Michael was buried in a suit I designed. It was a lightweight summer suit, in a wool gabardine. At the time, the suits were baggier, and it was in the zoot suit direction, kind of 1940s, kind of Cab Calloway, but modified to look contemporary. It was a cream color. I think we shot him in that suit—it looked so great on him—and he just loved it. Maybe he mentioned it to his mom, but when Michael's family told me that it was his favorite suit, I asked them to have it for the burial. You cannot imagine the dignity of that woman. She has a strength that is otherworldly. Sadly, that was her last look at her child, and he looked great in that suit. Nobody could ever wear it better. I never actually had that suit produced for market. That was one sample, and he had it, and that was it.

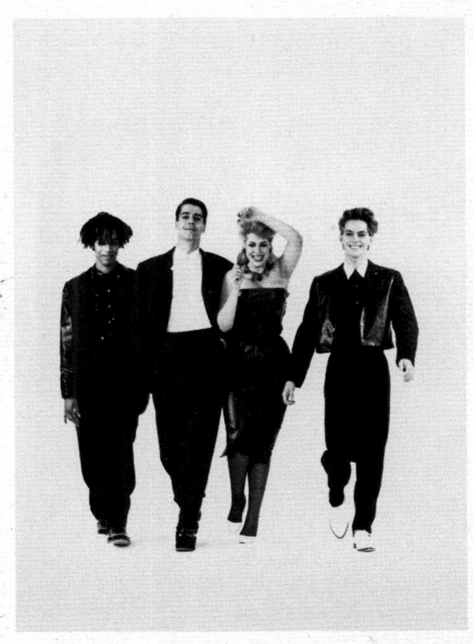

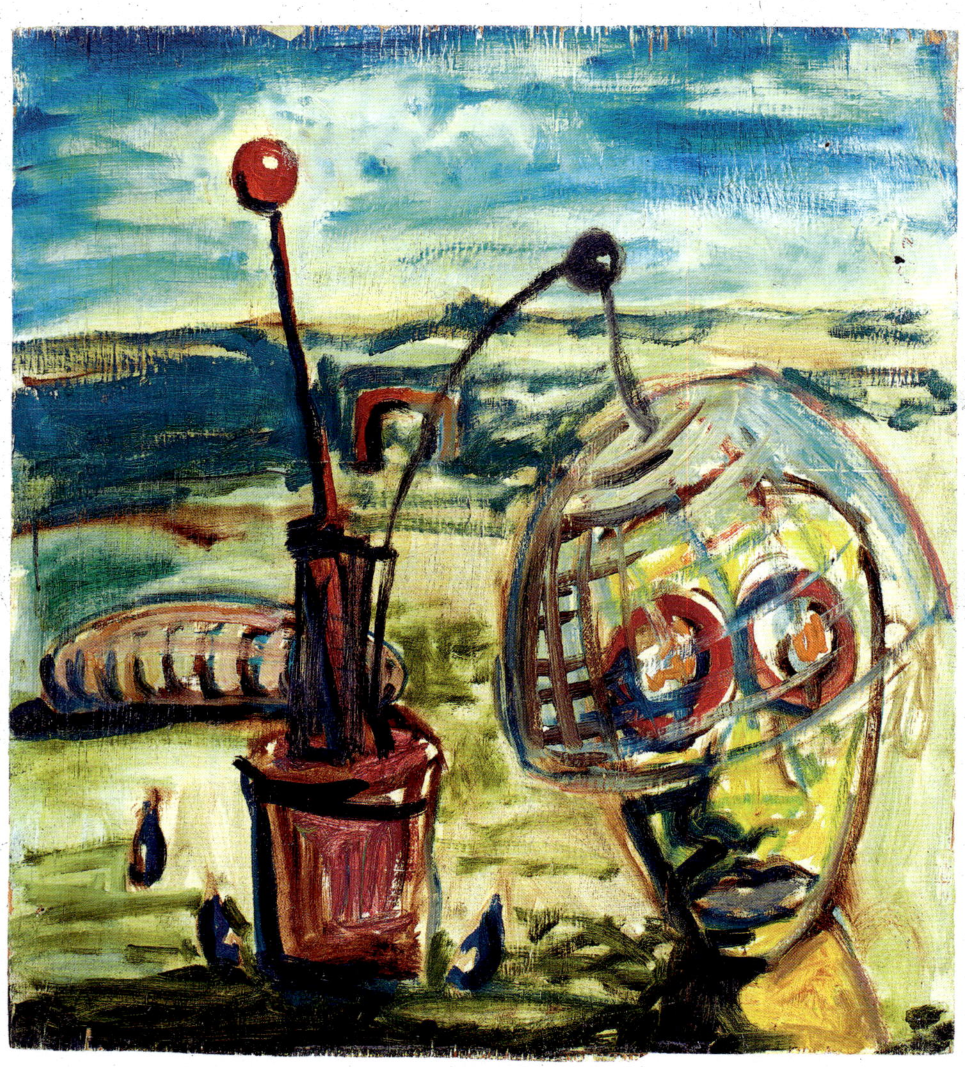

PLATE 15

George Condo

Portrait of Michael Stewart, 1983

Oil on wood panel

24 × 24 inches (61 × 61 cm)

Collection of the artist

George Condo
ARTIST

Jean-Michel was the first guy I met in New York City, because his band, Gray, was the opening act for my punk band, The Girls, for a show we played at the club Tier 3. We came down from Boston and I didn't really know New York, so he took me around to the Mudd Club and all these other places. We talked about music and our interests in art. He told me I needed to get out of Boston: "Nothing's ever going to happen there." I agreed and just quit the band and moved to New York. At least I knew one guy here.

Eventually I started working with Andy Warhol at the Factory, where I stayed for nine months. I did all this diamond dusting for him on the *Myths* series [1981]. After that I moved to Los Angeles with a girlfriend, and when I got out there, it turned out Jean-Michel and his studio assistant, Stephen Torton, were there too, because he was going to start working with Larry Gagosian. It must have been 1982 or '83. So we were hanging out in Los Angeles, driving around in this big, black gangster car that Stephen was driving. It had no brakes, so you basically had to pull over slowly on the side of the road until it stopped moving. One night we went to a Hollywood party that we were invited to, and we pulled up in the gangster-mobile, and the guy at the door said, "You can come in, but *he* can't"—gesturing to Jean-Michel. And I said, "Why?" And he said, "Because we don't let that kind of people in here." And I said, "This is Jean-Michel Basquiat. He's the most famous fucking artist in the world. What are you talking about?" At first Jean-Michel tried to say something to the guy, like that he spent more money on this suit than what you're wearing. He was obviously insulted and said, "Let's get out of here," because it happened a lot. So Jean and I went to a place called the Tail o' the Pup, which is a hot dog stand shaped like a big plastic hot dog, with little white seats around it. There we were, hanging out at midnight, talking about racism. Basquiat was constantly plagued with the problem of racism—it was awful. Later the painter Toxic and rap musician Rammellzee came out to L.A., and then Jean-Michel made the painting *Hollywood Africans* [1983] with those guys, which he showed with Larry.

Back in New York, I had some paintings in a show at Patrick Fox's gallery at the Anderson Theatre. Andy Warhol and Keith Haring went to the show, and they bought three or four of my paintings each, which to me represented a much more significant kind of appreciation than hearing from critics. Around this time I heard that Haring was having a party on Broome Street. I thought it might be a little presumptuous to just show up, given that I didn't know him yet, so I brought along Michael Stewart and Haitian Freddie. I'm trying to remember how or where I met Michael. You know, that's the part I can't really put my finger on. I think I must have met him through, potentially, my friendships with A-One, Rammellzee, Haitian Freddie, Toxic, or Jean-Michel. So I went over to Keith's thinking, "Okay, this guy bought some paintings, I probably could get in." But we got to the door, and he wouldn't let us in. So all of us just went wandering the streets, as usual. When Keith found out later that this was the night Michael was killed—after Keith and I had become best friends—he said that he wished he had let us in.

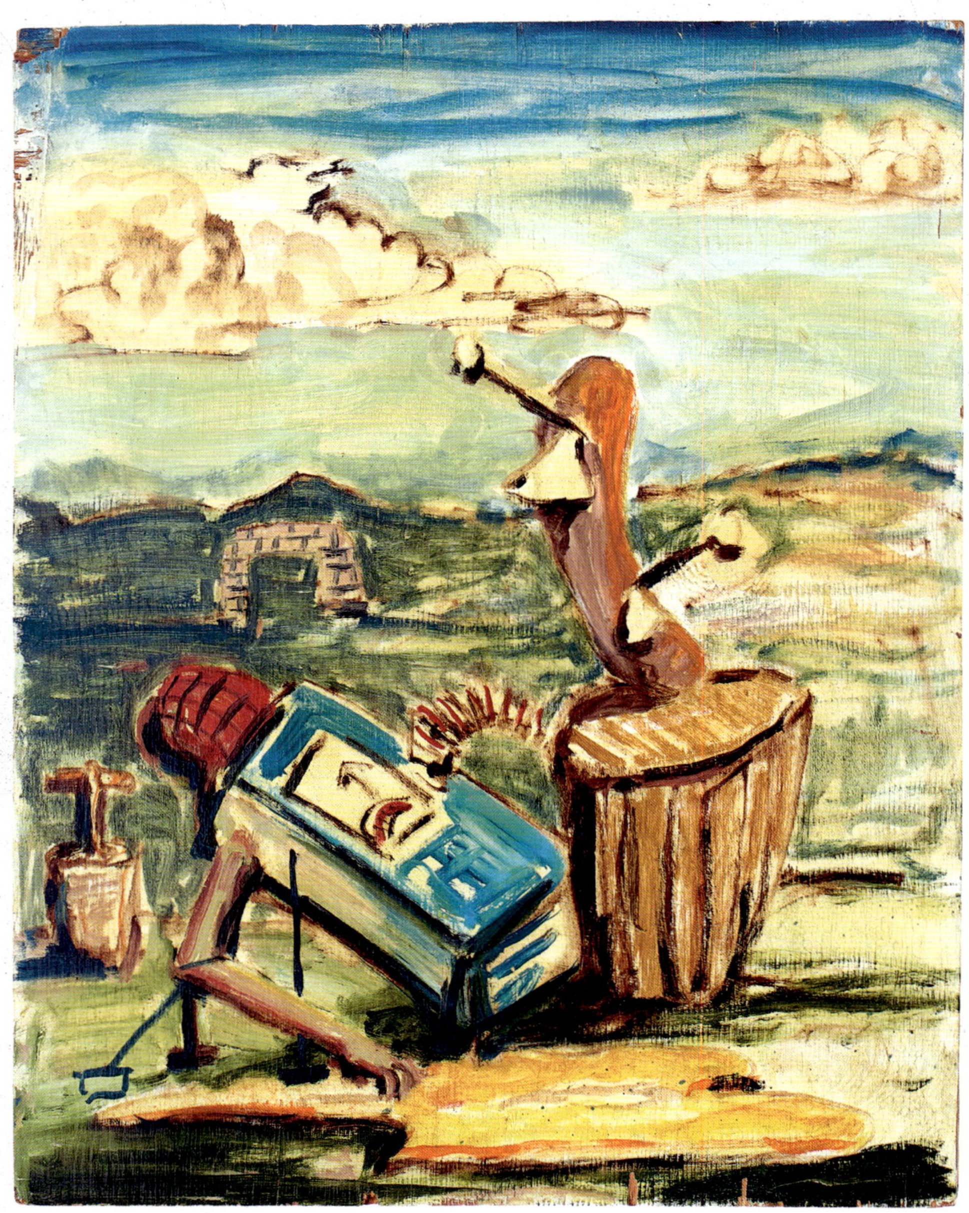

PLATE 16

George Condo

Automatic Still Life, 1983

Oil on wood panel

28 × 23 inches (71.1 × 58.4 cm)

Collection of the artist

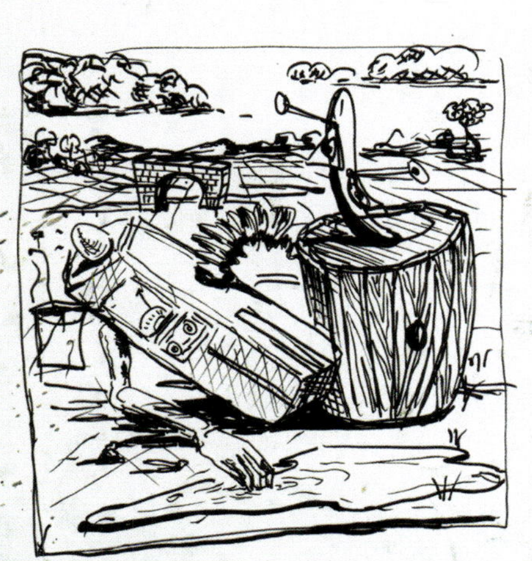

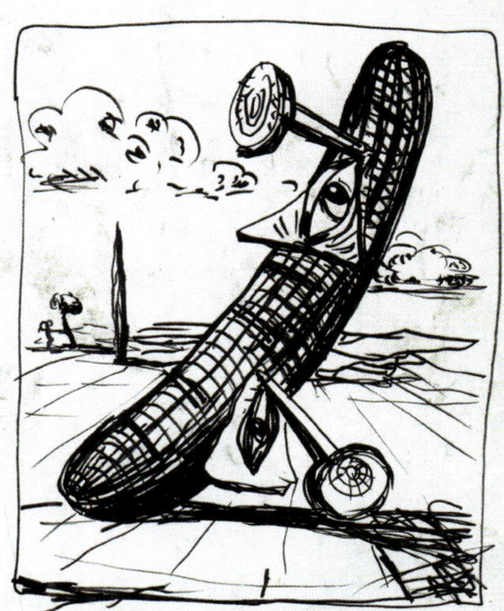

PLATE 17

George Condo

Studies for *Automatic Still Lifes*, 1983

Ink and charcoal on paper

22 × 29¾ inches (55.9 × 75.6 cm)

Collection of the artist

That night, we all eventually went to the Pyramid Club, and I saw Jean-Michel out front—this is why I really remember it. He was already making good money as an artist and was very touchy about people asking him for help, but I didn't have any money, so I asked him if I could borrow, like, five dollars. He gave me ten. And then I went into the Pyramid to have some drinks. We were all just hanging around. I remember talking to Michael a lot that night at the Pyramid, but I can't remember anything we said. All that was going on in my head was, like, "I feel so bad to have asked Jean-Michel to borrow five dollars, because we've been good friends for a few years, and everyone bums money from him." And I didn't want to be one of those people.

Michael was a very quiet guy. He wasn't at all like a provocative, confrontational, drug-dealing, drug-taking person. He actually seemed to be like a college kid, like an NYU student or something. So, we were all hanging around the Pyramid, killing time so we didn't have to go back home, wherever that was. And then he took off. What I think, without knowing any facts, is that he left around one o'clock in the morning to go to the subway station, and he was waiting for the train, and then the police beat him up and killed him. Clubbed him over the head. It was just shocking. They said that he had been putting graffiti on the walls, and when they told him to stop, he kind of answered back or was violent. And all of us thought, "That just can't be possible. That's just not him." There's no way in the world that I can even imagine—he was never even a graffiti artist. If anything, he would have been a little bit timid about even identifying as an artist, and maybe working really quietly on his art.

I don't remember an exhibition of Michael Stewart's work. I think that he would have certainly looked at Jean-Michel as being a really great artist and maybe would have tried to be yet another guy riding on his coattails, which was what was going on most of the time. But that may have not been Michael's thing. I think he wanted to be an individual and not be compared. He was very good-looking, you know? But the stupid thing is that the last thing he was was violent. The part that was so unnerving about the story was, of all people, why would they want to do that to him?

It traveled like wildfire. Everybody was shocked and saddened, and there was a lot of grief, and there was a feeling of wanting to make something, make some art. I made a kind of a portrait—this was when I was working on those old master-type paintings, with a surrealistic feel to them. And I painted a portrait of Michael on wood with this strange glass helmet that was connected to all these wires **[PL. 15]**. I think that it must have been my picture of him in the hospital, imagining him in this surreal landscape being kept alive through some sort of electrodes that were going in and out of his brain.

There was a lot of fear in the air after that. There was a fear that the police were out to get graffiti artists. Everybody was scared. There were two things that happened around this time: There was the death of Michael Stewart and there was AIDS, and both caused a distinctive paranoiac fear around the city. We felt that they were going to try to clean up New York, to gentrify it and make it an all-white city by killing innocent people. There was a police force that was out there to stop graffiti, stop black artists like Michael Stewart. And then there was this sort of scientific, medical disinformation about AIDS, which was fear-based, with people saying that it came from Africa and from screwing with monkeys or something crazy. That was also very racist. So there was this combination of two very dark, racist elements taking place. And it provoked an artistic response. There was a sense of desperation among the communities in the graffiti world; everyone suddenly felt there was a short-term lease on life. It brought you close to the idea that everything has to be done *now*. Everything has to happen quickly, because there's a wall of injustice moving in on our simple existence.

Michael Stewart was like a bright, shining symbol of the difference between innocence and power, like innocence being extinguished by power. Artists have a power that can't be taken away from them, which is their right to express themselves. Artists can tell the truth in their art, regardless of what is happening in the so-called real world. We can tell the truth the way we feel it and see it.

There were artists who were older than us, who were used to the protests of Vietnam and the antigovernment protests, but none of us really rolled with that generation. This was new for us; like it was a first attack on our generation. That's what it felt like. It may sound strange, but Michael Stewart became a catalyst for the idea of striking back against the empire. He was an enigmatic figure, nobody entirely knew him, but he symbolized a new revolt. In the '60s there were black superstars like Muhammad Ali, Jimi Hendrix, and many of the great jazz musicians whose art transcended racism, but there wasn't yet that degree of recognition in the art world.

Patrick Fox
GALLERIST

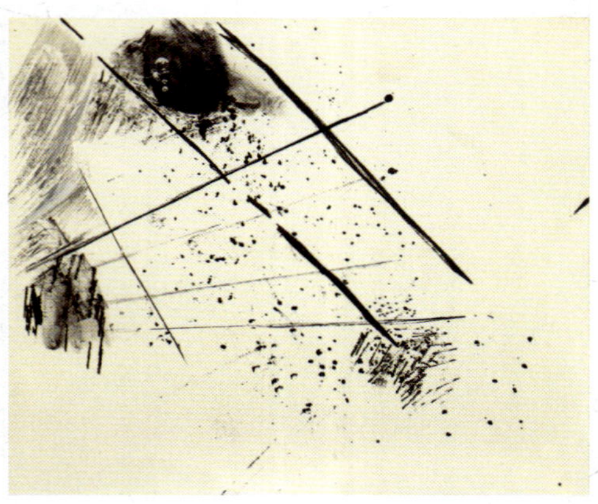

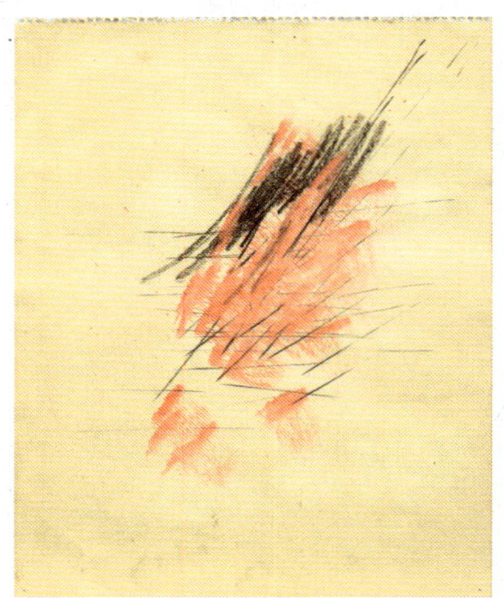

FIGURES 5, 6
Untitled artworks by Michael Stewart, ca. 1983.
Left: Collection of the Stewart Family;
Right: Collection of Patrick Fox

Michael's birthday was in May. He was heavily into numerology. I didn't know much about it but he did, and he liked to talk about how numbers directly related to people and affected their lives. He needed to know people's birth dates and used equations based on the letters in people's names. Jean-Michel and I were born in 1960—it was the first thing we discussed. We thought that was a cool year to be born, because it was truly modern, it was post-'50s greaser. As kids, we both liked the promise of space travel. Numerically, we both dug it; we liked the idea of being forty in the year 2000. Jean and I met at the restaurant Binibon on Second Avenue and Fifth Street. It's also where I first saw the beautiful and stylish Suzanne Mallouk working.

For all of its bad reputation, New York was actually much more civil than it is today. We created a new downtown society—a community of new artists. In 1981 I was living in the Anderson Theatre, which was at Second and Fourth Street, with my brother, James, and my then-boyfriend, artist Robert Hawkins. It was a vacant Yiddish theater, built in 1926. We occupied three floors above the lobby. On the first habitable floor, the marquee cantilevered over the sidewalk. It had four beautiful swivel windows that pivoted and you'd step out onto the marquee, which was our balcony. We often entertained "drop-ins" up there, since it hovered above the Second Avenue sidewalk, and we would barbecue. Michael took over the studio in the front, which had access to the marquee. Jo Shane had the back half. By then I lived on the top two floors. The mostly unused ground-floor lobby went beyond those living spaces and opened up to an 1,800-seat theater, with a huge chandelier, a balcony, box seats, and a giant proscenium. Electricity was limited since we ran lights from the theater. We didn't have running water, but we had the option of going next door and taking a shower and using the loo there. Otherwise, guys urinated in empty water bottles, and we had a fishbowl for girls.

I can't remember exactly how I met Michael; it may have been through Suzanne Mallouk or Jo Shane, or it could have happened at the Pyramid Club. He was such a beauty. Youth is beautiful, right? He was sinewy, and there was something just lovely about him, so of course I agreed to help him. Michael came to a party at the theater before he ever needed an art studio. Once space became available, Michael looked at it as a potential studio. I knew he saw the situation as far from ideal, but I also knew he was grateful that he had space—basically for free. We agreed to twenty-five dollars a month, but I never really tried to collect money for use of the space. Back then it wasn't really like that, you know—enforcing rent in an abandoned theater office wasn't the point. We shook hands on it, like, "Can you do twenty-five? Okay, great." One month he was short, so he gave me a couple of drawings. It was all very loose in that way, which seems inconceivable in New York now.

Once Michael's work got underway, I saw that he was creating abstract art. His drawings were slashes of color. I thought that he had something to prove—to himself. The marks seem to have been made because he was trying to leave proof of his very existence. You can see in their determination, there's a life force behind them. Michael didn't have a tag. I wasn't aware of one, and I was quite aware of graf writers at the time. I had an infamous glass doorway at the theater, painted black on the inside, that everybody tagged. I wish I'd taken it. I wish I had that door!

One late-summer evening, I was entering the building as he was leaving. We lifted the security gate together and exchanged a few words, not much. He seemed a little cranky. We all were a little cranky from time to time, given there was a lot we wanted to accomplish with little means. Also, that's just when we were becoming aware of our mortality. So I paid it no mind and soon went back out for the evening. The next day, the story of what happened to Michael swept through the East Village like wildfire. I was stunned to hear that the beautiful young man I anticipated seeing later that day was lying in a hospital, fighting for his life. I was afraid he didn't have enough fighter in him. His soul was too beautiful, too sensitive, to push back the brutal beating.

While Michael was still hospitalized, I remember going to Edit DeAk's loft to meet with her, Rene Ricard, Diego Cortez, Duncan Smith, and a few other people, including Suzanne Mallouk. Edit called the meeting to determine if there was something we could do to help. I brought three of Michael's drawings to the meeting to illustrate that this guy was not a graffiti artist, as the news reports were saying. The drawings were revelatory to them, since they'd assumed he was tagging because he was a young black man, and we were involved in the post-graffiti art scene.

Simultaneously, Haoui Montaug organized the huge Union Square protest for Michael and the Danceteria fund-raiser. Haoui was a practical guy and one of the smartest, nicest guys around. He was the fabled Danceteria doorman and emcee of the "No Entiendes" cabaret, meaning he continuously organized and promoted new shows. He was used to running a machine like that and could get flyers into the hands of important voices from the worlds of art, music, and fashion. He decided who got into the clubs and who didn't; he knew everyone. Haoui got the word out. What happened to Michael really galvanized our community. A young artist from our community was being accused of uncharacteristically bad behavior. The Michael I knew wouldn't provoke cops, and I knew the opposite must be closer to the truth—that it was the transit cops who were guilty of murder. Michael wasn't a graf writer; even if he had been, we didn't view graffiti, or tagging, as "bad." I was forever deeply affected by Michael's short life and brutal death. I mean, I saw a young man that day and then I didn't—he was gone. I was in a state of shock. Soon afterward, on November 21, I opened the Anderson Theater Gallery. It was weird for a long time, even after I moved out, because every time I saw the theater's heavy gate, I could see Michael opening and slipping under the gate, and leaving that last time.

Patricia Pesce

FRIEND OF MICHAEL STEWART

The first time I met Michael was at a club called Lucky Strike, where my sister was deejaying. We sat in the bar area and we talked. What did we talk about? I cannot remember exactly now. I know we probably would have talked about music and art, and getting to know each other. He was very gentle, almost timid—just, you know, quiet. You almost had to ask him to repeat himself. He had some of his artwork and asked me if I wanted to see it, and of course I said yes, and he showed me these black-and-white contact sheets that he had drawn over with marker. He had pages of them. We spent a few hours there and then left Lucky Strike. It was an early snow, and it was so beautiful because the city was quiet. We were near St. Marks Place and Third Avenue. We walked a few blocks and parted ways.

I had only really met with him two times—there was a connection—but I was with Michael that night, before he was attacked. I was not planning to meet with him, but he called me and said he really wanted to see me. It must have been around 12:30 a.m. I would have to go back to the court papers to see exactly what time it was, because I gave the accurate account in the testimony. Keep in mind that I've testified twice. First, publicly, at the criminal trial of police officers, and years later I testified for the family when the civil lawsuit was ongoing. I had to give my testimony again, but it was behind closed doors and I was by myself.

So, I met him at the Pyramid Club, and I got a drink, and we went downstairs to the VIP area, where we sat and talked. I remember that I sat on a cowrie shell, which was kind of a strange omen, in a club, on a sofa. I thought, "Wow, this is special. Okay." I kept it, and I still have it. I have it attached to this little bracelet I would wear all the time, with this soapstone cross that I've worn away from rubbing it. That was like my little prayer beads through all the events that we went through. It's a sacred memento.

After the Pyramid Club we walked. We must have walked around to Avenue A and up Third, because we sat on a stoop of a tenement building and kept talking. He asked if I wanted to see the T-shirt he designed. He was wearing it. He said, "Everyone's been trying to see it all day." While we were talking, I remember him telling me that he had ridden his bike across the Brooklyn Bridge that afternoon. At some point he told me that he was going to have a show, and he was very excited about it. After that we walked some more, a few more blocks. We must have gotten into a taxi on First Avenue, because I lived on Eighty-Second Street, between York and East End, and I said I would drop him off at the L train, because he was going to get the train to go home. The taxi stopped and he reached into his pocket; he had wanted to offer me money for the taxi, and I said no. I'm flashing back to giving testimony now and hearing that he had scribbled "RAS" on the wall in the subway, and John Fried, the assistant district attorney, asked if he had anything in his pockets. I remember commenting that his pants were so tight that he had trouble reaching into his pocket. I doubted that there was anything in his pockets they were so tight. And we kissed goodbye. It wasn't a romantic kiss. It was a kiss goodbye on the cheek. And he left the taxi and he went down the stairs. Technically, I was the last human being, the last caring individual, that is, who saw him alive.

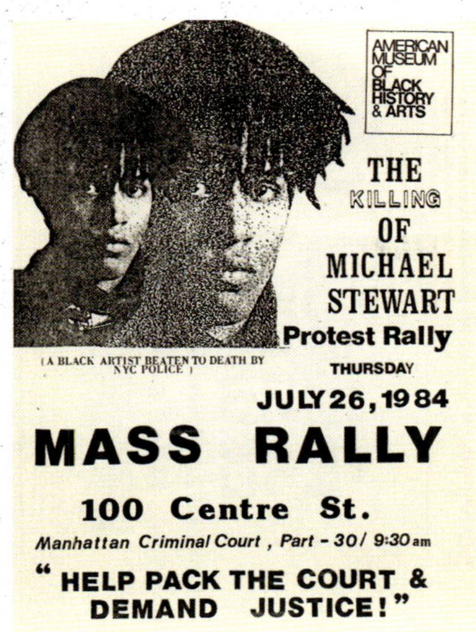

FIGURE 7

Flyer for protest rally at Manhattan Criminal Court, July 26, 1984. Collection of the Stewart Family

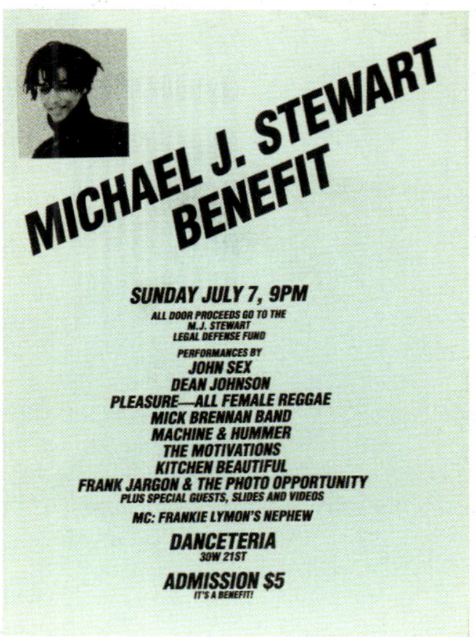

FIGURE 8

Card for benefit at Danceteria, July 7, 1985. Collection of Patricia Pesce, New York

The next day or the day after—I can't remember—I tried to reach Michael by phone. His brother John answered, and he told me that Michael was brought to Bellevue Hospital, and said, "My mother is going to want to speak with you." He sounded relieved in the sense that I represented a connection to events prior to Michael being delivered to Bellevue Hospital. When Mrs. Stewart called she told me—in her quiet and reserved and soft-spoken way—that Mike was taken to the hospital. He was delivered, chained and shackled, as an unidentified white male. And she said, "They didn't want Michael to resurface, if he ever came to. They left him for dead." I went to the hospital right away and saw him; his face was unrecognizable, it was so swollen. He was on life support. He was absolutely lifeless. He was brain-dead.

There was a group of us there and we let Mrs. Stewart know that we were going to do something about this, and that we weren't going to let it die. We formed this tight group of people. I remember meeting Suzanne [Mallouk] then, and I was a little curious about that because I didn't know that she was his girlfriend. He had never mentioned her. We all sat vigil at the hospital. It felt like we never left the hospital. We stayed. At this point we started meeting with the lawyers, Michael Warren and Clayton Jones. We all unified and started organizing protests. I remember going to the morgue over at NYU, on First Avenue, to protest when we learned that Dr. Elliot Gross removed Michael's eyes without the parents' permission. I remember protesting at the courthouse on Centre Street. We marched down Fifth Avenue, silent, holding hands. We had petitions signed; we got hundreds and hundreds of names. One was to elect a special prosecutor. We had a sleep-in at the World Trade Center in Governor Mario Cuomo's office. We sat there; we weren't leaving until Governor Cuomo assigned a special prosecutor. We were all determined to give voice to someone who lost his life in such a tragic way.

I've stayed in touch with Mrs. Stewart over the years, either by phone or by card. Something would happen, like when Eleanor Bumpurs was killed in her kitchen, and Mrs. Stewart would call. I do remember that we knew Keith Haring had painted something for Michael, illustrating what happened, and I took Mrs. Stewart to see it in New York.

Tony Shafrazi
GALLERIST

My friendship and working relationship with Keith Haring started from the time I met him. He had barely been in New York—he'd come in '78, I think. We met in fall of '79 or so. Around that time I was just forming a gallery on Lexington Avenue and Twenty-Seventh Street. The School of Visual Arts, where Keith had come to study, from Kutztown, Pennsylvania, was on Twenty-Third Street, where I had taught as a guest lecturer in the early 1970s. When I started that gallery on Lexington, there was a lot of work to do, and I needed to paint the walls. Bill Beckley, a very good artist and one of the pioneers of photo-narrative art, who was also a teacher of Keith Haring, asked me one day, "Oh, do you want a couple of people to help you?" I said, "Yes, sure," so Keith and his childhood friend, Kermit Oswald, came in to paint. As soon as they started, I noticed that Keith's way of "painting" and "working" was extraordinarily organized; I was very impressed. Keith was extremely mobile, his movements, body, ability, and working habits were meticulous. When he finished, all tools were washed and put in a beautiful row, including pairs of shoes. Many sneakers and various tools, in a pure, orderly row.

Whereas a lot of people would come around the gallery waiting, almost begging, for an opportunity; "Can you look at my work, can you help?" that was never the case with Keith. It was I who had to ask, "Keith, why don't we talk a little? What is it that you do?" And soon after I asked him, he gave me an announcement card he had made with hand-drawn figures for two shows that he was having, one at P.S.1 and the other at P.S.122. And that's how it began. That was about 1980. The gallery moved downtown in 1981 to Mercer Street, where we had many exhibitions over the next twelve or thirteen years.

We heard what happened to Michael Stewart. Everybody heard about it. It was a tragedy. Suddenly this very handsome, black young man, twenty-five years old, was beaten, and he had died. It shook the art world. He hadn't exhibited yet. He was very sweet and promising, and many artists of his generation knew him. Keith made the painting *Michael Stewart—USA for Africa* **[PP. 70–71, PL. 13]** in 1985 as his response, it's absolutely clear, he was addressing Michael Stewart's torture and death. It was remarkable that he was able to make such a serious painting that entered art history. A large painting on a canvas tarp, a major artwork, one of his largest, with a tremendous variety of color elements.

Once the tarp was put on a wall, Keith would start painting immediately, with no preparatory drawing, nothing. He would just start from one place and continue going. The composition, the idea of what goes behind what, and its complexity, how many figures, it all comes together while he's working. *USA for Africa* is an incredibly unusual painting in terms of what his peers were making. To this day there's been no other artist who's ever addressed the issue of politics, the issue of justice, in the same way as Keith Haring. Practically every single artwork that he did dealt with the subject of protest, the subject of injustice of all kinds—racial, religious—misconducts of every kind, criminality employed in every form. He made it his work, his job, to depict whatever was unjust. Drawing on black advertising panels in the subways, purposely choosing a public arena where everybody traveled, Keith was absolutely concerned with addressing the broader public.

USA for Africa was a central painting of an exhibition Keith had in my gallery, a one-man exhibition, which the whole art world came to see—it was the best we could do at the time, in terms of a voice responding to the tragedy. I would suggest whoever's interested in the painting go bloody well study it, look at the painting and make note of the fact that there is no indication of any hesitancy. There was no sketch, no preparatory marks, and there are no mistakes. It's a very determined, very focused way of addressing both subject matter and process in painting. Jean-Michel painted over things. With him, he loved mistakes. He worked with mistakes. He did takes and mistakes and overtakes. And with Keith, there were no mistakes, because it required a different energy. It was about everything falling in the right place in the right way; he believed in a sort of synchronicity.

I remember *Defacement* when it was part of a wall, before it became a painting, so to speak. Keith's relationship with Jean-Michel was inseparable. Absolutely respectful, from beginning to end. And the fact that Keith rescued a small part of a larger wall where Jean-Michel had painted, cut and actually separated and rescued it into art, as well as the fact that he kept it above his bed, shows the respect Keith had for Jean-Michel, which was mutual. Keith felt very strongly about Michael Stewart. This is a painting that Keith Haring saved for all of us.

Keith Haring was committed to representing the politics of the time, and Jean-Michel addressed different matters. He addressed history and learning and the history of black people, the glorious nature of jazz and black culture. He wanted to address the whole history of art, to move on from graffiti, although I consider every mark, every word, everything that he wrote to be absolutely unique. The voice that came out of those writings on walls was remarkably original, outstandingly, and different from every other graffiti artist. And soon after, he stopped doing it, purposely.

I can't remember going into Keith's bedroom and seeing *Defacement* above his bed, I might have. But at that time, '89 or so, we were so moved and concerned with his condition. He had AIDS and was frail, yet Keith never complained about his life. I would say hanging *Defacement* above his bed—Keith remembering the painful, tragic death of Michael Stewart along with so many other people who had died, never himself complaining about his illness—was remarkable.

Keith had Jean-Michel's *Defacement* as a commemoration of love and affection, an appreciation of the beauty that they shared, of the love that they had for art and their commitment, which was this extraordinary, glorious magic, and of the miracle that was Jean-Michel Basquiat, above his head. Those memories—the painting and Michael Stewart and that period, their lives—as he was ready to go to join them in the other world. That was a remarkable thing.

Michelle Shocked
MUSICIAN

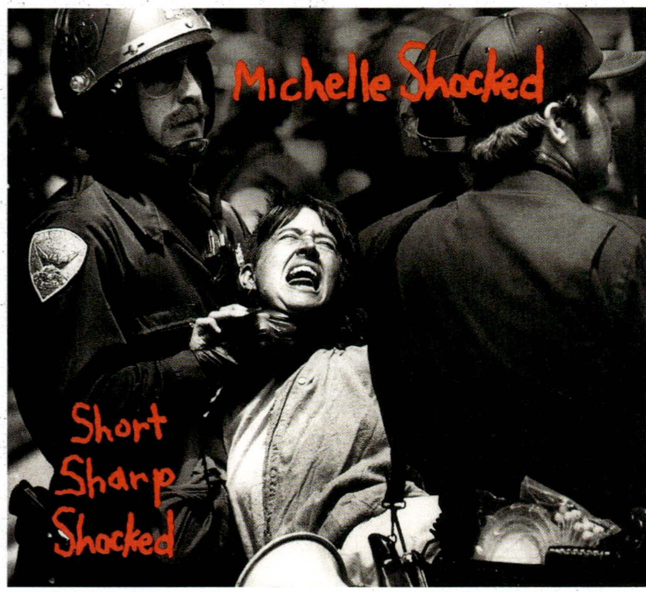

FIGURE 9
Cover of Michelle Shocked's album *Short Sharp Shocked*, 1988

I want to provide a context for the culture wars taking place on the ground, in the streets, at the time I arrived in New York in late '84, fresh off the boat from the West Coast hardcore scene. On the East Coast scene, bands like Reagan Youth and Bad Brains were influenced by the same political punk and second-wave anarcho-feminism coming out of Berkeley and Oakland. In San Francisco I was a squatter, part of an entourage of a hardcore band, MDC—Millions of Dead Cops. Their logo was a portrait of a hooded klansman and a uniformed cop split right down the middle. Rock against Racism, originally from England, arrived stateside in '83 as Rock against Reagan. It coalesced into an alternative youth culture engaged in resistance, around the same time as the nascent hip-hop culture. It was especially exciting when graphic and street artists joined the fray. It felt like the critical mass we needed.

In my song "Graffiti Limbo" there's an interlocutory part—I say, "Now, I wrote this song for Michael Stewart. Michael Stewart was a young, black graffiti artist who was arrested while writing graffiti on a subway wall in New York City. While under arrest, in the presence of eleven white transit cops, Michael Stewart was strangled to death. When his case was heard by the grand jury, you know, not one cop was found guilty. The coroner had lost the evidence and those cops are on the street again." When insufficient oxygen is the probable cause of death, a coroner removes the victim's eyeballs, dissects them, to determine whether the veins, the blood vessels in the victim's eyes, were constricted to the point of bursting. That is the science behind the coroner's art. So, when the coroner told the grand jury it was Michael Stewart's own eyes that he had "lost"—what I was really trying to say is that justice can be very blind indeed.

As an activist/organizer, I arrived in New York appearing, for all intents and purposes, like a punk. I had a Mohawk, a ring in my nose, rode my skateboard, went to Sunday hardcore matinees at CBGB. I wanted to be right there in the Lower East Side with my bohemian tribe, where all this action was happening. And that probably tuned my ears to Michael Stewart's epigrammatic case of police brutality. It isn't punk. Hilly Kristal's son, Dana, told me CBGB OMFUG meant "Country, Blue Grass, Blues (and Other Music from the Underground)," and that's the music I had brought on my vagabond sojourn from Texas. I was playing country, bluegrass, and blues with a punk, antifolk spirit.

I heard about a place in the East Village where Michael Stewart used to hang out, called the Limbo Lounge. That's what inspired the title "Graffiti Limbo." By writing a song about this artist, about this underground culture, I was participating without necessarily fitting the stereotype. When people say "Graffiti Limbo" is a protest song, I don't agree—for me, it's the blues. In my song, I invoked the Limbo Lounge, the Pyramid Club, the underground places where you could make the scene, where there was a Village vibe. Michael Stewart and Jean-Michel Basquiat were both part of that scene, all part of that underground culture we were creating.

Seth Tobocman
ARTIST

I never met Michael Stewart. My understanding was that he was a young man living in New York, aspiring to be an artist, studying in an art school, who may or may not have done some kind of street art. All those things would have been a pretty good description of myself at that time. I was living in New York, studying art at Pratt, and doing all kinds of odd jobs—you know, bussing tables, working as an usher at a movie theater, off-the-books construction, foot messenger—all while hoping to make a career for myself as an artist. Michael Stewart was a waiter at the Pyramid Club. That's what I was told.

So, when this event happened, I realized immediately that there were only two significant differences between myself and Michael Stewart. The first was that he was black and the second was that he was dead. That was an eye-opener for me and I think for a lot of people in the downtown, Lower East Side art scene. Because a lot of us came from communities that were more conservative—I came from Cleveland—and people felt that the Lower East Side was this more enlightened, more progressive place. We didn't imagine that this could happen to somebody in our scene. It was shocking, and it made us very aware of the white privilege in the scene, even if we thought that we were much more progressive than that.

I remember that Michael Stewart's girlfriend held a meeting of artists in the Lower East Side. Sabrina Jones, who later coauthored a comic strip about Michael ["The Ghost of (Michael Stewart)," 1984], and I went to that meeting and learned that they wanted artists to produce some kind of political art to bring up to Harlem for a congressional hearing on police brutality that was taking place the next day. So we went back to Sabrina's apartment, and the two of us stayed up all night making placards. In the morning we got up early and went to Harlem, and we found that we were the only people from downtown who'd gone up there with any artwork. We were pretty much the only white people in the room except for the congressmen. We heard one person after another get up and testify about how they were hassled by police as part of their daily experience. I became aware that this was a really common occurrence for black people in New York City, that it was just part of navigating the environment.

I had quite an intense experience of feeling the anger in that crowd, and after that I became a lot more involved in issues of police brutality in New York. I began to work with an organization called the December 12th Movement, which was basically a Marxist, Leninist, womanist, black nationalist contingent that was agitating against police brutality. They called themselves the December 12th Movement because on December 12, 1987, organizers came together to plan a shutdown of the New York City subway system in protest against police brutality—which took place later that month. It was also referred to as the "Day of Outrage."

I am primarily a comic artist. I'm the founding publisher of the magazine *World War III Illustrated*. But I also did a lot of poster art, some murals, some painting, and a significant amount of illustration. Most of my work on police brutality tended to be poster format so we could get it up in a lot of places. I would paste them around the city, and organizations would repaste them. The artwork moved very quickly out of my hands into the hands of other people. We tended to produce artwork that was extremely easy to reproduce and that meant that it was also easy for somebody to photocopy it from the magazine and reproduce it themselves.

There were three murals that related to the Stewart case in the garden La Plaza Cultural, at Ninth Street between Avenues B and C: mine **[FIG. 10]**, one by Etienne Li, and one by Chico. I was urged by my friend the writer Charles Frederick, who said, "Don't just do a victim image. Do something uplifting, do something inspiring." So I drew inspiration from a political protest called "No Business as Usual," which was a national antinuclear day of action, in which a number of people confronted police on horses. The way I painted it, there's a dead body under the feet of the police horse, which could symbolize Stewart or could symbolize everybody who's been killed by the police. But the main focus is the young man who seems to be floating in midair in front of the police horse made of weapons, which is jumping out of the surface toward the audience.

Also, the slogan "We Remember Michael Stewart" continued to be very important on the Lower East Side. It was one of the slogans used in the riots in Tompkins Square Park in 1988, following the confrontation between police and neighborhood residents over the imposition of a 1 a.m. curfew in the park. His death was an important event in the history of this entire community. Everybody knew about Michael Stewart; everybody knew what this signified.

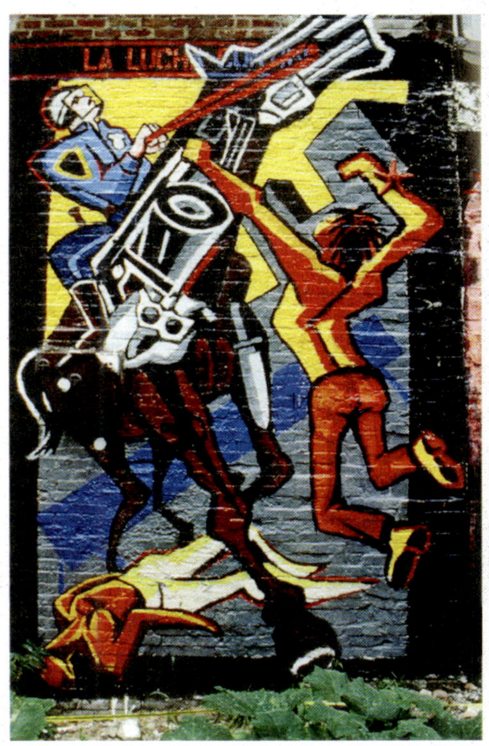

FIGURE 10
Seth Tobocman, *Young People Stand Up to Police*, 1985. Mural, approximately 14 × 7 feet (4.26 × 2.13 m). La Plaza Cultural, New York (no longer extant)

Carlo McCormick
WRITER AND CURATOR

It was so raw and sensitive then. Whenever someone did a tribute to Michael, I think it made everyone feel a little better. There was a feeling then that he wouldn't be forgotten. There was this real sense—even pre-AIDS—that there were people who were always going to be disappearing and always going to be forgotten, and that our culture needed to be much richer and more inclusive. We were informed by the hippies' motto "Don't sell out," but also by the punks, who proclaimed, "Don't be co-opted." We had inherited all these values, and for a lot of us, if we'd been given more ammunition to boost our career, we'd just find another way to shoot ourselves in the foot. At the time, I think that we all had really bad attitudes toward success, and I believe that wore heavily on the people who were successful—on the Basquiats and the Harings—because back then you were automatically suspect if you were playing on that level, because you were playing with the man and for the man. But of course, we were all really young, ambitious kids who wanted to be big and successful as well.

Maybe it is just my mind-set, but New York was a particularly haunted place, and it was a place that was always about memory. It's a place that no matter when you arrived on the scene—and that arrival might have been the day you got off at Port Authority or it might have been the night you didn't get home until six in the morning and your parents freaked out—you felt that you had just missed it. New York has always been haunted, and it always seems like it was better before. Back then it was like, "Oh, man, you missed the '60s." Or, "Oh my God, when Weegee lived here," or whatever. So we always had this sense of missing things and of disappearance. Michael Stewart is absolutely a part of that feeling of haunting. The trauma of it lingers. But it's in the work, Jean-Michel's, Keith's, Andy's, David's poster—it's all there. While the portraits are moving as memorials, it is Basquiat's painting and Wojnarowicz's poster **[FIG. 18]** that viscerally strike us in the gut for how they convey the atrocity and brutality of Stewart's being beaten to death. It's the sort of thing that's with you forever, that haunts New York forever. Legendary bouncer Haoui Montaug was slightly older than the rest of us. He had some kind of activist background, schooled in '60s protests. Haoui knew how to motivate and amass crowds, not just to hang outside the door of the Palladium or Danceteria, but to actually engage them in something meaningful. He's so hard to describe because now we all carry an insane amount of information; we're basically walking around with computers disguised as phones in our pockets. And Haoui was the type of guy who would say, "You know, Carlo, you should talk to that guy," and off the top of his head would give me the phone number. He knew everyone and he didn't have a Rolodex. He held an insane amount of information in his head, and Haoui parsed it out in the most democratic way. He was the consummate doorman. And he was the one who brought people together for Union Square protests against the assault of Michael Stewart. It was a fitting thing for Haoui to do, because of his background as an activist, and the scene, which is what our lives were about at that time.

There's actually this beautiful history of benefit concerts and benefit auctions in New York, because artists turn out to be the most generous people in the world. Now they're benefited out, because they gave so much work away to an unregulated

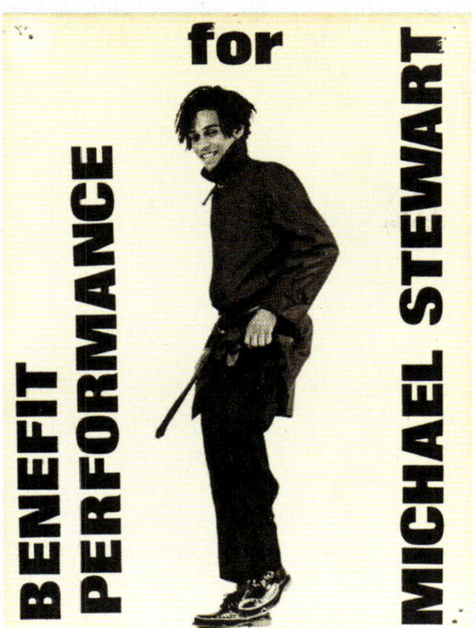

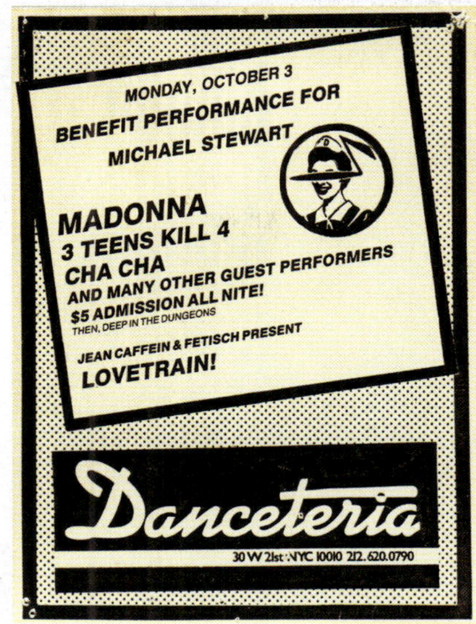

FIGURES 11, 12
Card for benefit at Danceteria, October 3, 1983. Collection of Franck Goldberg

market. But at that time there was no social safety net for any of us. Even though we lived below the poverty line, the nature of bohemianism wasn't to get on food stamps or Medicaid or anything like that. When people got hurt or got sick or got in trouble, the community took care of them. And this was an amazing, connective thing that I don't think people realize. If someone got cancer or arrested or something else, there would be, like, three nights of music at this club, where everyone, even those with no money, would pay to get in—even if you had a head cold and couldn't stay very long. The community found its own economic means to support itself. A lot of people were estranged from their families; some left home because they couldn't tell their parents they were gay, or something like that. So it wasn't like they could call mom and dad for help. Somehow, without a lot of organization, there were always people who stepped forward. The Danceteria benefit for Michael **[FIGS. 11, 12]** was actually not an anomaly, because benefits were happening all the time, for one reason or another.

I don't think I ever forgot Michael Stewart, and I don't know why, because there were a lot of fuckin' precious people who we lost because of drugs and because of AIDS. And some of them I probably don't remember so well. I do think that when something like Michael's death happened, when someone got ripped right out of the fabric, it wasn't like a loose thread, it was like someone had literally stabbed into the ligaments of what made up downtown culture. And it felt like an unraveling. One of the sad things when you lose a huge chunk of your generation is that every person you know constitutes a link in that memory, and then it's gone. So every time someone dies now, it's like, "Oh, that's one less person who knew Haoui Montaug." "That's one less person I can talk to about Michael Stewart, and what that meant at the time." It was a trauma that happened to our generation. We just lost way too many. I can do a pretty good job describing the party, but what's really hard to articulate is what happened when we stopped going to parties and we just went to memorial services. It was such a bewildering thing that left everyone at sea.

Franck Goldberg

FILMMAKER

I spent my teenage years in a small town in France watching movies. I was working as an actor, but when I ended up in New York, acting was difficult because of the language, so I started getting involved with film. At that time I was a squatter on Seventh Street between Avenues B and C, and housing was really the most important thing in my life. We were just trying to survive. The person who introduced me to the squat was the filmmaker Stephen Torton—who also worked as Basquiat's assistant for a period. He was living upstairs from me and I had acted in his film called *Watch Being Watched* [1981]. So I was hanging out with these people who were just starting their careers in the arts and in film: Jim Jarmusch, Nan Goldin, the members of Colab, and Liza Béar, for instance. She was the person who told me about Michael Stewart and encouraged me to start filming things in relation to his death. She asked me to shoot a rally at Union Square where a lot of people were talking about the Michael Stewart case. And that's how it started. I kept following the story, because I was really outraged by what happened. I was also witnessing what seemed like the collision of two worlds. There were all these young white kids who had no idea, who for the first time understood that there was police brutality, and it was racially motivated. Being from France, I had all these ideas about the racism in America, so I wasn't surprised. But it was a surprise to see the white kids being surprised by it, which really annoyed me and might have been a reason for why I didn't focus too much on the art kids in the documentary. Looking at the outtakes, I realized that the attitude of New Yorkers on the street at the time was like, "Yeah, that shit happens all the time." It's amazing how many people all say the same thing. They were almost blasé about it: "Yeah, this stuff happens. And that's what cops do."

DCTV [Downtown Community Television Center] let me use their equipment for free, and I called myself an artist-in-residence there, but I don't know if that was an official title, or if I even had a title. I often think what I did to make this documentary wouldn't be possible today. I was fearless. I was thinking and acting like a real reporter, and I was doing my job. The only thing I didn't have was a press card. I was really thinking I was a journalist covering the Michael Stewart case. But now looking at the outtakes, I could see that I was a bit of a pain in the neck. Because I was kind of crazy. I was videotaping everything. It was like I was a camera. Suzanne Mallouk and the Stewart attorneys helped introduce me to people, but a lot of other times, it was just me going to the official events, picking up the phone and saying I was calling from cable TV. I called the MTA spokesperson more than once. It is in the film. I interviewed Robert Rodriguez, who was an auxiliary police officer, and he witnessed the attack on Stewart because he was working at a Blimpie that was across the street from the First Avenue subway station. He was adamant that the cop pushed Stewart to the ground at the top of the stairs, though the police claimed he fell. I think Robert Rodriguez testified about this at both grand juries. Honestly, I really don't know what the story was behind his testimony. I gave the attorneys my footage of his interview, but I don't know if it was ever used.

I had a very brief conversation with Basquiat about the Stewart case, and,

BENEFIT FOR MICHAEL STEWART

VIDEO PROGRAM

90¢ FOR A LOUSY RIDE.... by FRANK GOLDBERG

LYNCH: WHO KILLED MICHAEL STEWART... by FRANK GOLDBERG
WORK IN PROGRESS

THE DAY THE KLAN MARCHED... by PAULA MANLEY + JIM CULLERS

THE ALGIERS INCIDENTS.... by JANET DENSMORE

NO SELL OUT...... words by MALCOM X
WORK IN PROGRESS music by KEITH LE BLANC
video by SHABAZZ SEVEN

VISITOR.......... by ZOE BELLOFF

SLIDES.......... by SCHMIDLAPP

READING......... by KAOS

PROCEEDS GO TO THE MICHAEL STEWART JUSTICE FUND AND THE ALGIERS JUSTICE FUND

FIGURES 13, 14

Program for benefit at Tin Pan Alley, February 22, 1984, with cover art incorporating Michael Stewart's arrest report. Collection of Franck Goldberg

basically, he said that he was not going to do anything for it. Suzanne was very upset because he was saying that he did not want to be political. So I'm surprised that he made a painting about it. But, on the other hand, I've always wondered if the graffiti that was on Houston Street that read "WHO KILLED M. STEWART?" was by Basquiat **[FIG. 2]**.

I originally called the film *Lynch: Who Killed Michael Stewart*, and showed it on the cable show *Cast Iron TV*, co-founded by Liza Béar and run by Milli Iatrou. But I also showed it at events as part of the club scene, some of which were fund-raisers for the Stewart case. I showed it at Tin Pan Alley **[FIGS. 13, 14]**, where Nan Goldin was bartending. The film was in progress continuously, until at one point it was no longer in progress because I couldn't get funding. I had made the decision not to focus on the story of Michael Stewart's life. My viewpoint at the time was that it didn't matter if he did graffiti or not. It didn't matter who his parents were. He was just a young man who five minutes before he got in the train station was with a beautiful girl in a taxi, and then half an hour later, he was dead, or in a coma. So I decided to stick to the events unfolding around his death and the cover-up. And that's a decision that cost me funding.

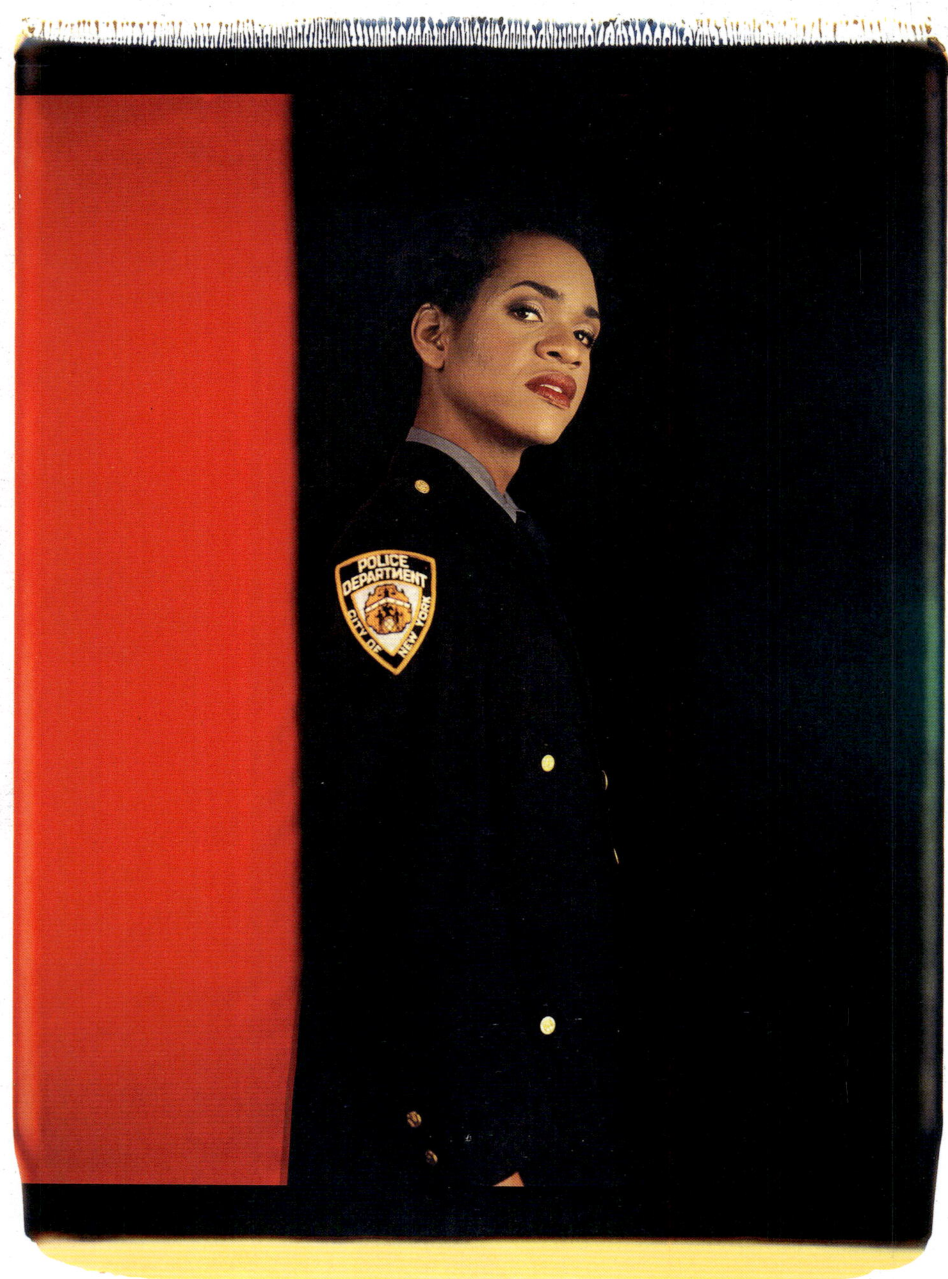

PLATE 18

Lyle Ashton Harris

Saint Michael Stewart, 1994

Polaroid

24 × 20 inches (61 × 50.8 cm)

Collection of Michael and Susan Hort

Lyle Ashton Harris

ARTIST

It was during the early fall of my first semester at Wesleyan when I found out Michael Stewart had died. There was a certain social consciousness at the university, where I was studying with Hazel Carby, a feminist scholar; Robert O'Meally, a Billie Holiday expert and Ralph Ellison scholar; and Bill Lowe, a specialist on the history of black music.

The story of Michael Stewart and, in many ways, the self-portrait that I later created, *Saint Michael Stewart* [1994] **[PL. 18]**, were connected to a larger narrative around double consciousness and the local and collective global trauma against black bodies. Although I was growing up in New York, I lived in Tanzania as a child during the mid-1970s. My mother married the South African revolutionary Pule Leinaeng—he's the subject of my brother Thomas Allen Harris's film *Twelve Disciples of Nelson Mandela* [2005]—and often our home would be a hub for South African exiles. At any given time there were people in my home, whether in the Bronx or Dar es Salaam, who were involved in the African National Congress. I remember what it felt like to return to New York after having lived in Tanzania, a country in the robust stages of its recent independence, under the leadership of president Julius Nyerere's African-centered Ujamaa, a practice of social and economic development.

Spending those formative years in East Africa deepened my understanding of the Pan-African diasporic experience. It was quite revelatory for me as a young child to be part of a group of thousands of students walking five miles to the international airport to greet foreign dignitaries. This particular experience of collective community engagement and African consciousness on a cultural and political level was eye-opening for me as a young boy, and in stark contrast to a racially stratified United States. Not that Tanzania didn't have its own issues, but when I returned to the U.S. with my family, I had a difficult adjustment. Puberty had sprung amongst my classmates in New York, and somehow the idyllic adolescence of my Tanzania years was radically jarred. I left the U.S. a young child and returned a faggot. That was a double layer of trauma I had to deal with—the external but also the conflict within.

During my sophomore year at Wesleyan, in 1985, I went to visit my brother, who was living in Amsterdam on a postgraduate fellowship from Harvard; I left a wannabe-IZOD-prep economics major and returned with orange hair and a miniskirt. While in Amsterdam, I came across Allan Sekula's seminal book *Photography against the Grain* as well as an article featuring Andres Serrano's photography, and that planted a seed. Upon return, I took a semester off and waited tables at Patisserie Lanciani. There I met Robert Mapplethorpe, signed up for a photography class at the Fashion Institute of Technology, and started hanging out in clubs. That same year, I met Basquiat with my cousin Alexandra on our first night at Area, the Wednesday before Basquiat was featured on the cover of the *New York Times Magazine*.

I saw *Defacement* for the first time in Francesco and Alba Clemente's home in the early 1990s, while hanging out with Iké Udé and Luigi Ontani, whom I met through Jack Tilton. My encounter with the painting was visceral, as there was a heightened sense of Basquiat's ghost in the room. I felt it very strongly—his aura as well as those that consumed it.

On the heels of completing the Whitney Independent Study Program in 1992, I developed a series of photographs collectively titled *The Good Life* [1994], which includes the unique Polaroid *Saint Michael Stewart*. It evokes the spirit of Stewart, summoning and disrupting, in a Fanonian sense, the uniform of oppression. The red, black, and green background refers to Marcus Garvey's 1917 UNIA [Universal Negro Improvement Association] conference. There's a synergistic relationship to the Pan-African flag, which connects to my childhood in Tanzania and the Bronx, and my family's relationship with the African National Congress.

The civil rights narrative has often been coded in a masculine, heteronormative voice, occluding black female and queer contributions to the movement. By extension, the Pan-African flag was associated with a heterosexist notion of identity. Appropriating it gave space for a certain elasticity, interrogating and expanding notions of masculinity and blackness.

Saint Michael Stewart was a way to work through layers of historical trauma that extend beyond my individual experience. It is an exorcism, a way to process the violence against young black bodies, be it physical and/or psychological. The trauma of what happened to Michael Stewart was so deep, it galvanized the East Village, and I believe contributed to the energy that eventually transmuted into AIDS activism. His violent, unjustified killing at the hands of the police was so traumatic for Basquiat that he traveled to West Africa in 1986 as a way to escape the onus, the trauma of his own body. It's evident that Basquiat was engaging with and working through his own exposure and vulnerability through *Defacement*, because, regardless of his status as an artist at that time, his 1983 response to Stewart's death says it all: "It could have been me. It could have been me."

Eric Drooker
ARTIST AND ILLUSTRATOR

I was doing lots of street posters during that era—still am, for that matter—but this was one of my early posters from 1984: *Remember Michael Stewart* **[FIG. 15]**. There was an urgency to it. I was taking it personally, not only being an artist myself but having grown up on Fourteenth Street, on the very corner of the First Avenue L train station where Stewart got picked up for allegedly doing graffiti. I put the posters around the neighborhood, especially right on that corner, right around that subway station, literally the scene of the crime. As far as I know, it was the first printed poster, even if it was only printed in an edition of fifty or a hundred. I don't remember seeing others before this other than just one-off things. Back then, in that neighborhood, people would often just do graffiti murals, or do a big poster and put that on the street, just like a one-of-a-kind painting. The poster had "Criminal Court" and a date written on it. It was trying to get people to go down to the court when they were sentencing the policemen who were charged with . . . I don't think they were even charged for murder. Cops rarely are—if it's a black person. I think maybe they were charged with manslaughter in 1983. So my first Michael Stewart poster was meant to induce people to go down and pack the courthouse at 100 Centre Street, to be there when the sentencing occurred. One way I tried to do that was to include in the poster editions the criminal courthouse address and the time and date of the hearing. To this day, that's how it's often done. If packing the courtroom doesn't necessarily help sway the judge or the jury, at least the media will be there, at least they'll hear people screaming and protesting.

I was in the courtroom when the judge very blithely, without any fanfare, announced, "That's it, not guilty," and the cops got up, and they were chuckling and kind of laughing out loud, and just walked out of the courthouse. That's when a black woman, maybe it was Michael Stewart's mother, started screaming, "Is this America? Is this America?" It was so outrageous. Just seeing his bereaved parents, who were right there. I'll never forget his father's expressionless face. He was a very gentle, very elegant, tall man. His mother was doing all the talking to the press, who had been in front of the courthouse. And his lawyers were there. And that's when I first made contact with them. I think I gave them a copy of the poster and one of the lapel buttons I had designed that said, "Remember Michael Stewart," which I had been giving out in the neighborhood.

About a week after I had met his family and the lawyers, the phone rang and it was one of Stewart's lawyers, Michael Warren. He said, "Listen, it was good to meet you. Thank you for the poster, I really like your poster, and it means a lot not only to the family but for our case." They were still working on the case, trying to get justice for Stewart, even though the cops were found not guilty. He wanted to get more of the buttons. I had only made a few dozen of them, to give to people in the neighborhood and to give out to everyone down at the courtroom. It was not such a big group of people, maybe a couple dozen folks who were in the inner circle, who were so distraught. The lawyers commissioned me to manufacture more of the buttons. They wanted me to make five hundred or a thousand of them, but larger.

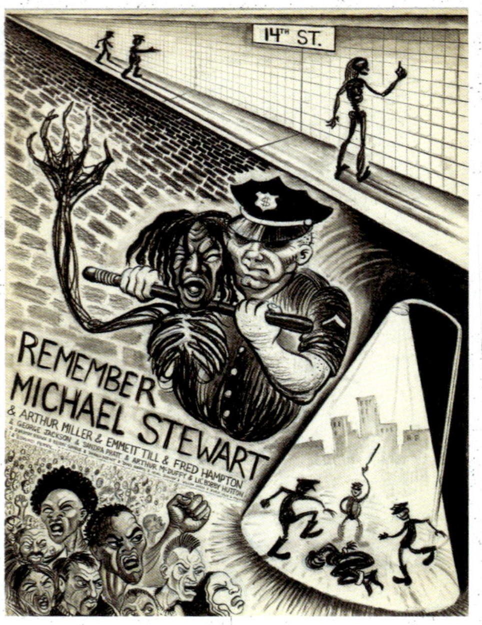

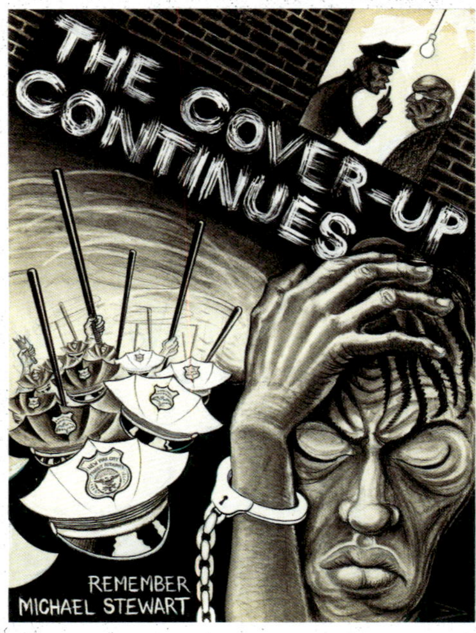

FIGURES 15, 16
Original artwork by Eric Drooker for protest posters. Left: *Remember Michael Stewart*, 1984; Right: *The Cover-Up Continues*, ca. 1984–85. Collection of the artist

And so I got right to work. I had them made at a button factory in Chelsea, and within a couple of weeks, Michael Warren met me at Astor Place, right in front of Cooper Union, handed me a check, and I gave him this bag of buttons, which showed a photograph of Stewart with the words "Remember Michael Stewart" in sans-serif font, in just black, white, and red **[FIG. 17]**.

It was right around that time that Warren started talking to me about the poster I had made. He was very moved by it but was concerned about its unintentional message. I had depicted Stewart in the subway, in the Fourteenth Street-First Avenue stop, and he's drawing graffiti on the wall. It was drawn in charcoal in an almost German Expressionist style, like in the style of Max Beckmann, George Grosz, and Otto Dix. You see him kind of innocently drawing something on the wall, and then below that you see that he's in a chokehold. So it was narrative; it was almost sequential. The policeman has a nightstick and is choking him with it. And Stewart's screaming and reaching out his hand, which is looking so sinewy and Expressionist that it almost looks like you could see his muscles and bones right through the hand. Michael Warren said it looked a little morbid, which didn't occur to me. I was trying to make it look as Expressionist as possible without being sensationalist. I was just putting all of my grief and emotion into it. But he very gently explained to me how the fact that I depicted Stewart drawing on the wall of the subway gave truth to the police alibi—that they busted him for defacing the station. He asked me to do another poster, because he and his legal team were now appealing the case, and they were trying to keep the story alive. I think the legal case was now expanding to not only be about the police, but they were charging the city with covering up the crime. Not only police, but the chief medical examiner, Dr. Elliot Gross, who they claimed was concealing evidence of strangulation. So Warren suggested that I create a second poster in another light:

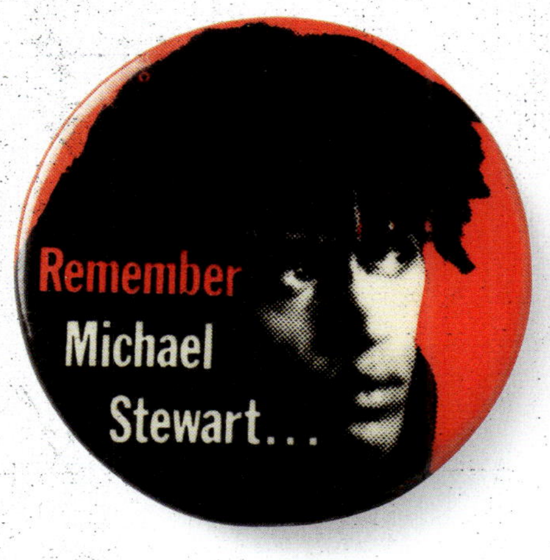

FIGURE 17
"Remember Michael Stewart" button, 1984. Design by Eric Drooker. Collection of Patricia Pesce, New York

The Cover-Up Continues **[FIG. 16]**. That's why, on the upper-right corner of the new poster, you see a cop saying "Shh" to a bald guy with glasses—he's the chief medical examiner who hid crucial evidence after the autopsy. The idea was to explain the conclusion that we all felt was happening, by suggesting a hypothetical conversation as, "This is a cover-up. I won't tell anyone if you don't tell anyone. The story is, we busted him for doing graffiti. And then when you told him to stop, he became violent, and he attacked you, and you had to subdue him. But you didn't strangle—you didn't have him in an illegal chokehold. No, no—he was flailing about. And then you threw him in the police van and took him to Union Square, where he continued to flail about. Oh, and he was very intoxicated, and he was high on marijuana, and he was drugged, and he must have just banged his head really hard or passed out from intoxication." That was the official story. He didn't die at the hands of police. It was somehow his fault.

So these were the details that jumped out at me at the time and so horrified me as a young artist. It was so appalling that I felt like I had to at least make a couple of pictures and post them on the street. I had to at least get involved in the capacity of an artist. I had some of the facts at my disposal, but most of the facts I'll never know. So I used my imagination. I was also aware that I was in an artistic tradition of Social Realist political art by Jewish artists, especially on the Lower East Side in New York City, for a hundred years. Emma Goldman lived on East Thirteenth Street a century before. It was part of my artistic heritage, and cultural heritage, as a third-generation New Yorker. My grandmother was born on the Lower East Side, and I was from that neighborhood and was aware that there was a rich tradition of not just artwork but artwork that had strong social content. I felt like I was part of that historic wave.

Kenny Scharf
ARTIST

Originally we were oblivious to the police. We felt like the city was so bankrupt, and there were murders and drugs and needles everywhere. So we just thought, "What do they care about us? We're just making some crazy art in the street." This changed for me with Michael Stewart and my own experience with the cops. That happened sometime in the summer a few months before Michael's death. I was in the street making a painting—it must have been around rush hour because there was lots of traffic on Twelfth Street and First Avenue. And I heard some screaming, like, "Get over here. Yo, come over here." I immediately hopped on my bike, and I went the other way against the traffic. I don't know who was yelling at me, but I saw this car. I didn't look inside. The whole night went by, me riding my bike and spray-painting all over. It must have been seven hours later, around three or four in the morning, when I was coming back, and I saw the car again and the car saw me. I immediately start racing for my apartment, which was on Ninth between First and Avenue A, but the car caught up, came up next to me, and while I was racing, they opened their door on me and knocked me to the ground. They ran over my bike a couple of times, back-and-forth. When they got out, it was the first time I knew they were cops in an unmarked car. Then they knocked me down again, and it was very violent. One guy had me behind the back and was holding my arm as if to break it. The other one was shoving his gun down my throat, like, simulating a blow job. They took me to the Ninth Precinct station on Fifth Street, where they proceeded to yell at me. They were calling me stupid over and over again. Then they took me down to the jail near City Hall, and I was in a crowded cell. At around six in the morning, a lawyer said, "If you plead guilty, they'll just let you go." I asked, "What am I pleading guilty to?" And he said, "Assaulting an officer." I thought, that's weird, but I did it anyway because he said they would let me go, and they did. When I was exiting the City Hall jail, the cop who was doing that thing down my throat with a gun was there waiting for me, and that was kind of weird and creepy. And he grabbed his crotch and said, "Thank you."

Then, lo and behold, a few months later, Michael Stewart gets killed. I knew it was the same precinct, and I was convinced it was the same cops because they were really sadistic. I first thought that if I were black, they would have killed me. If I had been Michael, they would have killed me. I swear that was my first thought. We were all dealing with it in our circle, but what I thought at the time and still think is that they were probably killing other young black men, and we just didn't know about it. And these other boys were not connected to a broader art world like Michael was. It just seemed routine for the cops, the way they were acting, like it was just kind of a fun night out.

Murder was something that we were not accustomed to—we were sort of oblivious to the other police-brutality cases. And for our little downtown East Village community, it obviously made quite an impact. It was a big shock.

I remember the protest in Union Square, especially since I had never seen such a group of all these people being organized in the daytime. Up until then, it was all about nightclubs—just music and dancing. I was used to seeing them at three in the morning, and at the protest they were in the bright light. I walked over to the protest, and I remember Union Square being totally packed. Everyone from the neighborhood was there, together for a cause. For me, all of it was very personal because of my own experience with the police.

Keith Haring was upset about Michael's death. He was always civic-minded and very involved in the community, and would address different topics that he was concerned about it. In a way, Keith set an example by being involved in causes that he felt strongly about. He was sort of a ringleader, and, in fact, I used to call him "The Mayor" because he could go anywhere with a piece of chalk and start drawing, and within five minutes there would be a huge crowd. He'd give away buttons and T-shirts and hats, and I would say, "Wow, you should really run for office," which he thought was funny. Michael Stewart and the case were a huge part of our conversation at that time. I think Keith's response to what happened [*Michael Stewart—USA for Africa* (1985) **(PP. 70–71, PL. 13)**] was more literal. The work that I did about it wasn't so literal; I can be literal, but not usually. I might have taken the angst and the anguish and channeled it somewhere, into an expressive face or something.

Michael's death was a huge thing for our circle. I had a lot of conversations about it with a lot of people, and though I can't remember, "Oh, [performance artist] John Sex said this or that," there was a shared horror about what had happened. What happened to Michael Stewart was so shocking and scary. But we barely had time to process it before we started having to go to funerals for AIDS. After a certain point, that's all that we did—go to funerals—but that nonstop onslaught of death kind of started with a murder. And people want to know why the '80s were so fun, and I say, no, actually it wasn't so fun. I don't know what you're talking about.

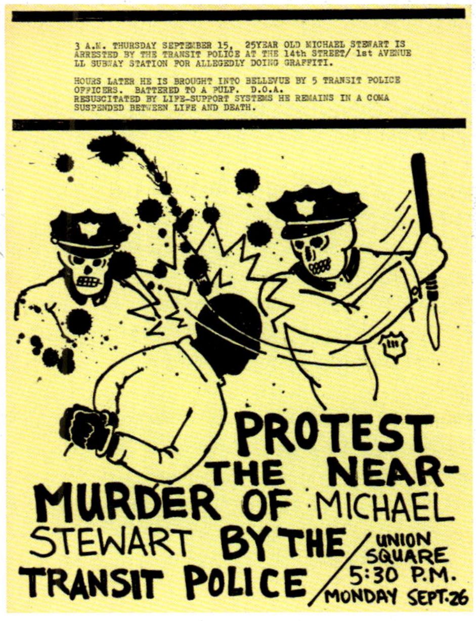

FIGURE 18

Flyer for protest at Union Square, New York, September 26, 1983. Design by David Wojnarowicz. Collection of Luc Sante

Leonard Abrams

PUBLISHER AND EDITOR OF THE EAST VILLAGE EYE

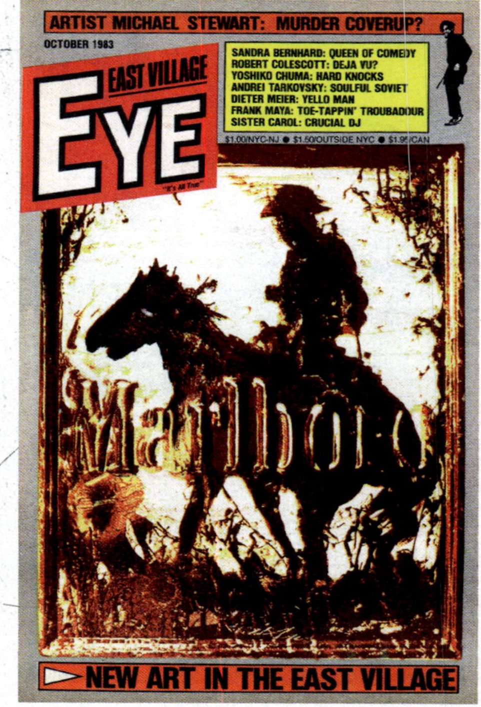

I had been living in the East Village in the early '70s, and once I saw what was going on downtown, I realized that it was just a matter of creating the right vehicle to encompass this energy as a way to represent it. So I started the *East Village Eye*, with the first issue coming out in May 1979. Basically, I went around telling everybody there was this paper starting and asked if they wanted to be a part of it, and a lot of people did. After the first issue came out, even more people wanted to join, so it was just a matter of keeping it alive, of feeding this machine that we had created, and we kept going as far as we could. The last issue came out in January of 1987.

The *East Village Eye* was, in my mind, going to be mostly about pop, underground culture, and rock and roll. I didn't know much about art history, but when this explosion of art making happened in the East Village, Tribeca, and the Lower East Side, we were there to express the energy of what was going on. This was completely outside the mainstream. The artists, independent curators, and new gallery owners were taking control of the mechanisms of display. The energy that they created was like a nuclear chain reaction, and I think that's what had such a great effect on society at the time. You had graffiti artists, you had rappers, you had break dancers—you had these kids who were otherwise segregated from the rest of society. The artists from downtown New York took the lead in introducing them to galleries, to collectors, to venues, and institutions where they could show their work and present their music. I heard of the story of the early rap group Treacherous Three. My friends and I went to the Mudd Club to see them and they didn't show up. They were late, and they were running to get to the venue, and the police saw these three young black kids running and they arrested them.

Michael Stewart was part of this scene, and he epitomized a situation in which a person of color was seen as crossing into the mainstream. At the time, things were a lot more segregated in New York City than they are today. And here's this person: he's good-looking, he's sophisticated, and he's mixing with all kinds of people. And then, instead of being accepted, his crossing over caused outrage by white

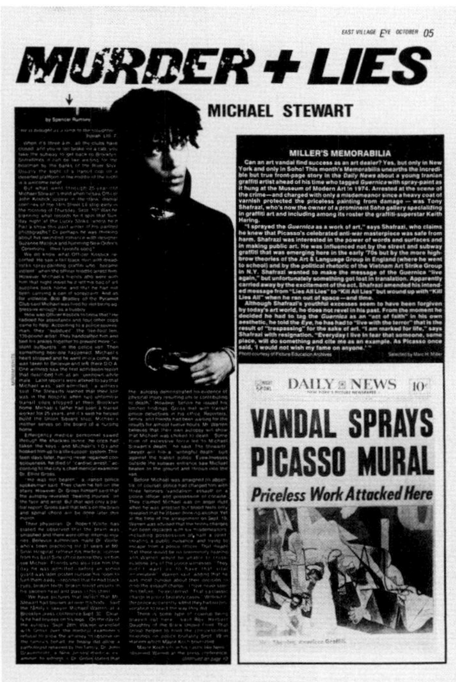

EAST VILLAGE EYE OCTOBER 05

MURDER + LIES

MICHAEL STEWART

MILLER'S MEMORABILIA

Can an art vandal find success as an art dealer? Yes, but only in New York and only in Soho! This month's *Memorabilia* unearths the incredible but true front-page story in the *Daily News* about a young Iranian graffiti artist ahead of his time who tagged *Guernica* with spray-paint as it hung at the Museum of Modern Art in 1974. Arrested at the scene of the crime—and charged with only a misdemeanor since a heavy coat of varnish protected the priceless painting from damage — was Tony Shafrazi, who's now the owner of a prominent Soho gallery specializing in graffiti art and including among its roster the graffiti-superstar Keith Haring.

"I sprayed the *Guernica* as a work of art," says Shafrazi, who claims he knew that Picasso's celebrated anti-war masterpiece was safe from harm. Shafrazi was interested in the power of words and surfaces and in making public art. He was influenced not by the street and subway graffiti that was emerging here in the early '70s but by the more high-brow theories of the Art & Language Group in England (where he went to school) and by the political rhetoric of the Vietnam Art Strike Group in N.Y. Shafrazi wanted to make the message of the Guernica "live again," but unfortunately something got lost in translation. Apparently carried away by the excitement of the act, Shafrazi amended his intended message from "Lies All Lies" to "Kill All Lies" but wound up with "Kill Lies All" when he ran out of space—and time.

Although Shafrazi's youthful excesses seem to have been forgiven by today's art world, he does not revel in his past. From the moment he decided he had to tag the *Guernica* as an "act of faith" in his own aesthetic, he told the *Eye*, he has had to "live with the terror" that is the result of "trespassing" for the sake of art. "I am marked for life," says Shafrazi with resignation. "Everyday I live in fear that someone, some place, will do something and cite me as an example. As Picasso once said, 'I would not wish my fame on anyone.'"

Photo courtesy of Picture Education Archives — Selected by Marc H. Miller

DAILY NEWS 10¢

VANDAL SPRAYS PICASSO MURAL

Priceless Work Attacked Here

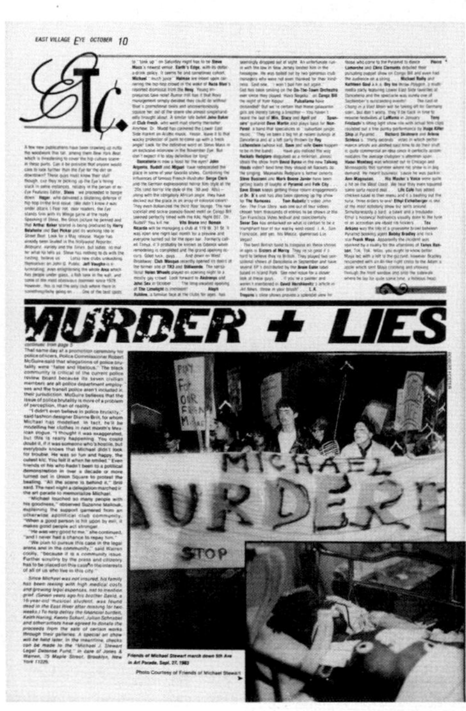

EAST VILLAGE EYE OCTOBER 10

Etc.

MURDER + LIES

continued from page 5

That same day at a promotion ceremony for police officers, Police Commissioner Robert McGuire said that allegations of police brutality were "false and libelous." The black community is critical of the current police review board because its seven civilian members are all police department employees and the transit police aren't included in their jurisdiction. McGuire believes that the issue of police brutality is more of a problem of perception, than of reality.

"I didn't even believe in police brutality," said fashion designer Dianne Brill, for whom Michael has modelled. In fact, he'll be modelling her clothes in next month's Mexican *Vogue*. "I thought it was exaggerated, but this is really happening. You could doubt it, if it was someone who's hostile, but everybody knows that Michael didn't look for trouble. He was so fun and happy, the cutest kid. You felt it when he smiled." Even friends of his who hadn't been to a political demonstration in over a decade or more turned out in Union Square to protest the beating. "All the scene is behind it," Brill said. The next night a delegation marched in the art parade to memorialize Michael.

"Michael touched so many people with his goodness," observed Suzanne Mallouk, explaining the support garnered from an otherwise apolitical club community. "When a good person is hit upon by evil, it makes good people act stronger."

"He was very good to me," she continued, "and I never had a chance to repay him."

"We plan to pursue this case in the legal arena and in the community," said Warren coolly, "because it is a community issue. Further scrutiny by the press and citizenry has to be placed on this case in the interests of all of us who live in this city."

Since Michael was not insured, his family has been reeling with high medical costs and growing legal expenses, not to mention grief. (Seven years ago his brother David, a 16-year-old musical student, was found dead in the East River after missing for two weeks.) To help defray the financial burden, Keith Haring, Kenny Scharf, Julian Schnabel and other artists have agreed to donate the proceeds from the sale of certain works through their galleries. A special art show will be held later. In the meantime, checks can be made to the "Michael J. Stewart Legal Defense Fund," in care of Jones & Warren, 75 Maple Street, Brooklyn, New York 11225.

Friends of Michael Stewart march down 5th Ave in Art Parade, Sept. 27, 1983

Photo Courtesy of Friends of Michael Stewart

people in power who couldn't accept that—in this case, the police. So here in New York in the '80s, instead of being accepted, Stewart was literally beaten to death. This was the essence of everything that the *East Village Eye* was fighting against. It was the perfect story for us in that it illustrated the conflict in our trying to promote a new, more open vision of the world and the reality of that world. That's why we covered it as much as we did.

FIGURES 19, 20, 21

East Village Eye, October 1983, featuring Spencer Rumsey's article "Michael Stewart: Murder + Lies." Courtesy *East Village Eye*

Reverend Herbert Daughtry

PASTOR AND ACTIVIST

It was a time of turmoil and tension, particularly with the black community and the police. There were a number of police killings and police exonerations. Never were they held accountable. The President's Commission said that in 1967, when the cities across America were going up in flames, almost all the riots were precipitated by police violence.

Ricky Bodden was only ten years old in 1972 when killed by the police in Staten Island. Clifford Glover was only ten years old when he was shot in the back by the police in 1973. He was walking with his father in Jamaica, Queens. In 1974 fourteen-year-old Claude Reese was killed in Brooklyn. And then there was fifteen-year-old Randy Evans, who was shot in the head in 1976. And in November of 1977 the jury sentenced Robert Tornsey, Evans's killer, to two years of psychiatric treatment, with weekends home. The community was furious. We decided we had to do something more lasting than just demonstrate for a moment, cool off, then go back to business as usual.

We came up with the idea of trying to do something that would be sustainable. We launched Black Christmas '77, an economic boycott. We threatened to shut down NYC. We didn't think that people were going to stop shopping during Christmas, but we wanted to make a statement. We knew that we would be able to sustain a boycott in Brooklyn, and from it we would build a lasting movement that would empower the people. During the boycott we had to awaken the people to their powerlessness and discrimination, and how we could change things.

We did about a year's boycott of the downtown stores. In fact, we were on the street boycotting the downtown Brooklyn stores in June 1978 when we heard that Arthur Miller was killed. He was choked to death by the police. That added to the momentum that was building, which led to the forming of the Metropolitan Black United Front. Then in 1980 we formed the National Black United Front. There were over a thousand delegates from across the U.S.A. and five foreign countries. One of the top items on the agenda was police brutality and the empowerment of our community—politically, economically, et cetera.

We started with just four of us: Assemblyman Al Vann, Jitu Weusi, Sam Penn, and myself. We would meet every week for two hours, going from home to home. We studied personalities, who would be with us, who would be against us, who controlled NYC—Brooklyn, in particular. We studied the demographics. We studied why black people, with such large numbers in Brooklyn, coming from many parts of the world, were so powerless. And how deep and pervasive was racism. So when Randy Evans was killed, and the jury pretty much acquitted the officer, we were ready with a plan, how to set goals and objectives, and how to strategize effectively.

The police have killed so many, before and after Michael Stewart. As an organizing strategy, the National Black United Front would form committees in the name of the person who had been killed, for example, the Michael Stewart Justice Committee, the Michael Griffin Justice Committee, the Arthur Miller Justice Committee. Calling out these police killings in the name of the person who had been killed helped to garner more support. Hence, with the case of Michael Stewart, we organized demonstrations, rallies, workshops, panel discussions—in fact, we have a photo of

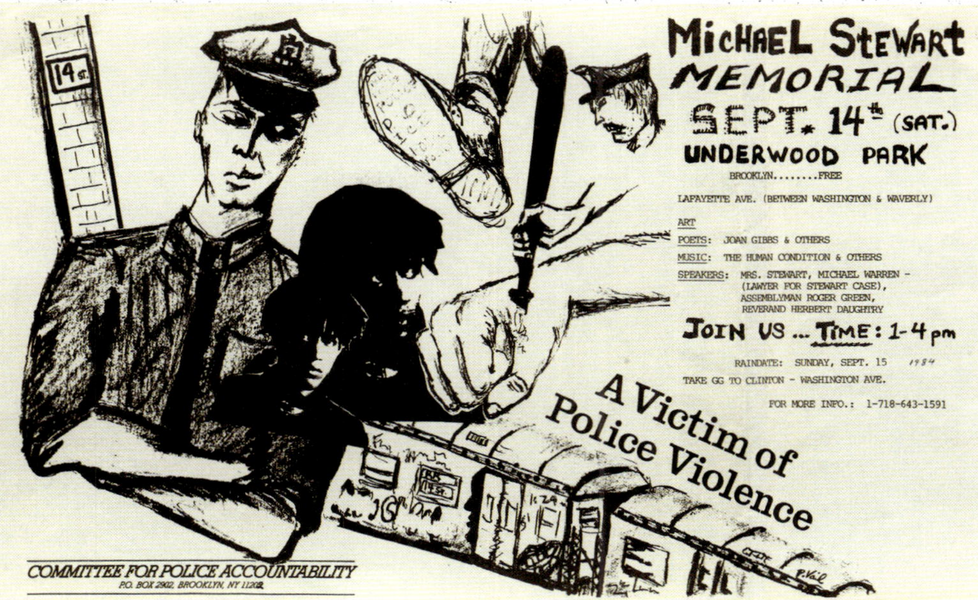

FIGURE 22

Flyer for Michael Stewart memorial at Underwood Park, Brooklyn, September 14, 1985. Collection of the Stewart Family

our doing a candlelight memorial here at the church for him and others. Also, we have a picture of a demonstration with me carrying a picket poster that read, "Michael Stewart brutalized. Dead at 25." And a much larger banner that had to be held by three persons, which read, "Michael Stewart's Justice Committee." On the banner there were drawings of bullets with victims' names on them.

By identifying the victims when we had rallies, meetings, demonstrations, we usually had wide support, particularly from the community with which these persons were associated. With Michael Stewart it was the art community. We also went to strategic places or timed our rallies to coincide with a person's birthday. For Michael Stewart, it may have been in a subway station or the transportation headquarters. For Arthur Miller, we even went to Wall Street on Black Solidarity Day, which is the first Monday in November. We marched into Wall Street to make the connection between what was happening in the black community to those working in the financial industry, because, in some sense, they were directly responsible.

Each case had its own identity. The killing of these people did not happen in isolation; they were not some isolated individuals. They were living, breathing human beings with families, associations, and networks. When a person was killed, that meant that not only were potential generations killed, but it was also a significant loss in the community.

An important part of what we did was to make early contact with the family of the victim, to ask them what they needed. We were there to help with everything, including funeral arrangements, transportation, and counseling if necessary. We didn't just protest and investigate the police, we always offered to find legal help. We would assign someone to always be available to the family. And we'd provide the strategy and encouragement to the family to be as involved as they wanted to be. It was my experience that the more involved the family was, the more they were able to manage what had happened. We maintained contact with the families long after the victims had been laid to rest and the media had found something else to do. That's why, as I said, we held the memorial for Michael Stewart in 1984 or '86.

Years later, we are still in touch with the families. Moreover, occasionally, when families finally settle with the city or police, they move to another area. I'd like to emphasize—and I'm glad to be able to say—we never received a dime, a penny, from any of the families that we represented, no matter how much money was given to them. The families never offered us any kind of remuneration, and, in some cases, it cost a lot of money. But my church was very compassionate and generous, and so was the community.

Another very important thing we did was to establish scholarships in memory of the victims. For example, we established the Randolph Evans Memorial Scholarship, which is now in its fortieth year. For most of those years we gave $1,500 to ten college-bound students. The last few years we have not been able to sustain the $1,500 scholarship, but we have been able to give something every year. One of the demands we made on the business community during the boycott was that they support the scholarship program, which they did for fifteen years while speaking highly of the program. In fact, they only agreed to fund the program for five years.

At the time, we were able to get pretty extensive press coverage. Our organizing had become rather, I must say, efficient. We knew that if you put enough people in the street, the press would come. In addition, we would meet with the press—particularly the black newspapers like the *New York Amsterdam News*, the *Daily Challenge*, and the *Big Red*, and radio—Percy Sutton had purchased WLIB and WBLS. We would have monthly breakfasts and bring them up to date on what was going on in the community and what we proposed to do.

By 1983 we had gone from a local organization to an effective national organization. We made police brutality a national issue. The fact that police killings were happening across the country demanded a national organizational response. Thus, the National Black United Front answered the call.

The police killings before and after Michael Stewart proved it was systemic. That was our argument. It wasn't that the police suddenly got angry at a victim who had done something to the police, or who was caught in a criminal act, and the police had to respond. No, what we were able to prove and demonstrate is that the police killings were not sudden acts, or police defending themselves, but that the killings were deep and pervasive, and, almost exclusively, the victims were black or Latino.

Ronald Fields

MEMBER OF THE FIRST GRAND JURY

What happened to Michael J. Stewart? I was on the first grand jury, in 1983. We were informally discussing the news and this specific event, which looked outrageous. Why was nothing being done? I said, "Well, we have the power to investigate—any grand jury has the power." All it takes is for twelve of the twenty-three people to have a majority vote in order to recommend a case. So, we took the vote, we decided, and we called the district attorney in and said, "We want this case." The assistant district attorney said that the Manhattan DA's office was looking into it and they're not ready to do anything. I said, "Well, we voted that we want the case, and if you don't start it in the next two hours, we will ask the governor for a special prosecutor." Then we had their ear and their attention.

I believed, at the time, that the autopsies were being politicized. The former medical examiner had been removed and replaced by someone who appeared to mislabel deaths at the hands of the state. If somebody dies at the hands of the police, prosecutors can't do anything unless it's deemed a homicide. So when Dr. Elliot Gross conveniently said that Stewart died of cardiac arrest, there was no case. If you looked at Rikers Island, 117 people that year died of cardiac arrest, which simply means their hearts had stopped beating. Well, what was the cause or manner of death? Was it a drug overdose? Was it a beating by the guards or fellow inmates? If you don't signal a homicide, there's no investigation.

The point that I had to get across to the grand jury, and to the judge, was that citizens do not wear blinders on a grand jury. This is different from a petit jury, where one has to stick to the law and to the evidence as presented to you. If you discover something outside, you cannot use what you found to make your private determination, but you can bring that to the grand jury body and then have the body bring the person in, subpoena the person, to have direct testimony. That's the difference: you can start your own investigation. If you gather some facts, you can bring back what you think might be useful to the jury. But again, you're just one of twenty-three votes.

Around this time, I experienced some major coincidences—what I would call God's way of remaining anonymous. I prayed one night to have a conversation with the supervising judge of the grand jury off the record. So, I boarded the 6 train to go pick up my son from swimming class, and there was an empty seat. And who's sitting next to it? Judge Shirley R. Levittan—the day after I prayed. We had a wonderful talk. In another instance, I was trying to find Dr. Michael Baden, the former medical examiner, but nobody knew where he was. I walked by a newsstand where the *Daily News* and the *Post* were sitting outside, and on both front pages were pictures of people arrested at a fraternity melee at Columbia. A couple of people had been hospitalized, one of them being Judson Baden, son of the former and much esteemed medical examiner. So I went to see him at St. Luke's Hospital and asked, "Where's your dad?" That's how I made my connection.

Why did I want to speak to Dr. Baden? I didn't want to discuss the Stewart case specifically, but when prosecutors spoke about the manner of death, I wanted to understand the physical mechanism involved. What happened to Stewart was that he was actually drowning. His lungs were filling up, or being coated, with liquid, so that the oxygen could not transfer. By the time the police had him at Union Square, he was flopping around on the sidewalk like a fish out of water; he was not getting oxygen. And the cops, seeing that behavior, seeing the kid in dreadlocks and all of that, figured that he was on drugs of some kind. So they hog-tied him, put him in the back of their suburban, and took him to the hospital.

Could these cops have performed better? Sure. That's why it was ruled a crime of omission rather than commission. In other words, the cops didn't do anything, specifically, to create the situation, but they did not attend to him—he was in their custody—and they failed to keep him alive. But they were not the ones who killed him. The decision to make the case about *these* cops protected the real perpetrators of Stewart's death. The actual crime was at First Avenue, not at Union Square. We tried to focus on that fact, but the ADAs kept on blocking it. They didn't want it to go in that direction. So what happened? A young white lady was with Stewart, and she gave him a kiss and left in a cab. A lone cop followed him down the stairs. And then you have this dead youth with dreadlocks, who got arrested by the police. It's not really clear what took place in the station, so they *tagged* him a graffiti artist. Of course, having half an ounce of a brain, you're in a grand jury and you ask the policeman, "Well, okay, he was doing graffiti, can you show us a picture of his graffiti? Where's the magic marker? Where is the paint?" There was nothing there. It was an excuse. There were two partial witnesses. There was the subway booth clerk—and yes, according to the testimony, which is sealed since it was before the grand jury, Stewart did not pay his fare. But the cop didn't know that, so it had nothing to do with the arrest. He was beaten up in the stairwell and then dragged upstairs. Upon leaving the subway, there's a slab that you step off of. Stewart was bound there, and an emergency service cop came. Obviously, Stewart was already in a bad shape, and this cop—according to the other witness, Robert Rodriguez, who was a Hispanic auxiliary police officer—saw him pull up Stewart, look at him, and then let him go. And when Stewart's head went back it hit the step. Rodriguez saw something that was terribly wrong, and he went to his precinct to report it. He did everything an auxiliary police officer was supposed to do and was told: "Your job is to observe, log what you observe, and not to get involved." At trial, the defense discredited all of his testimony because he claimed he saw the police vehicle with Stewart in it go north to Bellevue Hospital. Of course, it didn't go to Bellevue Hospital directly but via Union Square. But how would he have known that? The ADA was able to say, "Well, there's no case here; it happened in Union Square."

For the first grand jury, all the charges were thrown out based on my alleged misconduct, yet I had voted against indicting those cops. They were indicted by the ADA's manipulation, yet I received all the credit for it. The case was re-presented to a second grand jury with the same outcome for those hapless police officers. Two years wrongfully under the spotlight, with the inevitable outcome exculpating them. Meanwhile the guilty party was not even brought to justice.

Lou Young
REPORTER

In New York City there was an "us and them" survival mentality in the early 1980s. In other words, the city had lost control of graffiti on the subways, and the crime rate was soaring. If you did nothing but cover murders, you could fill an entire newscast. It was unbelievable. I once heard a quote that really stayed with me: the police had shot somebody in the Bronx, and someone at the station said, "Getting shot by the police in that part of town is death by natural causes, so we can't cover it." At that point the news was being criticized for too much mayhem, too much blood. Like, "If it bleeds, it leads." So shortly after, they began to say, "We've got enough violence. Find some other kinds of stories." People simply wanted the police to do something about crime, and they really didn't want to give a lot of thought to how they got it done.

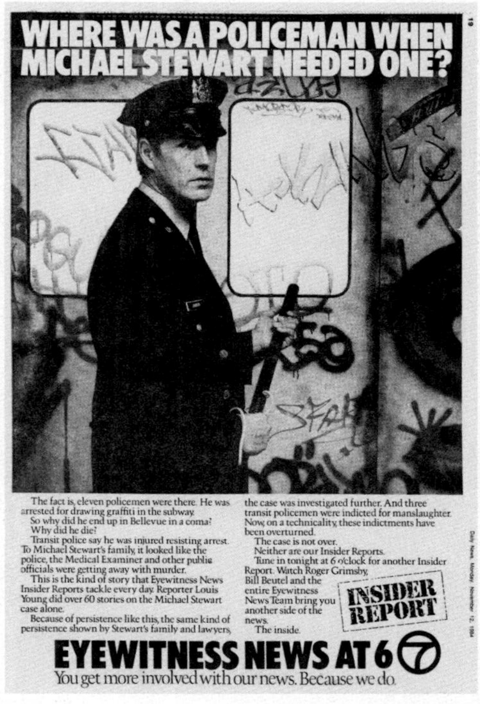

FIGURE 23

Advertisement for WABC-TV's *Eyewitness News*, in *Daily News*, November 12, 1984

With the Michael Stewart case there wasn't much sympathy in the beginning. The idea that the police had roughed up somebody who was defacing the subway and caused his death didn't really alarm people. The legendary reporter Gabe Pressman, on Channel 4, jumped right on the story. I was a young reporter then. I had moved from Tampa to *Eyewitness News* on Channel 7 in December of 1981. I saw the Stewart story as compelling and wanted to get involved, but who was I to want to do the story that someone of the caliber of Gabe Pressman was on? Howard Doyle, the senior executive producer at *Eyewitness News*, listened to my pitch and then gave me more than I asked for. "You do the story every day until I tell you to stop," he said, and we did . . . for *years*. It was remarkable—we set out to screw around with the very people who were trying to reel the story back in. We had an expanded way of treating the story; we called it "Insider Report." We'd put a couple of producers, a reporter, a couple of crews on it for a day, to check all our sources, and then we'd use the words "Insiders say. . . . Insiders look at it this way. . . ." We used to call it an RDF, Rapid Deployment Force, which was a military term at the time. I worked on several Stewart RDFs in 1984, and then we did periodic Stewart updates. At some points I would end up just calling people. I'd call Dianne Brill and say, "Hey, you hear anything? Anything going on?" I did stories with the attorney Michael Warren about him filing papers for a deadline. "That was the whole story, right?" We'd wait, follow him in, and he'd sign the papers, and then he'd turn and give us a sound bite and walk away. I'd somehow fashion a story around that; the idea was to keep the story on the air. Then, of course, there was the trial and the whole thing about the first grand jury being thrown out. I covered every day of the trial—I didn't miss a second of it. And it was painful. They took all the prosecution witnesses apart one by one: the lone eyewitness to the arrest at the station, Robert Rodriguez, was an auxiliary cop. He had a kind of zealousness about being an auxiliary cop and being included, but he was a man of limited vocabulary, so they kind of ripped him apart and made him into a fool. It was like watching a lopsided boxing match; he was not equipped to be cross-examined like that, and it came off as cruel. Then the pathologist who the family hired to contest the autopsy turned out to be an admirer of fringe presidential candidate Lyndon LaRouche. So the pathologist was trashed because he was a LaRouche follower.

There was always a dramatic push to make the cause of death anything but a homicide. If the defense could muddy it enough, they could suggest that Stewart had some medical problem or that he was very drunk or maybe there were drugs involved. In the end all the cops were found not guilty, because there was no forensic evidence to tie any one person to any one act. It was a maddening case; clearly something happened to Michael Stewart. I would love to talk to arresting officer John Kostick about what happened, in his opinion. This is only recollection, but I think Kostick had volunteered for an extra shift that night, a one-man patrol in the station. For the other cops who were called, Stewart was this "Afro-beatnik," or whatever, pain in the ass, who had now interrupted their coffee break with a 10-13 [police code for "Officer needs help"]. The transit police at that time were not a well-regarded group—just this side of thugs, in some respects. They spent their entire professional lives underground, patrolling train yards and subway stations, and were not even close to the NYPD in quality or training.

I thought that somebody had killed the kid, and clearly, they were not being forthright. Clearly, something was amiss. I did other stories about police brutality involving cases in which people had allegedly beaten themselves to death in the back of police cruisers, as if they had had a seizure and banged their head a lot. I was of the opinion that there was a blue wall of silence, and they weren't dealing with these deaths. The issue of homicides in police custody was under investigation. There was a history of recent deaths in police custody that were being challenged by black activists. And Elliot Gross, the city's chief medical examiner, was already having problems. When he announced that Stewart had died from a heart attack, we wondered what was it that *made* his heart stop. I told Michael Warren, "It's like saying he died to death." The fact that a man died in police custody after he was apparently beaten up was the thing that nobody wanted to look at. At the time, society needed to believe that police would not do this. Today, what happened to Michael Stewart would get more attention, but the thing that I heard back then was, "Cops just don't do that." Remember, this was before Rodney King, before there was video of cops doing these sorts of things, and since there wasn't refutable evidence, people wanted to believe that it wasn't true. They weren't willing to accept Stewart's battered body as evidence, but it was obvious that he had been beaten. They wanted improbable explanations but seemed willing to settle for no explanation at all.

As a public figure, Stewart became more sympathetic over time. In the beginning he was portrayed as a vandal. But, as you met Michael's family and the people who knew him, and saw the reaction in the community, he became less of an outsider. Michael didn't grow up in the public housing projects. He was a handsome guy. Light-skinned. He wasn't an immigrant. His parents weren't immigrants. They were just so . . . "American." The Stewart family seemed like next-door neighbors. Everything about him—the more you looked into him, the more sympathetic he became. The sense of tragedy has only deepened as time passed.

Michael Warren
ATTORNEY

At the time of Michael Stewart's death, I was in a law practice with Louis Clayton Jones at 75 Maple Street in Brooklyn. Prior to that I had worked with Alton Maddox on a project in Harlem, at the National Conference of Black Lawyers. Many of the legal cases we handled had to do with very serious criminal matters, like homicides, so we knew the system really well. Clayton, on the other hand, was a corporate lawyer. I thought that the three of us would be the perfect combination for Michael's defense, so we merged. Clayton knew Mrs. Stewart and her husband, Millard, because they were all from Kentucky. They agreed that we should represent their interests and their son's interest in the case.

The police had alleged that Michael wrote something with a Magic Marker on the subway wall in the early morning on the 15th of September 1983. There was never any concrete evidence of that; a marker was never found on Michael's body or entered as evidence during the trial. But let's humor them for a moment, and let's say that Michael did do this. He was an artist, and that's what they do, you know? Artists make art. And at that time, if you were confronted by a police officer for doing something like that, it would have been an offense requiring you to come to court at a later date and face charges. You could take your summons and go on about your business, and you would come back to court on whatever date was designated on that summons. But John Kostick decided that he was not going to give Michael a summons. Instead, he decided to handcuff and arrest Michael. Kostick was responsible for having Michael transported to Union Square, but it didn't end there. We, the lawyers, surmised that Kostick was a part of the group that beat Michael at Union Square, where he sustained fatal injuries. It was apparent to us that we were dealing with a terminal case because of the nature of the injuries. When he was delivered to Bellevue Hospital at around 3:30 a.m.—I wouldn't say "arrived" because it was really a stone-cold heartless delivery—Michael was hog-tied and not breathing. Fortunately, there were two nurses who were in the emergency room, and I was able to locate them and speak with them. One of the things you have to do in these cases is to find people who were there,

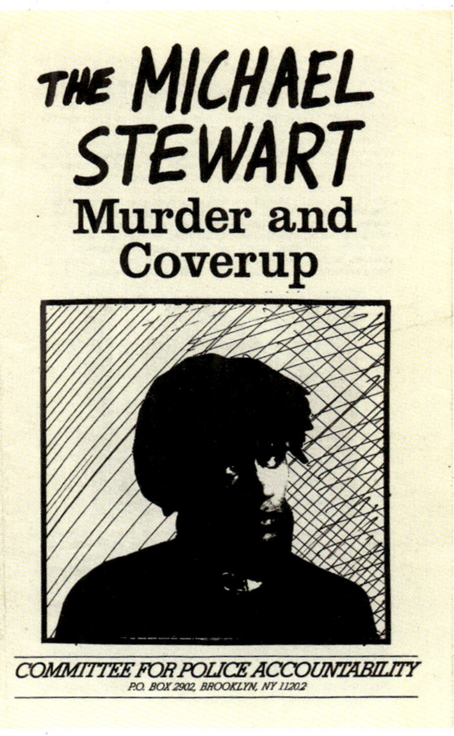

FIGURE 24
Pamphlet, "The Michael Stewart Murder and Coverup."
Collection of the Stewart Family

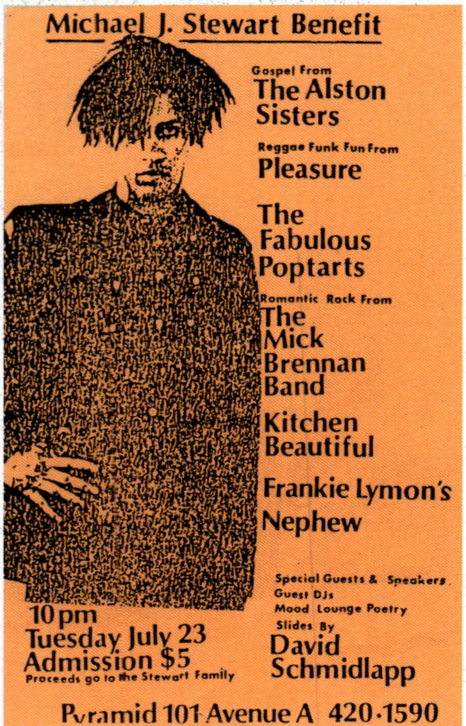

FIGURE 25

Flyer for benefit at Pyramid Club, July 23, 1984. Collection of the Stewart Family

who had firsthand knowledge of what took place, otherwise, you're operating within the realm of hearsay, at the very least. I learned that he was listed at the hospital as an unidentified male, although he had identification on him. It raised our suspicions that there was clearly a cover-up going on, with the hopes that Michael would die right away and be transferred to the medical examiner's office. And the medical examiner would do his thing, as part of what we, the lawyers and Michael's doctors, believed to be an institutional-scale cover-up. And the matter would be open and shut quickly.

It was quite clear, early on, that we were dealing with a terminal case, which meant that we had to act quickly. It's difficult to say that there was a step one, two, and then three because a lot of things were happening simultaneously. We got a pathologist, Dr. John Grauerholz, immediately on board, who was brilliant. We went to the hospital with our physician, Dr. Robert Wolf, to see Michael, because Bellevue is a city hospital, and they knew if we were able to establish liability, there could be a lawsuit down the line. We were concerned about the possibility of a cover-up from the get-go and knew that opportunities were ripe for it as Michael lay in the hospital bed, dying. When we got the call on September 28 that he had expired, we knew that it could have happened at any time, but it was still one of those things that we felt hard, very much so. Less than two weeks in, we were committed to Michael, and to the family. We had to mobilize quickly because this was now a homicide, as far as we were concerned.

I know the paperwork account of what happened—the time lines, ours and what the police alleged—but the thing that I can't imagine, and what no one can really imagine, is what Michael sustained in that hour in the custody of John Kostick and the New York Transit Police, and the terror that he felt, as he probably knew that he was going to die. As Michael's lawyers, we knew we were going to be in for a tremendous battle, but we were ready. We knew that God was with us. Clayton, Maddox, and I prepared for it every day, as though we were preparing for war. We knew this was child's play with respect to what we could expect next.

The incident that shifted everything for us was the removal of Michael's eyes. We followed the dissection of the eyes after the autopsy because the removal of the eyes had occurred without Dr. Grauerholz present, which tacitly went against the agreement that we had struck. Michael's eyes had been placed in a bleaching solution, again, without our doctor present, in what we collectively felt was an attempt to eliminate the existence of petechial hemorrhaging, which would have clearly indicated strangulation. After that happened, we understood that the entire apparatus of the system could not have been clearer about its intentions to cover up the case.

From the beginning, we strategized about how to reach the public. One of the first things that is done in a case like this is for law enforcement to assassinate the victim's character. It becomes even more vicious and ludicrous when the victim is deceased. For Michael, the police were essentially saying that he had beaten himself to death by thrashing about and hitting the sidewalk, cutting off his own air supply, and causing his own cardiac arrest. So before Michael died, on September 28, we went to the public immediately. We first began working with the black press, who we knew would report the story fairly and give us an opportunity to explain what happened and not just give sound bites. Plus, we already had working relationships with them from other police brutality cases we had helped with. The *Daily Challenge*, the *New York Carib News*, and the radio stations owned by Percy Sutton were a few of the outlets that we worked with. I remember their publishers being very keen to help mobilize the black community. From the coverage generated by the black news press, the white press got wind of it, and Gabe Pressman at WNBC Channel 4 got in touch with me, and then we began working together. Then came Lou Young at WABC Channel 7, who stayed with the case longer than any other TV reporter and was sympathetic to what was happening. We also began holding community forums in churches to talk about who Michael was as a person, what kind of family the Stewarts were, and to tie what happened to Michael to some of the cases of black men who had died at the hands of the police in the late 1970s, which were still on everyone's minds.

Gabe Pressman really understood the racist dog whistling that was happening with Michael being labeled a graffiti artist when there was no real evidence of such, and the way that the standard press was using that in a covert way to drum up public support for the police. There were a number of different journalists involved. The standard news accounts were not helpful at all. They ran the standard lines, and they digested the unholy food given to them by the police as if it were gospel. But there were others, for example, Peter Noel with the *New York Amsterdam News*, who was covering the policing beat, and we became close to him. We trusted him, and he did great work. So far as I know, he was the only journalist who stayed with the story from start to finish, from 1983 to 1990. We also trusted Gil Noble, who had a weekly show on WABC called *Like It Is*. He was quite essential in covering the case and one of the first black journalists to do so.

I also recall Michael's friends—a close-knit artistic community on the Lower East Side. I remember Eric Drooker; I believe that he made the "Remember Michael Stewart" buttons for us **[FIG. 17]**. I also recall Franck Goldberg. Franck was a very tender, spirited soul—one of the most tender souls that I had ever met. We established a good relationship right away, and he introduced me to other folks in the community. I know that Michael's circle of East Village friends were very actively involved in promoting his case; they were involved in spreading the news when and where they could to bring about justice. I heard that they were organizing protests and benefits, but I don't ever recall going to any myself. But they were a close community, and they experienced enormous pain as a result of Michael's death. Their friend was taken away from them and was no longer able to partake in the beauty that he had been creating with them.

In terms of the case itself, there were numerous problems with the first grand jury. Witnesses were being turned away or never called, and a juror, Ronald Fields, was conducting his own investigation. He had written to a Columbia law professor inquiring about the powers of the grand jury, and he suggested that new witnesses be called before the grand jury. Since grand juries are supposedly independent, their rules of evidence are much looser than governing trial juries, and none of this was actually illegal. But the first grand jury was dismissed, and the process began all over again, and a second grand jury was called. Miraculously, we got an indictment in the second grand jury, which led to the trial in 1985. We felt Michael in the room, so to speak, especially when we got the indictments on the cops.

We took this case and stayed with it for years because of our collective, fierce sense of justice. It was a mission for all of us. But we—Louis Clayton Jones, Alton Maddox, and I— weren't involved when Michael's case entered the civil arena for monetary damages, although the legal groundwork had been diligently laid by us based on our previous involvement. We didn't receive a dime nor ask for one or recoup any legal costs, billable hours, any of that. That wasn't the point. We were trying to create the basis for a strong federal case for a precedent, while educating the public about how a cover-up takes place. We considered ourselves to be instruments that would expose these types of injustices so that they wouldn't happen again, or if they did happen again, they would happen to as few people as possible. The men who we believed were responsible for Michael Stewart's death got off with an acquittal, but as the lawyers, we knew this case was never going to go away. In our eyes, and for many people, they were innocent only in a flawed court of law, and we had to trust that history would take its course and tell the complete story. I'm enormously pleased, in the autumn of my years, to see that this is happening. It's a justice that supersedes the courtroom.

Fighting the good fight has been hard work. I can't speak about how it affected Clayton and Alton over the years, but I know how it affected me. I know that it affected Dr. Wolf as well, because, remember, he was essentially watching Michael Stewart deteriorate and keeping us apprised of that in medical terms, since we couldn't trust the hospital. All of the cases that we took stayed with us, but particularly this one. You become close to those you represent, especially in these types of cases. I've always had a problem with erasing the spirits of those that I have represented, that I have swum with in this ocean called life, on many occasions, in quite turbulent waters. And a lot of the swims have been tough, and they've been against very rough waters and high tides. But if you're sincerely involved, at least from my standpoint, you never forget it. It becomes innately a part of you and shapes how you are and how you function in life thereafter. This frontline work has been, over the years, quite taxing on many levels. It's a consequence that you fully accept when you make a commitment to this type of work. Do I still consider Michael my client? The answer is yes, after all these years, the answer is still yes, very much so.

Peter Noel
JOURNALIST

At the time, I was a young whippersnapper reporter for the *New York Amsterdam News*. I attended these important forums where the four black attorneys Louis Clayton Jones, Alton Maddox, C. Vernon Mason, and Michael Warren would report to the community about what was going on with the Michael Stewart case. They had a running debate going on with Robert Morgenthau, the Manhattan district attorney, as to how the case should be handled. A major point of contention was the identity of the cops: all we knew was that they were white. We *did not* know the names of the police officers who had killed Michael Stewart. So, I was calling Morgenthau's office almost every day. Why were they being kept secret? Even though the officers were suspended, black residents of the city feared they still might be roaming the streets. Police officers were, of course, considered suspect by the African American community, and for very good reasons. Even me, a reporter—they would stop me, take my press card, and rough me up for reporting while black.

One day, out of the blue—pun intended—Mr. Morgenthau called me to his office to give me the names of *all* the police officers. It was a big scoop for me. I remember talking to Mrs. Stewart about it, and she just held on to me—she was always holding on to me—and she said, "I see something. And it's his name. It's Michael's name. I see his name." That's all she kept saying to me. I didn't ask her, "What do you mean by that?" But I knew she was only a mother wanting some type of closure, and finally knowing the names of the people who allegedly killed your son gave you something at least to hold on to. After I published the names in the *Amsterdam News*, she read it and called me and said, "I believe I can see these police officers beating Michael. I believe I can see them right now doing it. And they're all white cops. I can place the names. Every baton."

Police brutality was rampant then. Unfortunately, Michael Stewart became a victim. September 15, 1983—four days before the actual police brutality hearings began in New York City. Most believe it was because he scrawled graffiti on the subway wall. But based on what was happening at the time, in terms of race relations, the allegation was that a transit police officer, John Kostick, saw him kissing a white woman. And at the time, it was still taboo to be seen walking down the street with a white woman. I'm told he was just kissing her goodbye on the cheek, or holding her hand and saying something. But in those days, police officers were totally opposed to that type of racial mixing. Michael Stewart, being who he was—I mean, the avant-garde type, how he looked, his hair—he was really one of those Village guys. The story goes that they asked Michael Stewart for some ID, and he allegedly pulled his hand away, and then they beat the hell out of him and then choked him. It was Louis Clayton Jones, the main attorney for the Stewart family, who found out this information, because he and the other lawyers interviewed the woman and two witnesses who claimed to have seen this.

At that time these four lawyers were articulating black rage in a way that very few people attempted to do or were brave enough to do. They said that the medical examiner was covering up the killing and that the Manhattan district attorney was also part of the so-called cover-up. It certainly raised doubts in the minds

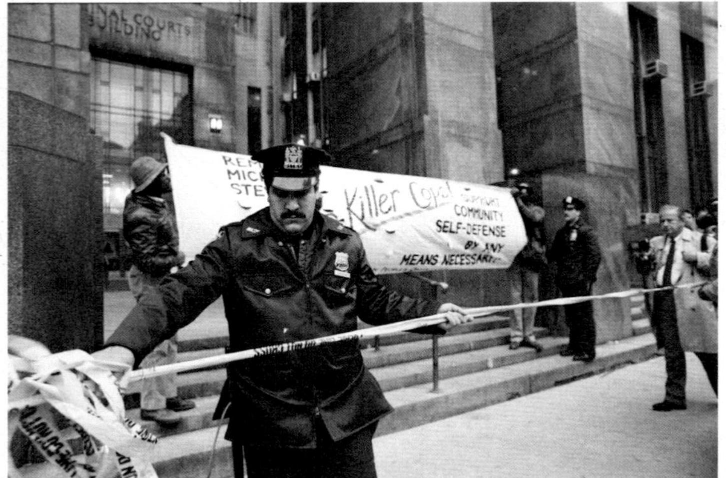

FIGURES 26, 27
Demonstrators protest acquittal of six transit police officers in the death of Michael Stewart outside Manhattan Criminal Court, November 25, 1985

of the African American community, which was subjected to the most brutal type of behavior by police officers. Hey, what happened to Michael Stewart is consistent with the way they treat us. He was not the first black man they had choked to death; prior to the Stewart case, people went to the lawyers for any police brutality incidents during the early 1980s. The most vocal among them was Alton Maddox. He was a member of the National Conference of Black Lawyers, and had defended a lot of young black kids. Maddox and his colleagues were largely responsible for whipping up "Day of Outrage" protests, and that's how they brought people's attention to the cases. Michael Stewart could have been another statistic: nobody would have known his name were it not for these lawyers, who said, "Look! He's not just another statistic." These four lawyers would not let this man die in vain.

I was kind of embedded with these attorneys. They were out there making all these allegations, and people ran to the *Amsterdam News* for that type of controversial coverage. And that's how I cut my teeth as a young, black reporter, covering the police brutality beat. I called my type of journalism "BAJ": Black Advocacy Journalism. Initially the white press, especially television, didn't want to talk about Michael Stewart. The lawyers would call news conferences and the cameras would refuse to show up, or they would show up and can the story. They didn't really care about Michael Stewart's background. But these lawyers became relentless in getting the word out: a black man was killed, and that was it. When the white press found out who his parents were, and their quiet, middle-class background, they began to take notice, acknowledging, though cautiously, that even the son of black, middle-class, law-abiding people could become a victim of police brutality. The lawyers came up with ideas about how to break news around the case. It was because of their daring, their persistence, that we got slightly favorable coverage in the mainstream media. John Johnson of WABC was very good to the cause; he was one of the most trusted black faces who came into our homes in the evening. But like any other black reporter at the time, the pressure was on him to put the spotlight on the police version of events. News editors, who heavily influenced the final scripts, got their information directly from the NYPD. It was canned news, all ready to go, and they just put a new top on what we call B-copy. It went something like this: "The police department tonight is refuting allegations. . . ." That was their lede. After a while, Johnson and others refused to parrot what the police department was saying, and at some point, the slant of the stories began to change, because the lawyers' genuine pleas for justice led the story. They led the six o'clock news: "Alton Maddox today charged that Dr. Elliot Gross is hiding blah-blah-blah."

Or Clayton Jones would make a statement that might have sounded ridiculous, like, "Elliot Gross, the medical examiner, dug out the eyes of Michael Stewart." But he knew what he was saying. Gross, Jones insisted, was hiding the eyes. Exposing this scandal was a major part of the lawyers' strategy. They were very savvy. *Extremely* savvy. They had gotten an independent medical examiner, a pathologist, who said that something was very suspicious. Without the eyes, which would have shown the petechiae, the particular hemorrhaging caused by strangulation, the case remained unproven. Jones and the lawyers made a big argument around these petechiae; they hammered it. It became part of the lexicon of the reporting, on a daily basis. All the lawyers also spoke with Diane Thompson, who had an afternoon radio show on WLIB, to report to her devoted listeners about what was actually going on with the trial. It became required listening. The police department came to hate WLIB, because it was the voice of the people, the black community. It was the flagship station of the Inner City Broadcasting Corporation, which was owned by Percy Sutton, who was the former Manhattan borough president.

Even today, all issues surrounding police brutality still evoke Michael Stewart's death. He was strangled to death, which is the most egregious way of dying, perhaps the most personal. You cannot talk about Eric Garner, who was also choked to death by the police, without mentioning Michael Stewart. His name is very easy to remember; it easily rolls off the tongue. "Oh, Michael Stewart, we heard of that case." You only have to mention Michael Stewart in two lines, or just drop his name, and people associate a particular case with police misconduct. Things began to change with such awareness and with the advent of the iPhone. There are young people, white folk, who are saying, "We understand this. We know we are part of this now." And, "I'm a witness. I saw you strike this young black man who is handcuffed behind his back, and that he had mouthed off something to you, and I heard you say, 'What did you say?' and you slapped him." Or, "You did something to him." Their testimonies are very important at this time. Michael Stewart changed the way people looked at police brutality. In a way, he came back. Michael Stewart is here, ever hovering over all of these cases—his presence, his ghost, whatever you want to call it. "I'm here, use me as an example. I have been sacrificed in some way. My name, you invoke all the time, to talk about police brutality in this great city of ours. Here, use me." And it's here we feel the presence and acknowledge the role of Michael Stewart. That is his contribution to the Movement for Black Lives.

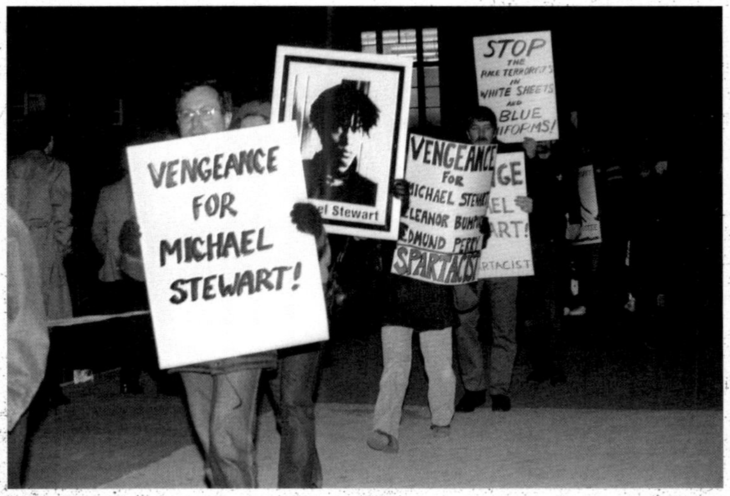

Carrie Stewart
MOTHER OF MICHAEL STEWART

Michael was tall and thin. His and his father's statures were alike. In terms of his facial features, I think he looked a lot like both of us. Have you heard the statement "Still waters run deep"? Well, they both had a quiet side; they were observers, ever vigilant about what was going on in any space. With them, you just didn't rock the boat. As a little boy, Michael would draw childlike prints, but in elementary school his interest in art started to become obvious. He would write imaginary stories and illustrate them. He started sketching on paper napkins or drawing on top of photographs, or doing strange kinds of things that maybe you really wouldn't call painting—or even artistic—but he started making things that seemed strange to other people but made sense to him.

I think he started going to the East Village when he began working as a deejay for WPIR, the Pratt radio station. Maybe that's when he started to make friends in the Village with music groups. It was just not the way I had expected that he would be enjoying his adult life: dancing all night, coming home at the break of dawn, and drinking. As the mother of an adult son, it was out of my control. Whatever I thought didn't really make a big difference because he was going to do what he wanted to do. He was an adult. I couldn't say, "Don't go there, don't be there." He would leave with his portfolio. There are those who said they would see him on the subway sketching, and he would always have a portfolio with him. I can't say that he ever talked about having long-term career goals. Back then, it was hard for me to accept the idea of modeling as an actual career, because they were posing in strange-looking buildings with everyone in all black and odd-looking things that I didn't really go along with. Music and modeling might have been the connection with the East Village, not graffiti. My understanding of what graffiti is, or was, was not clear. I was thinking of the way they marked the trains, or the way they drew on windows and buildings, and I never knew Michael to do that kind of thing, at that age, as a young adult; it just never made sense to me that he would have been involved with that. My impression was that the arresting officer just needed something to put on the ticket, so he claimed that Michael was writing, and that was a quick way for him to say why he was giving him the citation. It was painful to us for him to be described in that way.

When we found out what happened, we were at home in bed. It was early morning. Someone rang our doorbell and told us that we needed to get to Bellevue. We thought someone was going to wait and take us there, but the person left. We will never know, unless someone finally comes forward this many years later, who that person was. By the time we got to Bellevue, on our own, we found out that Michael had been left there, registered as an unknown white male. But someone had to have known where he lived, and who he was, to come and tell us. I was working at that time at the Marcus Garvey Nursing Home on St. Marks Avenue in Brooklyn, but Millard, my husband, had just retired from his job at the New York City Transit Authority, and we were looking forward to that. As the events unfolded, I was finally dropped from the job. I didn't go back after that.

All the coverage showed pictures of the victim alone rather than any photos of the person who caused his demise, which was why we wanted the hospital picture

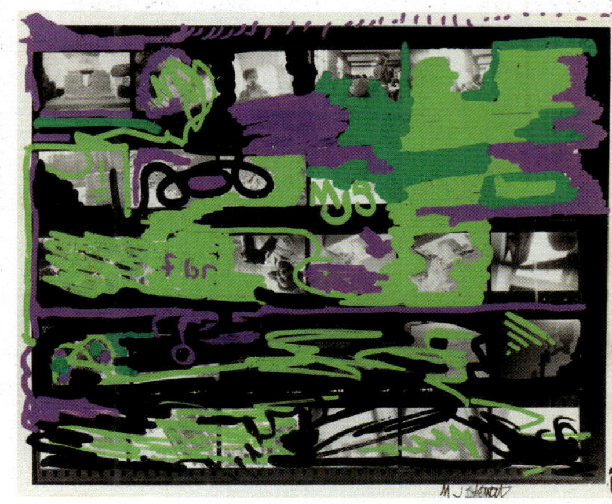

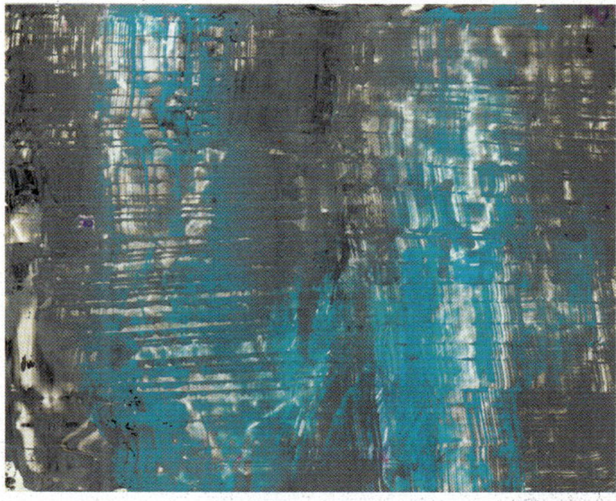

FIGURES 28, 29
Untitled artworks by Michael Stewart, n.d.
Collection of the Stewart Family

to go public. We knew we were breaking rules, but we wanted people to see what had happened to Michael. Let's just say it was our decision—that we wanted someone to know the condition that he was in, because of the way he was neglected, the way the arrest took place, and all the details were being swept under the rug. We wanted it to go public that this is how he ended up. There was always a police guard outside his room, as if he were under arrest. The handcuffs had finally been removed, but the injuries were prevalent. He was in a coma. We knew we were breaking the rules. We knew we shouldn't have taken the photos, but we did it anyway.

We wanted to know more. How did Michael end up in this situation? It was our decision to find out what happened, and we didn't want it to be kept a secret. We wanted everyone to know what happened. The legal support was organized quickly. Louis Clayton Jones was the brother of my pastor's wife, Sylvia Jones Harris. So my pastor and my lawyer and the other partners of Louis Clayton Jones all came together to find out what happened—what caused this. The other reason that it came together quickly is because of Reverend William Augustus Jones, who was also a brother of my pastor's wife and was a civil rights activist. When we were trying to get attention from the State of New York, in order to get a special prosecutor, Reverend Jones organized a sit-in at the World Trade Center in Governor Cuomo's office. After the governor refused to see us in his New York office, we decided to go to Albany to see if we could have an audience with him there. That did take place. The thing that stands out most in my mind now is that when they finally let us have an audience with the governor, I remember saying to him that my son was the same age as his son. It could have been him. I can't remember how he responded, but the outcome of that visit was that there would be no special prosecutor appointed for the case.

I suppose my greatest hope was that Michael's death would serve as an example for anyone who had doubts about what was happening with the police department, with arrests, and with brutality. That we would be an example of trying to fight back.

GUGGENHEIM PROJECT TEAM

Advancement

Mary Anne Talotta, Senior Director, Individual Development and Campaign
Corinne Gocsall, Director, Corporate, Institutional, and Global Partners
Andrea Petrini, Associate Director, Institutional Development
Kate Stichnoth Randi, Senior Major Gifts Officer
Judy Cuker, Manager, Corporate Development

Art Services and Preparation

David Bufano, Director, Art Services and Preparations
Elisabeth L. Jaff, Senior Preparator
Colin O'Neill, Senior Preparator
Chris Williams, Senior Preparator
And team

Conservation

Lena Stringari, Deputy Director and Chief Conservator
Julie Barten, Senior Paintings Conservator and Associate Director of Conservation Affairs
Jeffrey Warda, Senior Conservator, Paper and Photographs

Curatorial

Nancy Spector, Artistic Director and Jennifer and David Stockman Chief Curator
Joan Young, Director, Curatorial Affairs
Terra Warren, Curatorial Assistant

Director's Office

Richard Armstrong, Director of the Solomon R. Guggenheim Museum and Foundation
Lindsey Cash, Senior Assistant to the Director and Manager, Director's Office Affairs
Lydia O'Connor, Specialist, Board of Trustees and Director's Office Affairs

Education

Kim Kanatani, Deputy Director and Gail Engelberg Director of Education
Sharon Vatsky, Director, School and Family Programs
Christina Yang, Director, Public Programs
Jennifer Yee, Senior Manager, Public Programs
Rachel Ropeik, Manager, Public Engagement
Carolyn Keogh, Manager, School and Youth Programs
Alan Seise, Associate Manager, Public Programs
Laili Amighi, Public Programs Associate
Blake Myers, Public Engagement Coordinator

Exhibition Design

Jaime Krone, Director, Exhibition Design
Lucie Rebeyrol, Junior Exhibition Designer

Exhibition Management

Clare Bell, Director of Exhibitions
Kim Bush, former Director of Licensing and Traveling Exhibitions
Lauren Robbins, Associate Manager, Exhibition Management

Exhibition Services

Paul Bridge, Senior Manager, Exhibition Installations
Mary Ann Hoag, Head of Exhibition Lighting
Mark Argue, Manager, Exhibition Construction
And team

Fabrication

Christopher George, Director, Fabrication
Peter Brayshaw, Chief Cabinetmaker
Peter Mallo, Chief Framemaker
Steven Ott, Cabinetmaker
Marcel Walker, Cabinetmaker
Ross Caudill, Fabricator
And team

Facilities

Peter Read, Director, Facilities
Michael Zall, Associate Director, Facilities Operations
Ian Felmine, Chief Engineer
Richard Avery, Senior Manager, Facilities
And team

Finance

Marcy Withington, Chief Financial Officer
Lesley Lana, Director of Budgeting
Anna Shadbera, Senior Accountant

Global Communications

Tina Vaz, Deputy Director, Global Communications
Sarah Eaton, Director, Media and Public Relations
Lauren Van Natten, Associate Director, Media and Public Relations
May Yeung, Publicist

Graphic Design

Jae-eun Chung, Director, Graphic Design
Janice Lee, Associate Director, Graphic Design
Brette Richmond, Designer

Information Technology

Sergey Filkov, Acting Director, Information Technology
Josh Meehan, Associate Director, Information Technology
And team

Interactive

Laura Kleger, Director, Interactive
Robert Duffy, Associate Director, Interactive Technology and App
Maria Slusarev, Associate Director, Website and Interactive Experience
Caitlin Dover, Senior Editor, Interactive
Stephan Knuesel, Digital Media Producer
Josie Rubio, Interactive Producer
Grace Tung, Manager, Interactive

Legal

Sarah Austrian, Deputy Director, General Counsel, and Assistant Secretary
Marianna Horton Mermin, Senior Associate Counsel
Ronni Weinstein, Assistant General Counsel

Marketing and Social Media

Holly Campbell, Director, Marketing
Alex Barber, Senior Manager, Digital Marketing
Essie Lash, Senior Manager, Marketing
Harineta Rigatos, Digital Marketing Manager
Alexa Revans, Marketing Associate
Elizabeth Cosgrove, Digital Marketing Coordinator

Photography

David Heald, Director of Photographic Services and Chief Photographer
Allison Chipak, Photographer and Studio Manager
Susan Wamsley, Digital Asset Manager

Publishing

Diana Murphy, Publisher
Melissa Secondino, Associate Director, Production
Elizabeth Zechella, Managing Editor
Shiori Kawasaki, Assistant Production Manager
Cullen Gallagher, Editorial Assistant

Registrar

MaryLouise Napier, Director, Registration
Eliza Stoner, Registrar, Collections and Exhibitions

Retail

Gigi Loizzo, Director of Retail Strategy and Operations
Katherine Lock, former Senior Manager, Merchandise and Product Development
Kristin Rae, Senior Manager, Museum Store and Operations

Security and Visitor Experience

Trevor Tyrell, Director of Operations, Museum Facility
Emily Schluter, Associate Director, Security
Jonita Luti, Senior Security Manager
Emily Johnson, Senior Manager, Group Sales and Box Office
Nicole Fernandez, Manager, Visitor Experience
Brian Wilson, Manager, Visitor Experience
Kai-Ti Kao, Associate Manager, Group Sales and Box Office
And team

Published on the occasion of the exhibition
Basquiat's "Defacement": The Untold Story
Solomon R. Guggenheim Museum, New York
June 21–November 6, 2019

Funding for this exhibition is provided by the National Endowment for the Arts and The Keith Haring Foundation.

ISBN 978-0-89207-548-5

First printing

PUBLISHED BY
Guggenheim Museum
1071 Fifth Avenue
New York, NY 10128
guggenheim.org

AVAILABLE THROUGH
ARTBOOK | D.A.P.
75 Broad Street, Suite 630
New York, NY 10004
artbook.com

DISTRIBUTED OUTSIDE THE UNITED STATES AND CANADA BY
Thames & Hudson, Ltd.
181A High Holborn
London WC1V 7QX, United Kingdom
thamesandhudson.com

DESIGNED BY Loidë Marwanga
PRODUCTION BY Shiori Kawasaki, Melissa Secondino
PRINTED AND BOUND BY die Keure, Belgium

TYPESET IN Titling Gothic, Berthold Akzidenz Grotesk, Letter Gothic
PRINTED ON 135 gsm Magno Volume

Greg Tate's essay "Black like B." was originally published in Richard Marshall, *Jean-Michel Basquiat*, exh. cat. (New York: Whitney Museum of American Art, 1992). The text appears here in slightly modified form by permission of the author.

PAGE 1: Jean-Michel Basquiat, *Untitled (Biography)*, 1983 **[P. 55, PL. 9]**, in inverted black-and-white design treatment

ILLUSTRATION CREDITS

All works by Jean-Michel Basquiat © Estate of Jean-Michel Basquiat. Licensed by Artestar, New York.

All other works © the artist or the artist's estate. The following credits apply to images for which separate or additional credit is due. Bettmann Collection/ Getty Images: p. 150. Courtesy Dianne Brill: pp. 106, 107. Photo: Allison Chipak © The Solomon R. Guggenheim Foundation: pp. 17, 40 (both), 114 (both), 125 (both), 127 (both), 132 (both), 133, 135, 139, 145, 146, 153 (both). © Eric Drooker: p. 132 (both). Courtesy *East Village Eye*: pp. 41, 136, 137. © Franck Goldberg: pp. 98, 103. © The Keith Haring Foundation: pp. 70–71. Photo: Nancy Elizabeth Hill, courtesy The Keith Haring Foundation Archive: p. 23. Courtesy Gordon Munro: p. 57. Photo: © Camille Perrottet, Artmakers Inc.: p. 123. Digital Image © The Museum of Modern Art / Licensed by SCALA / Art Resource, NY: pp. 44–45. Album cover courtesy Michelle Shocked / Campfire Girl Publishing; featured photo: Chris Hardy: p. 120. Photo: Smithsonian American Art Museum, Washington, DC / Art Resource, NY: p. 75. © The Estate of Michael Stewart: pp. 40 (right), 114 (both), 153 (both). Photo: © Ivan Dalla Tana, courtesy The Keith Haring Foundation Archive: p. 48. Courtesy WABC-TV: 143. Image and Artwork © 2019 The Andy Warhol Foundation for the Visual Arts, Inc. / Licensed by ARS: p. 21. Courtesy *Workers Vanguard*: p. 151

Cataloging-in-Publication Data is available from the Library of Congress.